RURAL HUMAN SERVICES

RURAL HUMAN SERVICES
A BOOK OF READINGS

edited by H. Wayne Johnson

The University of Iowa

F. E. PEACOCK PUBLISHERS, INC.
ITASCA, ILLINOIS 60143

Preface

In recent years a new interest in the rural community has emerged in social work education and practice. A body of literature is developing on the subject, and a number of related workshops and institutes have been and are being conducted. The 1971 edition of the *Encyclopedia of Social Work* was the first to carry an article on rural social work. As recently as 1976 the initial book on this subject in recent decades was published by Ginsberg.[1] Rural topics now appear with frequency at the annual program meeting of the Council on Social Work Education, and a rural caucus has come into being. It is clear that the rural community is a concern of a growing number of people in the human services.

My interest in editing this book undoubtedly reflects in part having been reared in a hamlet of 200 people. A four-block walk in any direction from our home brought one to fields or pastures. Hence at age 48 I have long been involved in this subject and developments of the 1970s pertaining to rural social services attracted me. Although the limited literature that has so far accumulated has tended to focus on certain geographic regions to the exclusion of others, this volume is not restricted to any particular section of the nation. It is my hope that it reflects the rural situation more broadly and generally as a result.

There is a danger in generalizing on the rural community and making it appear that nonmetropolitan America is homogeneous and uniform when in actuality there is great diversity. There are many "rurals": New England, Appalachia, the Ozarks, the South, the Midwest, the Western Mountain, the Southwest, and the West Coast. These are still extremely broad regions, and each is divisible into a number of subsections with somewhat differing economic, social, and cultural characteristics, problems, and promises. Even a single state may encompass several rural regions differing in makeup. For example, within one state can be found rural coastal communities along a major body of water, farming areas with fertile land, and communities in rugged terrain in which most agriculture is not feasible.

It is important to understand what is meant by the term "rural." The U.S. census defines rural communities as those under 2,500 inhabit-

v

ants. But there are important reasons to view many communities that are larger than this as essentially rural too. Other writers and researchers have included areas with populations up to 50,000.[2] A reason to use the latter figure as the dividing line is that the Census Bureau classifies standard metropolitan statistical areas as units surrounding cities of this size and larger. Furthermore, the term "urbanized area" as used in the census consists of "a central city or twin cities with a total population of 50,000 inhabitants or more, together with contiguous closely settled territory (urban fringe)."[3] Obviously there are communities of 30,000 that are more urban in important respects than others much larger. But it is the editor's view that, in general, towns under 50,000 can be thought of as rural for social welfare purposes.

Rural cannot be equated with farm since there are nonfarm as well as farm areas in the nonmetropolitan world. And, as will be seen, the former is much larger in population than the latter in the United States at the present time.

While the United states is clearly an urban nation and has been so for a long time with the majority of the population residing in cities, a substantial portion of Americans has either remained in the country or moved there. At least one-fourth of Americans are rural dwellers, and depending upon the definitions used, the figure may be more than this.[4] According to the U.S. Bureau of the Census the population of the nation in April 1979 was slightly under 220,000,000; therefore either way the rural community constitutes many millions—far too many people to ignore when considering social problems and human services.

A word about the organization of the book is in order. There are three sections having to do with issues/problems, services, and working in the rural community, respectively. Not only are these divisions arbitrary but often the placement of an article in one section rather than another is equally arbitrary. There is considerable overlap between the sections, which is unavoidable given their interrelatedness. It is difficult to examine problems without considering possible or actual programs aimed at ameliorating the problem and vice versa. Similarly, both problems and services are intertwined in what needs to be known about working in the rural community.

Finally, the title. I considered several and debated especially between "Rural Human Services" and "Rural Social Services." The former was finally chosen because it is broader. Throughout the introduction to each section of the book both terms and "social work" are used interchangeably although it is recognized that in some contexts human services has a technical and special connotation. Probably the majority of readers will be social workers, but I am desirous of reaching any and all social welfare "helpers" who share my interest in the rural scene. If there is anything to the notion of a need for a generalist worker in rural communities as is discussed in Section III it would seem that the image of the worker should be broad and flexible rather than narrow and constrained.

NOTES

1. On the other hand, those of us who see ourselves as pioneers might do well to spend more time in the library. I recently came upon a number of items having to do with rural social welfare published between 1933 and 1941; for example, Josephine C. Brown, *The Rural Community and Social Case Work* (New York: Family Welfare Association of America, 1933).

2. For example, Leon Ginsberg who authored the "Rural Social Work" selection in the 1977 *Encyclopedia of Social Work* (Washington, D.C.: National Association of Social Workers).

3. *Statistical Abstract of the United States* (Washington, D.C.; Government Printing Office, 1978), p. 2.

4. Calvin Beale wrote in "A Further Look at Nonmetropolitan Population Growth Since 1970," *American Journal of Agricultural Economics* (December 1976), that he was dubious "that the rural population could ever go above 60 million people, but it now appears to be advancing toward such a level" (p. 957).

Contents

Acknowledgments

No book of readings would be possible were it not for the willingness of authors and publishers to have their work reproduced. To those persons I am particularly indebted for their cooperation in the development of this anthology.

The staff of F.E. Peacock Publishers has been consistently helpful and supportive, and I acknowledge with enthusiasm the value of their assistance and input. Beverly Sweet has worked diligently as typist and her work, as always, is of the highest quality.

I owe a great deal to colleagues and students, present and past, for ideas and encouragement of various types. These are far-ranging kinds of contributions which led to my own thinking becoming so enmeshed with that of many other people that it is virtually impossible to sort out to whom I owe what. To all I simply want to express my deepest appreciation.

Finally, it is my family to whom I owe the most. Hundreds of hours that might otherwise have been spent with my children and wife went into the preparation of this book. Their tolerance and understanding shall be ever cherished. It is in this spirit that the book is dedicated to Donna, my wife.

I.   Rural Issues and Problems

Two generalized views of the rural community appear to exist. On one hand, rural life is perceived by some to be an utopian situation free of the problems typically associated with the metropolitan center. Clean air and streams, abundant green fields, and open and uncrowded space beckon. In contrast to the picture of the urban center as a grim scene of compacted and overwhelming social problems and an environmental disaster, this idealized perspective of the rural community sees a kind of idyllic paradise. At the opposite extreme is the notion that the rural scene is one scarred by the exploiter of natural resources and a wasteland with regard to social institutions and human resources. The isolation of rural living is criticized, and the distances and lack of proximity to desired services are noted. This stance is one emphasizing supposed deficiencies of various kinds.

Between these two extreme positions reality can be approximated. However, it is important to recognize that there are attitudes such as those just described and that the existence of such attitudes has implications for the total society, rural and urban. What both of the composite pictures just sketched fail to consider is the fact of *change*. The rural community is not a static, quiescent place but, like its urban neighbors, it is undergoing profound transition. Many of these developments are recent and have not yet been fully incorporated into the awareness, thinking, and feeling of people broadly. Some of them deserve examination before moving on to the readings.

The decade of the 1970s marked a major reversal in the centuries old pattern of rapid city growth outstripping rural expansion in the United States. The Industrial Revolution brought the city into being and maintained its subsequent growth. For decades we were conditioned to the idea of persisting urban growth and the parallel notion of limited growth or even decline on the rural side. But while nonmetropolitan population increased by 6.6 percent from 1970 through 1976, metropolitan growth was only 4.1 percent.[1] Of the population growth occurring in the 1960s, less than 10 percent was in rural areas, whereas in the first half of the 1970s, nonmetropolitan locations received 37 percent of the national growth.[2] It is projected that if present trends continue nonmetropolitan areas could experience a net growth of 5 million people by 1985 and 15 million by the end of the century.[3]

One of the most noteworthy features of this development is that while some of the rural growth is spillover from suburban sprawl, much of it is not. Counties with the lowest population density are showing the greatest growth, and it is growth due to migration into the county. These are the same counties that as recently as the 1960s were losing population, largely because of people moving out.[4]

In view of this significant change in rural/urban population growth, it is important to understand that, within the rural sector, it is the nonfarm population that is growing. Farm population continues to decline in spite of the fact that the rate of loss has slowed.[5] The 1977 farm population was only 7.8 million, which is 20 percent lower than in 1970.[6] Another way to appreciate what is happening in the rural farm sector is to note what portion the farm population is of the total population. In 1960 the farm population constituted 8.7 percent of the total; in 1970 it was only 4.8; and in 1978 the preliminary figure was down to 3.7.[7] Substantial numbers of people are either leaving farms or discontinuing agricultural operations on the farm.

The changing U.S. Agriculture Department definition of "farm" is a recent factor in the 1978 drop in the number of farms. Between the early 1950s and 1978 a farm by definition had an annual agricultural output of $250 or more or $50 or more in annual commodity sales from a place larger than ten acres. The new definition used for 1978 requires that the annual sale of agriculture products be worth $1000 or more. Defining farms in this way led to a drop of about 302,000, with most of the decline in southern states. The remaining number of farms under the revised definition was 2,370,000.[8]

A few characteristics of farm areas should be noted since they have relevance for the existing rural problems and human services. The proportion of the rural-farm population that is black is steadily decreasing. Whereas in earlier times slavery and sharecropping tied most blacks to the farm, there is little place today for the nonlandowner.[9]

Two features of farm families have to do with size and age makeup. Farm families are slightly larger than nonfarm families and have more children under 18. There also are proportionately more elderly persons within farm families.[10]

Unemployment is lower for farm families. Income is also lower, but it is gaining more rapidly than for nonfarm families.[11] An interesting change that has occurred relative to hired farmworkers is that as of 1976–1977 most (79 percent) lived in nonfarm places whereas this was true for only 35 percent in the late 1940s.[12] On the larger rural scene one of the most striking developments is the growing role that nonfarm jobs is playing. Forty percent (4 million) of the new nonfarm jobs that opened in this country from 1970 to 1977 were in nonmetropolitan areas.[13] This is a reflection in part of the expanded industrialization and commercial developments in rural communities. The end result is a more diversified rural economy and way of life.

As far as social problems are concerned, rural America, farm and nonfarm, has most of the same concerns as do the cities. Problems related to health, mental health, education, leisure, the family, discrimination, crime, employment, and other life stresses are as real for people in towns and on farms as they are in the cities. In some respects the nature of the rural setting makes such problems even more trying. For example, to be poor in the country can be worse than in the city when it comes to needs such as transportation. There are other aspects of poverty for which the reverse is true.

With regard to poverty, it was Michael Harrington who noted the invisibility of much of this phenomena in modern America. He also recognized that a substantial segment of our poverty is rural and that its nonmetropolitan location is a factor in the lack of visibility. Poverty tucked away in the hills of Appalachia or in small towns in other parts of the country is real, and it hurts whether it is seen or not. Harrington pointed out that areas containing devastating poverty may even be perceived by those passing through as scenic, rustic, and quaint. The human misery may go unrecognized.[14]

Another problem related to poverty has to do with the kinds of employment found in nonmetropolitan sections of the country. Among farm labor is the migrant, one of the most severely deprived groups within America's poor and rural. Although there are changes in this group, too, the massive problems of second-class citizenship persist with deficient housing, education, health, and income for migrants. While there are other rural laborers, some farm and some nonfarm, who also represent abject poverty, the migrant is generally the most pronounced relative to this problem.

In addition to the generally found social pathologies, the nonmetropolitan world experiences problems that are specific to it and characteristic of it. An example is programming for specialized needs such as day-care, services for the developmentally disabled, and provisions for the chemically dependent in sparsely populated areas.

The needs are often genuine but so scattered that it is difficult (1) to persuade the community of their existence, and (2) once successful in establishing their presence, to take appropriate action to meaningfully intervene and provide necessary services. A retarded child in a small town requires assistance fully as much as a comparable youngster in a city. But how is the help to be provided if the boy or girl is the only handicapped child for miles around?

There is a national trend toward deinstitutionalization in such fields as mental health, retardation, and corrections. This trend depends upon and influences another, the development of community-based programs. Unless sparsely populated areas are considered in this process there is a danger that remaining institutions will be populated largely with persons from rural locations. This would be unjust and discriminatory.

"New" social problems come into being when societal conditions perceived as problematic gain attention. The condition may have been present for years or even thousands of years, but somehow it is "discovered" and finds its way into television documentaries and social problems textbooks. Interestingly, often a bit later some of these recently defined, often supposedly nonrural problems are found to exist in the rural community, and it comes to be acknowledged that the urban world has no monopoly on the problem. This was clearly true for child abuse, and now the research and literature include content on rape and spouse abuse in rural locations, to cite some illustrations.[15]

Davenport makes the point that in a rural community if a rape occurs it is general knowledge and there may be pressure placed on the victim not to report the offense in order to protect the social fabric of the community. It may be necessary in nonmetropolitan areas to devise means of raising the consciousness of the community about problems such as rape in order that programming may be instituted or at least begun to be considered.[16]

Two age groups, young adults and the elderly, provide further examples of rural social problems and also demonstrate that conditions defined as problematic often have another side—assets and strengths. The departure of youth and young adults from small communities and their migration to the cities is frequently bemoaned, and this is often seen as part of the demise of the towns. It is argued that the rural community goes to great expense to educate young people only to have them leave when they reach adulthood. On the other hand, this is one of the groups that is currently involved in the reverse migration back to smaller communities. A set of values and expectations motivates and accompanies this move to rural areas, and hence the stage is set for still further social problems as the new environment may not be found to be entirely satisfying. A specific issue for the near future is what will happen if and when the energy crisis is such that fuel for auto transportation is either unavailable or too expensive, or both, to continue the drive from rural dwellings to urban places of employment.

The aged are a significant group in nonmetropolitan society. A major concentration of the elderly is in the Midwest, one of the principal rural areas of the United States. In 1970, of the seven states possessing the highest percent of the population age 65 and over, only Florida, at the top, was not in the central part of the nation. All of these essentially rural states exceeded by far the national figure of 9.9 percent of persons 65 and over.[17]

While the problems usually associated with being elderly in America also apply in rural areas, there are in addition such added complications as transportation. Many retirement communities are nonmetropolitan, often in the Sunbelt. An interesting situation to watch in the near future is the extent to which the elderly in the northern states remain in that part of the country in retirement and how many move south. In the latter case, a question raised is whether going south will be a permanent arrangement or whether significant numbers will maintain two homes, one summer and one winter. The fixed and limited incomes of the elderly is a major factor in such determinations. Increased leisure for retirees is often a mixed blessing and is even defined by some as a social problem. On the other hand, life-experienced persons with abundant free time can be a particularly useful resource as volunteers.

So it is seen that social problems too develop and evolve and that most community and societal pictures are mixed—strengths and weaknesses, problems and solutions, with the "solutions" often carrying the seeds for further problems. Rural communities do present diverse and significant social problems and issues.

It is the thesis of the editor that change is a fact of the present social scene, not only for the metropolis as is so commonly acknowledged, but just as meaningfully for the rural areas that is generally unrecognized. Quite to the contrary, life in the towns and on the farms tends to be thought of as stable and static rather than dynamic and in process of undergoing extensive transition. The sociological and demographic data that have been cited are intended to demonstrate that the past decade or so not only brought about impressive modification in previous long-term trends but may well be the threshold of a new era. While we may speculate that there is undoubtedly a degree of faddism operative in, for example, some of the movement of people to the countryside from the city (part of the "back-to-nature" move for some perhaps), there is reason to believe that this development is deeprooted. Genuine value changes appear to have occurred as millions of Americans now express a preference for living in nonmetropolitan areas.[18]

It is professionals in social work and the human services in part that attempt to assist people in coping with change. Individuals, families, groups, organizations, and communities all need help in adapting. For example, older people account for much of the recent rapid growth in nonmetropolitan counties.[19] How do they take to this change in lifestyle? What problems are encountered? What are their expectations and how do these fit the new realities of their life situations? Change creates disequilibrium and often, on the personal level, anxiety, stress, anger, or guilt. This suggested orientation to thinking about rural problems and programs is both traditional and nontraditional—traditional in that social work has typically been identified with services for those experiencing change, and nontraditional in that the rural community has not been thought of as changing. It is changing and it is going to continue to change, probably much more than it already has, and important social work and human service functions exist as a result.

Articles in the following section describe some of the issues and problems observed on the contemporary rural scene. Kotz deals with poverty in the South. Problems of transportation in scattered rural communities are addressed by Kaye. Coughlin presents the paradox of how efforts to preserve or recreate the rustic past may destroy a way of life cherished by today's rural dwellers. We are able to take a look at the European situation and compare it with our own through Denman's analysis of rural problems in England. That natural disasters take their toll long after the immediate crisis has passed is seen in another article on housing. Two readings, one by Hill and the other by Rhenisch, relate women's rights and the women's movement to the farm and nonmetropolitan areas. Land can be a key to economic security for people, and Graber's article points up legal obstacles standing between many blacks and such security. The small item on IQ testing provides considerable food for thought about an urban bias in testing. Finally, Beale's article brings us back to the fact of change, the context of all rural issues and problems. In doing so we come full circle in this section and have a foundation for the next, which is concerned with rural social services.

NOTES

1. Council on Environmental Quality, *Environmental Quality* (Washington, D.C.: U.S. Government Printing Office, 1978), p. 222.

2. Ibid.

3. Ibid.

4. Ibid.

5. *1978 Handbook of Agricultural Charts*, Agricultural Handbook No. 551 (Washington, D.C.: U.S. Department of Agriculture, 1978), p. 34.

6. Ibid.

7. Ibid.

8. George Anthan, "Iowa's Loss One of Lowest in New Farm Count," *Des Moines Register*, February 28, 1979, p. 5B.

9. *Farm Index* (Washington, D.C.: U.S. Department of Agriculture, October 1976), p. 10.

10. Ibid.

11. Ibid.

12. *1978 Handbook of Agricultural Charts*, p. 35.

13. *1977 Handbook of Agricultural Charts*, Agriculture Handbook No. 524 (Washington, D.C.: U.S. Department of Agriculture, 1977), p. 33.

14. Michael Harrington, *The Other America* (New York: Macmillan Company, 1962), pp. 1–18.

15. For example, see "Rape Crisis Service in Rural Areas," a videotape by Joseph Davenport III, Appalachian Education Satellite Program, Lexington: University of Kentucky, 1978; and "Marital Violence in Rural America," *Response*, 2, no. 4 (February 1979), Center for Women Policy Studies, Washington, D.C., pp. 1–2.

16. Davenport, ibid.

17. U.S. Bureau of the Census, 1973.

18. *Environmental Quality–1976*, p. 297.

19. *Environmental Quality–1978*, pp. 223–224.

In the following article, Nick Kotz, a Pulitzer prize-winning writer who has concerned himself with social problems, again probes poverty, this time in the rural black South in Georgia. There has been progress in this part of the nation since the civil rights movement, but it is slow and painful, and injustice remains. Housing continues to be a major problem, and the black southerner as a farmer is disappearing. Problems and progress in education, criminal justice, civil rights, employment, and welfare are discussed. Although change is the order of the day, poverty and discrimination persist.

1

NICK KOTZ

The Other Side of the New South

Union High School in Sumter County, Georgia, which includes Plains, is in bad physical disrepair, with pigeons roosting in the rafters and rain dripping through the ceiling. The state fire marshal has declared the building hazardous and a state legislative committee had condemned it. A bond issue to build a new county high school recently was voted down, despite a tape-recorded message of support from Sumter resident Jimmy Carter. The schools that serve Plains offer a good example of what the experts call "second generation" civil rights issues.

The Sumter County school system is in trouble today because many whites have sent their children to the private Southland Academy, and no longer want to give the public schools their tax support. The county school superintendent, several school principals, and members of the school board—the key people in running the public schools—all have their own children and grandchildren in private schools.

Reprinted from Nick Kotz, "The Other Side of the New South," *The New Republic*, Part II, April 1, 1978, pp. 18–23, by permission of *The New Republic*, © 1978, The New Republic, Inc. and the author.

Things are better in Americus, 10 miles from Plains. Officials there support the public school system, as do the citizens of adjoining Lee County, which recently approved a bond issue to build a new $2.5 million high school.

School desegregation continues to be a problem in the rural South 24 years after the Supreme Court's first desegregation decision, and not only because of white flight. In Albany, southwest Georgia's principal city, 40 miles south of Plains, civil rights leaders return to court every few years as the public schools never have been fully desegregated. Fifteen out of 35 schools in the city are either 90 percent black or 90 percent white. Ten schools are virtually all black.

An even more pressing issue to Southern blacks today is how their children are treated in school. The American Friends Service Committee and Children's Defense Fund both have documented hundreds of cases in which black children have been "pushed out" of Southern schools under the guise of disciplinary action—action that is not taken against white students. In a recent and typical case in Terrell County, Georgia, two students were expelled after a teacher smelled liquor on their breaths and gave them a breathalizer test. The parents appealed the dismissals to federal court. Judge Wilbur Owens ordered the students reenrolled, ruling that the school system arbitrarily was throwing students out of school, inflicting an overly severe punishment, without any pretense of fairness or due process.

Leroy and Ida Mae Young moved from their farm in rural Worth County to Albany "so our kids could live in peace." The Youngs' oldest children, the first students to integrate the Worth County schools, had been shipped off to a juvenile detention center by white officials resisting integration. The final blow came 10 years later when their son was expelled from school, accused of "laughing like a dog" on the school bus. Young said, "I had to move before somebody hurt me or I hurt somebody."

Another new school issue in the rural South is the question of "tracking"—separating children of the same grade into different "ability groups." The track system, long used in Northern urban schools, was not introduced in southwest Georgia until integration. Some blacks support the track system, believing that both exceptional students and slow learners will benefit from being in their own tracks. Others strongly disagree, believing that system is educationally harmful and is used as a thin guise for resegregation. "It used to be when the schools were segregated, that we had smart black kids and smart white kids," said R.L. Freeman, a former assistant principal in Americus's black schools. "Now all too many black kids are assigned to the bottom track." His view is shared by Eugene Cooper, a black organizer in Sumter County and chairman of Sumter County Organization for Public Education (SCOPE). "Integration has not helped the typical black child," said Cooper. "They have completely lost their identity, their sense of community. I think it was designed that way."

Many parents and children, however, both white and black, believe that integration is working. And as long as that belief is there, it has a chance.

Veterans of the civil rights movement were not surprised to read recently in the newspaper about the "Dawson Five" case. Dawson, population 5000, and located 26 miles south of Plains, is the county seat of Terrell County, which became known during the 1960s as "Terrible Terrell," a rural area in southwest Georgia that even the boldest civil rights workers avoided, especially at night. Civil rights workers had been beaten in the county jail; churches and offices had been burned there; and four black people had died mysteriously. The "Dawson Five" case seemed just another chapter. Five local black youths were charged with fatally shooting a customer in a country store. The store owner did not identify them as the perpetrators until five days after the incident, even though several were regular customers at the store and had charge accounts there. The case recently was thrown out of court, but not before defense attorneys from Team Defense, a non-profit group opposing the death penalty, had shown that the defendants had been threatened with castration and execution and that the signature of one of them on a waiver of rights was forged. The list of citizens from which juries are selected was revised after the defense showed that few blacks were included, despite a 60 percent black population in the county.

Since the Dawson Five case, a federal court judge has issued an injunction to stop many violations of the rights of other black prisoners held in the Terrell County jail. These prisoners routinely have been held for months without being permitted an attorney, without a pretrial hearing or a chance to make reasonable bail. The prisoners were ill-fed, subject to beatings by other prisoners and denied medical treatment.

Millard Farmer, the Atlanta defense attorney who handled the Dawson Five case and others for Team Defense, does not believe that the criminal justice system has improved for poor blacks in the rural South. "Elitism and racism have only changed in small ways," he said. "In some ways, it was easier to fight in the 1960s, when things were visible and obvious." C. B. King, a black Albany attorney who has handled many civil rights cases, says, "There has not been a significant reduction in terrorism. I file as many civil rights deprivation cases now as I did at the height of the movement."

Individual blacks who measure their daily lives against earlier times see more progress than King and Farmer do. Virtually every black I interviewed said a major change is a reduction in the fear of what whites might do to black people. Lucius Holloway, 45, a black insurance agent, has been an important civil rights advocate in Terrell County since the earliest days of the movement. He can recall being jailed as a teenager, falsely charged with violating an 11 pm curfew for blacks. His early civil rights work got him fired from his post office job. "Today," he said, "black people feel freer to open up and move about Terrell County. There is less fear of the police. You can register and vote, although some people are pressured economically—told that they'll lose their job if troublemakers get elected."

Holloway is now organizing an NAACP chapter, which Terrell never has had. In the past, Holloway explained, blacks would give money to the NAACP, but only if they could do so secretly, without their names being recorded on any lists that might fall into the wrong hands. Much of the improvement in the county, Holloway stresses, has resulted from federal law and court orders. "I sure hope Judge Owens lasts," said Holloway. "He's providing justice to southwest Georgia."

Judge Wilbur Owens, 48, who serves the middle district of Georgia, is a Republican and former assistant US attorney, appointed to the federal district court by Richard Nixon in 1972. Civil rights lawyers call him a good "liberal conservative." He has ruled in favor of blacks on a variety of voting rights, criminal justice and employment discrimination cases. His role is crucial for black progress and not appreciated by white officials. "It seems to us that no one individual should have that kind of power," says Albany Mayor James Gray.

Blacks outnumber whites in "Terrible Terrell," but they have yet to translate their population majority into election of blacks to public office. They report, however, that white officeholders have improved their treatment of and services to blacks. Holloway pointed to his street, which was just paved, 15 years after he first petitioned for the improvement. He says that other city services have improved for black neighborhoods. "They're not doing this out of the goodness of their hearts," he said. "A lot of these things are being done with federal money, and we've got our eyes on them."

Holloway also believes there is less job discrimination today, a subject on which blacks in southwest Georgia and other parts of the rural South offer widely differing opinions. Holloway cited the employment of at least three black foremen at a local peanut processing plant, black foremen on all three shifts at the Yale Rubber Company, and blacks in inspection and clerical jobs at a Dawson textile mill.

Industrial development in the rural South has done little to improve job opportunities for blacks. The areas of most industrial development are not the areas with the largest black population. Industrial growth has been greatest in a channel down the Piedmont in the Carolinas, across central Tennessee and then across northern Georgia, Alabama, Mississippi and Arkansas. But the largest black population runs in another belt east and south of the new industrial development. Generally speaking, industry avoided the black population and opted for a better-trained, available and low-wage white work force.

A report last year by the Task Force on Southern Rural Development compared the recent gains of Southern whites and blacks. In the 244 Southern rural counties with the largest black population, 56 percent of blacks and 20 percent of whites lived in poverty. Blacks comprised 40 percent of the population but got only 16 percent of the new industrial jobs over the past decade—a smaller share than the 21 percent that blacks had gotten in the previous 10 years. Whites had a net gain of new industrial jobs over lost agricultural jobs of 287,000 jobs during the decade. Blacks suffered a net loss of 97,000 jobs.

The Delta Foundation, a nonprofit community development corporation in Greenville, Mississippi is one of the few very successful efforts to help poor blacks in the rural South. This cooperative enterprise grossed seven million dollars in sales last year, with a metal stamping company, a ladder company, a small electronic firm and financing of a black-owned radio station and several small stores. Measured against white business, this is a relatively small operation. But it is the 42nd largest black business in the country. Unfortunately, similar efforts in other southern rural areas, including southwest Georgia, have been far less successful.

Lack of success in these black community development businesses has been attributed partly to undercapitalization, partly to lack of management experience and partly to the difficulties of combining social idealism and business.

Albany, the chief trade center for southwest Georgia, has been a classic New South boomtown. Yet Albany blacks, 43 percent of whom live in poverty, seem to have benefited only marginally. More than 50 industries have plants in Albany, many of them lured there by subsidies from the city. Kroger, MacGregor-Firestone and Rockwell International are among the industrial names drawn to Albany during the last few years. The leading promoter of Albany is Mayor James H. Gray, who also directs the Payroll Development Authority, owns the city's daily newspaper and television station and has been president of the Chamber of Commerce five times.

Part of the city's sales pitch is an unspoiled non-union labor force.

As the mayor puts it, "We've got the working man out of the union hall. He's a homeowner, a church member, a social club member."

City Commissioner Mary Young, who is black, believes local blacks have been discriminated against: "We are paying for this industry as taxpayers, but whites from surrounding counties are getting the jobs," she said. "The city advertises a cheap, docile labor force and blacks in the inner city are not considered docile." A. C. Searles, editor of a weekly black paper and president of the Albany NAACP, points an accusing finger at Mayor Gray. "He doesn't have a single black reporter on his paper or visible on his television station," Searles said.

Albany blacks have gained jobs mainly as a result of federal action. Judge Owens ruled that the city government discriminated against blacks in hiring and promotion, and has ordered the hiring of dozens of blacks for non-menial positions. Blacks have also benefited from those much-maligned War on Poverty programs, especially a Head Start program, run for the last 12 years by Harambee Day Care Center, in which 28 teachers work with almost 400 poor black youngsters. There are many success stories, not only of children who went through the program but of teachers as well. Mary Jones, 44, for example, started 12 years ago as a teacher's aide. At the time she had only an 11th grade education, no job and dim prospects. Today, Mrs. Jones is a teacher in the day care program, has earned a college degree and owns a new $34,000 home in Country Club Estates, a suburban neighborhood in transition from white to black. Mrs. Jones and her husband, a stock clerk in a government supply facility, earn $18,000 between them. They have sent two of their children through college. But she still sees racial problems. "We struggled to give our children college educations and they can't get jobs here," she reported. "There is still awful employment discrimination."

In Americus, young blacks with higher education make the same complaint. Henry Lee Wilkerson, 28, who has a degree in behavioral science from Georgia Southwestern College, says he can't get a job in social work or as a salesman, yet sees his white contemporaries from college getting jobs.

The depth of poverty in southwest Georgia is indicated by the welfare statistics. In the Albany metropolitan area one out of eight people receives food stamps and one out of ten gets help from the welfare program for mothers and dependent children. The percentages are similar in Sumter County, and probably there are many more eligible people who have not applied. "The payment level is so low that many people prefer to do without, considering the harassment and red tape," said Patricia Johnson, Georgia director of the AFDC and food stamp program. She pointed out that the state's $147 monthly payment to a four-member family is only 65 percent of the state's 1969 standard of need. And even this welfare aid is not available to two-parent families, which are still in the majority among the Southern rural poor. If there is a bright spot in the welfare picture, it is that poor blacks in the rural South less frequently are being denied welfare benefits to which they are entitled. Fannie Lee Burnette, for example, lives outside Plains in a shack that lacks running water, a toilet or any heat other than a wood stove. But she has survived on $230 a month in old age welfare payments, supplementing that income until recently with food stamps. "Things are better," she said. "At least we get something to eat now. Not too long ago we didn't have anything to eat but bread, and had to beg like a dog."

Perhaps the bleakest story for Southern rural blacks today is the rapid disappearance of the black farmer and landowner. These blacks are suffering the same problems as small farmers everywhere in the country, but that explanation alone will not suffice. The 1974 agricultural census showed fewer than 50,000 black-owned farms remaining in the country. The decline has accelerated in recent years. At the present rate of black land loss—300,000 acres a year—there will be no black farmers left in 1990. This trend totally belies the glowing optimism of accounts of Southern blacks returning from the North to till the Southern soil.

In the four-county area around President Carter's farm in southwest Georgia, the number of black-owned farms declined by 53 percent (from 193 farms to 92) between 1969 and 1974, while white-owned farms decreased by only 14 percent. Even Homer Smothers, the largest black landowner in the area, the one picked as a model farmer, has had problems. Smothers, who farms more than 1000 acres and has a net worth of $700,000, recently was refused a loan by the Production Credit Association. Smothers was saved from difficulty by getting an FHA loan, which normally goes to smaller farmers. "I get a strong feeling that Homer was rejected because he was black," said Hugh Gleaton, the Sumter County FHA supervisor. "He might have become too successful for some of these white board members." James Mays, another black farmer, couldn't get a loan even though he offered over 2000 acres of land as security.

If Smothers and Mays can't get financing, black small area farmers don't have a chance. "Blacks are not going out of business because they don't know how to farm," said Joseph Brooks, Emergency Land Fund director. "They are simply not getting the credit and services white farmers get from the Agriculture Department."

The latest report of the Agriculture Department's own Office of Equal Opportunity noted that FHA farm ownership loans to blacks had steadily declined from 810 in 1971 to 166 last year. Only 44 percent of black farmers participated in Soil Conservation Service programs in Georgia, while 72 percent of white farmers did. The important county ASCS offices, which determine farm payments, employ only 15 blacks out of 753 professionals throughout the South. In Georgia there are two blacks out of 112 professional employees. There are no blacks serving on the ASCS county committees in Georgia and only seven black alternates out of 787 members and alternates. There are only three black committee members in the entire South. Only 11 percent of black farmers in Georgia received agricultural advice from the extension service. Only 51 blacks held professional extension service jobs in Georgia last year. This is three less than the equivalent figure in 1971.

Most black farmers in Sumter County, unable to afford expensive farm machinery, have been forced out of the peanut business. For a time, they can lease their valuable government price support allotments to white farmers, but eventually they will lose these as well, which will effectively bar them from profitable peanut production.

Joe Brooks's Emergency Land Fund is trying to save the black-owned farm by providing services that should come from the Agriculture Department. "I'm a boxed-in farmer," said Fred Bennett, president of a black landowners' association. "I'm limited in land, limited in assets, limited in knowledge of where the market is and how to reach it. I have some acres and can't get any more, but I can't leave it after working it all my life." Bennett hopes that some black farmers will survive by forming cooperatives. There are several black cooperative associations in the South which are fighting to buck the trend.

Southern farmland is growing increasingly valuable as industrial and residential development continues. Industrial development is beginning to edge toward the principal areas of the Southern black population. "We're in a holding pattern," said Brooks. "The question is whether there are going to be any black landowners left when that development gets there—or whether we're all going to be on welfare in Chicago."

Of course there has been progress in the rural South. But I was struck by how much progress today is dependent on federal civil rights laws, federal court orders, and federal assistance programs—ones that the neoconservatives today tell us did not work. Many of the newer problems in the rural South today have a familiar Northern ring to them—problems like "urban removal" of blacks as part of urban renewal, problems like resegregation and tracking in the schools. As one black leader recently told me: "I'll tell you about this New South. It's just like the Old North, and that isn't good enough."

Transportation is a fundamental human need. People require mobility for jobs, for the necessities of life such as groceries, for education, recreation, and many other basics of life. Lack of adequate public transportation in cities is often noted and criticized, but the absence of transportation in nonmetropolitan areas with greater distances can make life impossible. The next article is addressed to this pressing problem and its solution.

2

IRA KAYE

Rural America—You Can't Get There from Here—Yet

There is a growing awareness that one of the factors leading to the decline of rural life in America is the lack of mobility. In our society it has become increasingly difficult for people in rural areas to gain access to the basic services necessary to life.

Evaluations of health and welfare delivery systems, manpower training, economic development and other human resource programs show that such programs reach rural people in inadequate proportions. For instance, rural areas receive only 2.1 per cent of basic adult education funds, 5.5 per cent of health service funds, 10 per cent of manpower training funds and barely a trace of federal transportation funds. Such inequities create a self-fulfilling prophecy of the eventual doom of rural communities.

Since transportation is a commodity which must be bought, rural areas with their disproportionate number of lower income residents suffer most. Additionally, the rural aged appear even more likely to be without transportation.

Although there is a dearth of comprehensive data on the condition

Reprinted from Ira Kaye, "Rural America—You Can't Get There from Here—Yet," *Transit Journal*, May 1975, pp. 61–64, by permission of the author and the journal.

of public transportation in rural areas, the subjective evidence indicates that the rural situation is in as much—if not more—of a dilemma as the urban situation. In 1974 there were only 313 bus systems in towns not located in larger urbanized areas, with a population of under 50,000. In the last 15 years 146 bus companies have disappeared. Most were in towns of less than 25,000 people.

Urban mass transit is receiving increasing attention and resources. Although this is encouraging, there is no assurance that it will continue. The dominant view seems to be that until we achieve a national growth policy of rural development capable of reducing migration of young people, it is doubtful whether Congress will (or should) authorize the funds necessary to provide adequate public transportation for rural people. Recent advances in communication technology could lessen the need for transportation, although these advances will not eliminate it. What is required is a realistic appraisal of the transportation/communication mix necessary to properly serve rural people.

Until recently, among the few voices calling for improved rural transportation services have been representatives of the elderly. They have viewed the transportation problems of the aged as being closely associated with the absence of any effective national rural transportation strategy, and have called for a comprehensive attack on the problem. The 1971 White House Conference on Aging saw transportation as one of the top three problems facing the elderly....

The first significant Federal effort to provide public transit systems in small towns and rural areas were the demonstrations authorized by Section 147 of the Federal Highway Act of 1973, as amended. 102 projects funded at about $25 million were launched in a wide, varied area of rural America. The grants provided for the acquisition of buses or vans and the funds for operating the system. While the evaluation of these projects has not been completed, they have in large part been successful. Congress was sufficiently encouraged to provide a major program in the Surface Transportation Assistance Act of 1978 to aid states and local non-urbanized areas to establish public transit systems. $75 million has been appropriated for the first year and it covers purchase of vehicles and operating expenses. The success of the effort depends on the ability of the states and local governments to achieve the coordination of all of the categorical social service transportation providers with the public system. There are 114 federal programs out there providing resources for transporting people. The new program must be able to coordinate and consolidate these resources. If it only becomes the 115th program it will not succeed.

The American experience with most public utilities, indeed the experience of most industrial countries, indicates that total reliance on the private sector of the economy will not answer the need for adequate mobility in our rural areas. Just as it took federally subsidized financing and other assistance to organize electric and telephone cooperatives, a similar approach might be used to assist in the formation of rural transportation cooperatives. If this option were available, and if there could be assurance of the same type of long-term, low-interest support that the rural electric and telephone cooperatives receive, cooperative regional transit companies might well be part of the answer to the rural dilemma.

These cooperative institutions are an accepted part of the rural scene and it would make it easier for the transit authorities to achieve the degree of integration needed to assure the system its initial operating revenue.

An approach which has not yet been explored is the combination of the existing transportation and communication resources in multicounty rural areas and, with a systems approach, fashion a people-serving comprehensive system. The resources spent by the postal service to pick up and deliver mail, by the school system in picking up and delivering children, by the social service agencies to serve their individual clients, and by the military with their underutilized maintenance and training facilities represent a sizeable investment. If this investment could be restructured into a single system, it could provide a basis for a people transport system at affordable fares.

For example, Switzerland has a highly developed Postal Passenger Service (PTT). The Swiss PTT, and privately licensed companies under contract to PTT, provide public bus transportation and mail conveyance in areas where no railway service is available. Legally bound to keep its rates as low as possible, the PTT uses idle and reserve vehicles for extra trips, particularly for tourists, to generate additional income. The postal bus network extends over 4,700 miles, providing service to 1,600 villages. The average length of a route is about 7.5 miles. Vehicles are made to specifications of the PTT, and are flexible enough in design to be used for a variety of assignments. The PTT owns garages for maintenance and repair work. In the last few years, there has been more than a five per cent increase annually in the level of passenger service. With surprising directness, the PTT states, "It has always been one of the foremost duties of a government to promote good transportation facilities at reasonable charge." That philosophy seems to be the foundation which makes possible such a progressive transportation system.

The fossil fuel crisis is forcing many economists and political scientists to rethink issues and solutions. The Ford Foundation-funded Energy Policy Project, *Exploring Energy Choices*, found that Americans will be required to live closer to work, schools and shopping areas and employ more efficient transport to achieve a viable energy posture. This can only be achieved within the framework of a harmonious rural/urban balance.

What then needs to be done? In spite of the siren call to sacrifice human needs to reduce inflation, a full federal legislative program must be enacted to sponsor rural mass transit opportunities. This adequately-funded program should include the following points:

1. The authority and funds for planning, research and operating subsidies and capital assistance should be provided.
2. Multimodal transportation systems should be tied in.
3. Funding priority for an alternative to rail transit should be given to those communities harmed by rail abandonment plans.
4. Technical assistance and funding should be provided to grassroots organizations so that the consumer side of transportation planning can be presented.

In addition to the proposed federal funding, the following actions should be inaugurated:

1. State and local institutions desiring assistance in meeting the mobility challenge must have a clearinghouse they can rely on to obtain information, data, ideas and staff assistance.
2. Institutions of higher education must be encouraged to advance the state-of-the-art.
3. A well-designed group, dedicated to comprehensive rural development and balanced urban/rural growth, sensitive to the strengths found in people participation, is needed to oversee all activity in rural transportation.

Currently there is no organization which represents the comprehensive rural development approach. Without such an organization it is quite possible that special-interest, fragmented groups will advocate policies which may be conflicting, destructive, or just so expensive for a limited result that the desired fundamental change needed for a rational rural development policy may never be achieved.

Undoubtedly, institutional and functional trade-offs will be required. But, weighed against the human tragedy imposed by lack of mobility and widespread human misery in rural communities, none of these trade-offs seem insurmountable.

This is an era of nostalgia and back-to-nature. As such there is an emphasis now on preservation of the past, including rural life-styles. The question raised in the next article is whether we should destroy in order to save. A value conflict is pointed up. Mention is often made of the "price of progress." Too seldom do we ask whether it is actually progress and whether the price may be too high, considering human elements.

3

KENNETH M. COUGHLIN

Imitation of Past May Wreck Rural Present

The U.S. Forest Service wants to build a scenic highway traversing five rural counties in southwestern Virginia. The 63-mile roadway, say officials, will be the centerpiece of a larger tourist recreation area designed to preserve the rural character of the region. The theme of the recreation area will be "Rural America."

But according to 8,000 residents who have signed petitions opposing it, the highway will make a developer's paradise out of the rural land surrounding the project. In effect, say area residents, the Forest Service is knowingly destroying an authentic part of rural America in order to construct its imitation for tourists.

"You have to see the area to get an idea of what we are talking about," says June Slemp, a spokesperson for Citizens for Southwest Virginia, the group that has formed to fight the $60 million project. "This is going to pretty much destroy the rural quality."

The highway is part of the Forest Service's plans for the Mt. Rogers National Recreation Area (NRA), an elongated, 154,000-acre strip of public land lodged against North Carolina's northern border. It takes its name from Virginia's highest peak.

Reprinted from Kenneth M. Coughlin, "Imitation of Past May Wreck Rural Present," *Rural America*, Vol. 3, No. 8, July 1978, p. 1, by permission of the author and the journal.

The NRA was created in 1966 by a Congress searching for alternatives to other parks in the region which were becoming overcrowded.

At the time, the Forest Service set a goal for the new NRA of five million visitors annually by the year 2000. Thus far, however, visitations have fallen far short, and what is keeping tourists away, the Forest Service says, is poor transportation within the area.

"Traveling from east to west is a very difficult task," says Reggie Kinman, a Forest Service landscape architect. "There are just little farm-to-market roads that don't go anyplace in particular. A lot of the development sites are inaccessible." The proposed two-lane scenic highway, Kinman says, would solve the problem.

But some in the small towns around the NRA dispute this. "We have a beautiful scenic road system through our mountains," says June Slemp. "The new highway will create a lot more traffic than we have now. Our small roads are just not big enough for big campers. Our smaller roads will wind up being access roads to the scenic highway."

The highway's critics fear their towns will become replicas of towns like Boone, N.C., or Gatlinburg, Tenn., which underwent rapid commercialization because of their proximity to major parks.

"They used to be extremely nice places to visit," says Slemp. "They were small communities: they had character. Now you start running into what we like to call junk shops—motels, food chains."

In addition, say highway opponents, land values will increase, driving up taxes. Less well-to-do residents, unable to keep pace with taxes, will leave the area. The tax problem may also hasten the decline of family farms in the area. "This will effectively put the small farmer out of business," says Slemp. "They are barely making it now. They just want to hold on."

The Forest Service views all these changes as inevitable. According to its recently-released environmental impact statement on the NRA, "the general cultural drift of the area is already toward a more urban lifestyle, and the NRA will intensify this drift . . . Research indicates that the rural atmosphere which remains is just a remnant of a period that ended with World War II, when the family farm (a time of family self-sufficiency) began to fade from the scene."

Residents who want to preserve a rural lifestyle find this attitude particularly galling in light of the "Rural America" theme of the NRA. According to the Forest Service, the NRA will "restore, recreate, and perpetuate those elements of early rural America which have had a lasting charm and attraction."

"Living period farms" will be constructed along the highway, and grazing land will be preserved. With the help of a Roanoke architectural firm, Clay and Griggs, the Forest Service is designing all other buildings in the park to conform to the rustic theme.

"People will have a chance to get a glimpse of some of their rural heritage," says Michael Penfold, the supervisor of the national forest surrounding the NRA.

The irony has not been lost on area residents. "The conflict between the real rural America and the "rural America" theme is that on the border of the NRA is the real rural America, and that kind of life may not last," warns Bill Blanton, editor of *The Plow*, a local newspaper.

Slemp adds: "What they plan to do will destroy it for those of us who love it."

The Forest Service and Penfold are mystified by the reception the NRA has been getting in the five counties. "Where in the world people get this idea, I don't know—this idea that we are going to put rural people on display like monkeys in a cage," says Penfold. Few farms will be condemned to make room for the highway, he adds. "It's a poor farming area generally. In most cases, the farming in the area is very marginal."

The deadline for public comments on the scenic highway is early this month, after which the Forest Service will make a final decision on whether to go ahead with its plans.

Louise Pierce is one who will be waiting on that decision. With her husband, she owns 104 mountainous acres, most of which the highway will consume. The Pierces had hoped to eventually build a new house on the land.

"We agree with the Forest Service as far as some of their plan," Mrs. Pierce says. "We just can't see tearing up that whole mountain range. They will ruin everything they've been trying to preserve up here."

Similarity in problems between the United States and many other countries is marked as the following article from England demonstrates. Changing economic activities and concentration of elderly are among the social characteristics in England's rural regions as they are on this side of the Atlantic. Social policy developments aimed at still further change and possible remedies are discussed, and again parallels can be seen between the American and European approaches.

4

JACKIE DENMAN

Problems of Rural Areas

As the inner city was once the hub of trade and industry for a whole area, so the rural areas were centres of intensive economic activity: agriculture, mineral extraction, small skilled craft industry, local service industry all provided opportunities for local employment. Two factors have contributed to the decline of these relatively labour intensive industries: agriculture and extractive industries have become significantly mechanised, with great reductions in manpower requirements, and economies of scale and mass production have led to increased centralisation or closure of small enterprises and local services. The countryside which was once a hive of activity is now seen as a place of rest and quietness, and local job opportunities are very restricted. This massive reduction in the economic base of the rural areas has been combined with a significant rise in their attraction as centres for tourism and recreation, retirement and conservation of the natural environment. These trends have further restricted opportunities for development: conservationist attitudes die hard, and it is

Reprinted from Jackie Denman, "Problems of Rural Areas," *Social Service Quarterly*, Summer 1978, pp. 139–142, by permission of the author and the journal.

only recently that a more widely held progressive attitude towards development has become acceptable.

Coupled with this low level of employment opportunity are problems concerning the housing market. Prices are inflated by demand for retirement and second homes, difficulty is found in raising a mortgage on an older property, few housing developments outside 'key settlements' can obtain planning permission and there is considerable under-occupation of dwellings by high proportions of the elderly.

These two factors alone lead to a growing distortion in the age structure of the rural population: as opportunities for the young diminish, the proportion of elderly people in such areas is increasing. This process causes a spiral of declining opportunities for the young, and the resulting imbalance in the community is not only regrettable in itself, but also leads to increasing demands for services for the elderly as those who were once independent and mobile find themselves less able to cope with life in a remote and poorly served community.

Although there are opportunities in the rural areas which do not exist in towns, they are not always recognised or valued by those who live there. Young people in particular wish to experience a wide range of new activities, and opportunities for these are restricted in the rural areas. For instance, organised youth and recreational facilities are often remote from the small villages, and inaccessible to those without their own transport. For families, factors such as the location of the nearest primary school, the doctor's surgery, the post office must be taken into account in deciding where to live. As more and more services are centralised, the rural areas are left without many of their lifelines. Access becomes of great importance, and public transport services are poor.

The deprivation of the rural areas lies in a poverty of experience. Contact with other people is often restricted, choice is limited, the opportunity to do a number of things, particularly specialised interests, does not exist. The influence of the media means that young people have expectations of life which cannot always be fulfilled in their immediate environment. The challenge is to provide opportunities for those who do wish to stay in the country to do so, and to lead a fulfilling and satisfying life.

LOCAL LIMITATIONS

Attitudes in rural areas do not always help: partly as a result of being cut off from main centres, people are poorly informed and unaware of the implications of many important developments for their own immediate area. There is little knowledge of the functioning of local authorities and public agencies, and the bigger voluntary organisations have little contact with much of the rural area which they cover. Expectations are low and interests are parochial. Political leadership can often be remote from those communities which it seeks to represent: the task of maintaining effective contact with a scattered population is daunting. Minority groups are often scattered and seldom sufficiently organised to develop satisfactory aid and support. The statutory services are hardpressed to cover the wide areas into which they are organised. It is hard to develop good communications with the large number of scattered villages involved, and the development of new work is restricted by existing commitments.

There has been no comprehensive approach to the problems of rural areas by the Government: a number of government departments and agencies have a particular interest in the rural areas, but there has been little attempt to bring these together, or to harmonise their respective policies. Whilst the inner city areas have received considerable attention and there have been a number of government-sponsored schemes and programmes to tackle their problems, little consideration has been given to the rural areas. The main government agencies with a central concern for the rural areas are the Ministry of Agriculture, Fisheries and Food, the Development Commission, the Countryside Commission, the Forestry Commission, the Nature Conservancy Council and the Sports Council. A number of interests of the Department of the Environment are clearly relevant. Other government departments have some considerable impact on the rural areas, but mainly in a rather negative way by virtue of the fact that the rural areas are accorded low priority in their policies, thus exacerbating the problem of centralisation of services. The Department of Transport is an exception in that it is trying to examine particularly the problems of transport in rural areas, and is sponsoring a series of experiments to discover alternative means of providing a public transport service to the rural population.

POLICY REVIEW

In 1974 the Countryside Review Committee, chaired and serviced within the Department of the Environment, was set up to consider government policy as it affects the countryside. The main government interests in the countryside are represented on this committee, but they are essentially land use interests. The Committee is publishing a series of topic papers to generate discussion on the main issues, the first of which was concerned with rural communities. The comments of the Standing Conference of Rural Community Councils (RCCS) on this paper have been presented to the Department of the Environment. Their main concern is with the attitude of government policy to the rural areas. The Government sees the countryside as an area for food production, for the conservation of natural beauty and amenity and where the pleasures of the countryside can be made available to as great a number of people as possible. The essential questions concerning the future of rural communities are, according to the CRC topic paper, economic. The RCC response states that there are inherent positive strengths in small, rural communities which justify active policies to maintain them for their own sake. The CRC paper was nevertheless welcomed as a step in the right direction, particularly as it is an attempt to bring together a number of government agencies to look at policies towards the rural areas. A coherent and explicit government rural policy would be greatly welcomed.

The government agency with the most central concern for the social and economic wellbeing of the rural areas is the Development Commission (DC). Its Development Fund is at present being used to support three main areas of activity:

1. The construction of small factory premises in rural areas of England where diversity of or increased employment is needed to prevent or check depopulation or to meet other rural problems.
2. The provision through the Council for Small Industries in Rural Areas (COSIRA) of business management and technical advice, instruction and limited credit for small manufacturing and servicing industries in rural parts of England.
3. The work of voluntary, self-governing bodies which provide in areas of the countryside and country towns a wide variety of service designed to enrich social or cultural life for country people and their environment (e.g., RCCS, NCSS, etc.).

A full account of the work of the Development Commission is given in its current annual report.

For the sphere of work concerned with factory building the Commission has designated Special Investment Areas. These are largely marginal upland areas, but they also include some lowland farming areas such as Norfolk and Lincolnshire. 114 new factory units were approved during the period April 1976 to March 1977. In the Special Investment Areas the Commission has worked in partnership with the local authorities. An action plan has been drawn up for each area by the local authorities involved, specifying areas for investment by the Commission in advance factories and supporting action to be undertaken by the local authorities. This normally relates to housing, transport and service infrastructure. Joint committees have also been set up for each Special Investment Area, involving local authorities and other relevant agencies, sometimes including the RCC.

The Commission has also revised the policies for COSIRA to intensify services in the Special Investment Areas, and has asked the Small Industries Committee in each county to identify other areas, or 'pockets of need,' requiring special attention. Similarly, the Commission has suggested that RCCS should give consideration to putting similar priorities on their own work, and to becoming fully involved with the work which COSIRA are undertaking. They are seen to have an important strategic role as they are particularly knowledgeable of, and sensitive to, the needs of country people and are very close to the pulse of the community. Many RCCS are involved in working groups with COSIRA and other agencies to look at the needs of these areas and to identify action which might be taken. This partnership between the economic and social interests could prove very fruitful.

STIMULATING DEVELOPMENT

In their own work RCCS are seeking to involve the local rural communities as fully as possible in the decision making which affects them and in taking local action in response to particular problems which have been identified. Field officers funded by the Development Commission have been appointed to 25 RCCS, and have been involved in developing effective public participation in planning; encouraging the local community to consider its own situation, identify needs and draw up a programme of local action to tackle some of these problems; and working in general to raise the level of awareness of local people as to the nature of their problems and ways of achieving local solutions. Local community organisations are particularly important in this process, and the presence of local (parish) councils throughout the rural areas is a great asset in this work. This third tier of local government is an instrument of great potential, and the RCCS, with the County Associations of Local Councils, are working hard to develop and strengthen their role in local affairs.

The Development Commission is also sponsoring a series of projects to provide guidance on an effective range of methods for a general programme of work at a local level, each to be associated with one of the Special Investment Areas. These projects will be concerned with broad issues of social development and most will seek to create a constructive involvement of the local communities, both in drawing up a programme of priorities for action and in taking responsibility to tackle particular issues. As with the inner cities programme, the significant step in these projects is to encourage and develop a comprehensive approach to the problems of an area: to involve a wide range of local community organisations, public agencies and individual professionals in looking beyond their usual boundaries to take a wider view. Community participation and voluntary effort have great potential to contribute much of value to these projects. There is a need for experience and information about developments in different parts of the rural areas to be shared amongst those involved. With co-operation from RCCS the NCSS has begun to develop this role, and it is hoped to expand it further in the future.

The recently published Wolfenden Report on the future of voluntary organisations emphasises the importance of the role of RCCS as local intermediary bodies, and in particular their development role. The priority for imaginative development work for RCCS would appear to be in those areas of deprivation identified within each county, seeking ways of achieving a constructive partnership between local communities and local and central government.

How natural disasters create problems for people that may persist long after the disaster has subsided is examined in the following article. It is seen how sometimes one problem results in others and that action aimed at helping people cope may have its own negative consequences. The slowness of government's responsiveness to human needs when powerful business vested interests are present is also discussed.

5

Still in HUD's Lowlands

Receding waters of the 1977 floods in southeastern West Virginia left hundreds living in trailers loaned them by the federal government. Now, fifteen months later, more than 600 families still reside in the "temporary" housing, and the chances of their soon finding permanent homes appear slim.

The trailer-dwellers have been left high and dry because most suitable land in the area is corporation-owned. Many who would already have purchased their trailers and moved them to higher ground, or else have found other housing, remain mired because dry land is unavailable.

The state of West Virginia has taken upon itself the task of coaxing land from the corporations and now is claiming many victories in its negotiations with land companies. But critics in Mingo county, the area hardest hit by the flooding, say the state has made negligible progress. Even the state director for the Department of Housing and Urban Development (HUD), the lead federal agency in the recovery effort, has termed the land crisis a "major problem" in moving families from temporary to permanent housing.

Reprinted from "Still in HUD's Lowlands," *Rural America*, July 1978, p. 3, by permission of the journal.

The Tug Valley Recovery Center (TVRC), a non-profit group based in Mingo county formed to aid West Virginia flood victims, is blaming the state for failing to act boldly in buying land from corporate landowners. They contend that the state has the power to acquire land for private housing by condemnation, a claim the state has consistently denied. According to the TVRC, the state is showing more concern for absentee landowners than for flood victims.

At a state capital news conference held late last year, TVRC spokesman Jerry Hildebrand accused Governor Jay Rockefeller of "proceeding most timidly" in acquiring land under what Hildebrand called "the wide discretionary powers" given the governor in the flood relief bill.

At the time, a spokesman for Rockefeller announced that "massive negotiations" with landowners would bring "unprecedented results."

The state believes it has been making headway in these negotiations and spokesmen now boast that they have produced "major breakthroughs."

According to Brooks McCabe, the governor's housing coordinator, the state is closing deals with a Philadelphia land company; 100 acres in Mingo county may be available for housing this summer. McCabe said another 100 acres will be created from the landfill of a nearby interstate highway some time in the next two years, and a soon-to-be-stripmined mountaintop will be reclaimed by the state and used for housing within the next ten years.

But many in Mingo county are unimpressed by the results of the governor's negotiations. According to TVRC's Sister Mary Margaret Pignone, one of the new land acquisitions will displace at least twelve families now living on the land, and some of the land located near the interstate will be reserved for over a hundred people who are being displaced by the highway.

"The whole notion of stripmining a mountaintop" she adds, "is ludicrous. People here just laugh at it. Part of the agreement is that the company would be allowed to stripmine the mountain."

"They keep announcing this as the grand plan," Sister Pignone concludes, "but when you start analyzing, it's only 50 housing units. We are talking about a year and a half after the flood. The state has not moved expeditiously to buy land. It is basically the state's responsibility and the state is failing miserably. It is working hand in glove with industry."

Meanwhile, those still in the trailers have little idea where they will go. In the wake of the flood, many of the homeless were given two and three-bedroom mobile homes by HUD, with the understanding that the families could live in the trailers for one year free of charge, after which they would be assessed a small monthly rent based on their ability to pay. The families were also given a chance to purchase the trailers, with the proviso that the trailers would be moved to land above the flood plain.

Although HUD has set trailer prices as low as five dollars, only 110 families have been able to take advantage of the offer.

Most of the free leases will be up this month, and the families will begin paying rent. In a recent TVRC survey of county trailer residents, nearly half of those questioned had "no idea" what they would do if forced to find permanent housing.

*The women's movement is a conspicuous development currently.
But as the next article points out, women have had difficulty
deriving the benefits from the extensive contributions they have
been making on farms for years. They also are disadvantaged in
attempts to move into farming. Changes are beginning to take
place, and more women can be expected in agriculture in the
future.*

6

FRANCES HILL

Why Women Deserve More Opportunity in Farming

"Farmer" is a male noun to most Americans. Women have found
increased opportunities for meaningful and rewarding careers in many
sectors of the economy but not in agriculture.

Women held 17 percent of non-farm administrator and manager
positions by 1970 and 40 percent of the nation's professional and
technical personnel were women. But only about four percent of all
farmers and farm managers were women. The number of women listed
in the Census as "farmers and farm managers" declined from a high
of almost 308,000 in 1900 to only 63,000 in 1970.

During this period, of course, the number of farms and the number
of male "farmers and farm managers" also declined. However, the
number of male farmers declined by a small percentage from a larger
initial number. Women have sought greater economic opportunity the
past 15 years, not simply as wives but as independent economic actors.
Why hasn't agriculture provided opportunities for such women?

One common assumption is that women simply do not want to

Reprinted from Frances Hill, "Why Women Deserve More Opportunity in Farming," *Catholic Rural Life*, Vol. 27, No. 4, April 1978, pp. 8–10, by permission of the
author and the journal.

farm, My research among Midwest farm women, married and single, suggests that many women have a keen interest in agriculture. To the surprise of the Extension Service, women have flocked to programs on dairy production and herd improvement once they were invited to attend. What some see as a lack of interest in agriculture may instead be lack of opportunity.

A second reason for the limited number of women in agriculture is the idea that members of the "weaker sex" are too delicate for the physical demands of farming. Current research on physiology and the historical role of women on American farms questions this idea. Whether married or single, American women have always been welcome to "help" with the farm work.

Abigail Adams ran the family's farm while her husband John tried to run the country. Frontiersmen settled their wives and children on a farm while they roamed further west in search of opportunity, adventure, and amusement.

Modern farm women take pride in their ability to keep the books, drive tractors, and care for livestock. They resent the suggestion that men "farm" and women only "help." If the Department of Agriculture would begin collecting data on women's as well as men's contributions to farm labor and management, these basic realities of the "family farm" would be more widely recognized.

The hypocrisy of the idea that women are too delicate to farm is suggested by the 141,000 women the Census included in its "farm laborers and farm foremen" category in 1970. This total actually is higher due to the presence of large numbers of undocumented workers in American fields.

Official estimates indicate women currently account for 15 percent of agricultural laborers. In 1910 there were 1.5 million women farm laborers, which was 25 percent of the total farm labor force. This does not include wives, who have always been expected to donate their energy to their family and to the family farm.

Women have worked on farms but that work has been "hidden from history" by a screen of cultural myths about female delicacy and male gallantry. Historical data suggest that chivalry consisted of relieving women of the burden of owning and controlling property, not in freeing them from labor. Discounting the possibility that owning a farm would be more physically taxing then working on one, the reasons that there are few independent women farmers are the same as the reasons there are still few women professors or astronauts or independent businesspersons or bank presidents. Women have been denied the right to control the enterprises on which they have toiled.

A third reason, then, for the limited opportunities open to women in agriculture has been the limited credit available to women. Discrimination against women in granting credit did not become illegal until 1976. Women were always more than welcome to co-sign the mortgage but not to own the property, as farm women have begun to realize when confronting the estate tax laws.

Systematic data on loan application and the rate of approval for single women is not available. Most bankers or Farmers Home Administration directors or Production Credit Association managers will say that they do not discriminate against women. Those few women who have managed to establish their own farming operations agree. However, no one has yet studied women who were rejected for credit or women who wanted to farm but were discouraged in other ways. Most people I interviewed agree there is skepticism, at the very least, about a woman who wants to farm on her own.

Two factors suggest that more women may successfully seek to establish their own farms in the future. First, the agricultural colleges have, during the past three to four years, admitted a significant number of young women to production-related courses. These women will have proved that they are both competent and serious. Second, the struggle by farm women for change in the inheritance tax laws already means more widows are able to keep their farms and that young widows will be able to make careers as independent farmers. Their example may make it easier for single women to enter farming.

Like the previous article the following one also addresses the women's movement. A number of examples are provided of women of all ages instituting various activities to enhance their own situations and those of their families. While the degree of activism varies, most groups of rural women who are organizing are doing so in rather conventional ways and around traditional content.

7

LYNN RHENISCH

Is a Feminist Mood Rising in Rural America?

Signs are that rural women—traditionally an oppressed but poorly developed political force—have begun organizing and asserting their strength. New feminist groups can be found in every region of rural America. Their concerns are diverse, ranging from land reform and health care to agricultural policy and employment, but they appear to share a common perspective as rural women and to feel a common need to voice their grievances.

"The biggest problem for rural women today," notes Florence Rachwal of American Agri-Women, "is to be heard."

Intense isolation and lack of communication seem the most common problems cited by rural women throughout the country. Feelings of hopelessness and of "no options" exacerbate the limited education opportunities, poor employment chances and other social limitations facing 34 million women. Groups attempting to address these problems are themselves beset with special difficulties: long journeys on country roads, farm responsibilities, bad weather and child care obligations are formidable obstacles of the formation of stable groups.

Yet rural women are banding together to carve a more central place

Reprinted from Lynn Rhenisch, "Is a Feminist Mood Rising in Rural America?" *Rural America*, Vol. 3, No. 4, March 1978, p. 10, by permission of the author and the journal.

for themselves on the national scene. They come from what seem to be three major sources: a conservative, land-based, auxiliary-like movement devoted to farm market interests; social activists committed to local economic and political self-determination; and an admixture of people working on such issues as land trusts and cooperative health care in an effort to build social and personal alternatives.

Neille Pike is president of a group that represents the first type. She and her organization, Tennessee Valley Cotton Wives, have met twice yearly to put on banquets, fashion shows and fairs for the purpose of promoting cotton.

"We wanted to do something to help our husbands," says Ms. Pike. "They're too busy running the farms to do all this." Her group is concerned with such issues as parity and the rising farm costs that threaten to drive some farmers out of business.

Tennessee Valley Cotton Wives is affiliated with a large umbrella organization of farm women known as American Agri-Women. Formed in 1974, American Agri-Women is made up of 22 affiliates, with an individual membership of 3,000 women in 32 states. Members focus on such commodities as beef, dairy, fruits and vegetables, cotton and poultry. Their stated goal is to preserve the family farm.

Judy Gillan is a member of Women in Agriculture, Food Policy and Land Use Reform. The group, located in Northhampton Massachusetts, sees the disappearance of a small farm economy in New England as its major concern. Keeping their organization small, members offer technical assistance to other local groups and participate in state-wide policy planning aimed at reviving a decentralized, small-farm economy. One of their aims is to establish a New England Farm Institute, an alternative to the "bigger is better" land grant colleges, where people will be able to learn land-based skills—"not how the corn grows, but how to grow the corn."

Noting that 85 percent of New England's food comes from outside the region, Ms. Gillan says her organization worries about an attitude toward agriculture that turns "some of the most fertile land in the nation" into shopping centers, and "sees cornfields as logical building sites."

She sees women's involvement in national affairs increasing, "because they are no longer content to sit at home and live with the decisions. Historically, women have had to live with the consequences of past policies. They are the ones who are faced with a vast array of inferior food, for example. "Because we're women, out there doing things and talking," says Ms. Gillan, "we've made ourselves visible as competent people. And because women can see the consequences, they have been able to come up with the most holistic approach."

A group committed to self-determination is MATCH, Inc., a craft marketing cooperative that stretches over eight states with a membership of 8,000 families. It was started in 1974 as a spinoff project of CORA (Committee on Religion in Appalachia), in response to a need for a crafts market.

"In the 1960s," said Nina Poage, a leader in the Co-op, "we saw a lot of anti-poverty money come in to stimulate economic development. Various programs encouraged the production of craft items, but they never developed a marketing system for them. That's what MATCH was designed to do—a matching up of the producers with the market." The group holds fairs, publishes a catalogue and owns and operates a retail store in Lexington, Kentucky.

"Eighty to ninety percent of our members are women," Ms. Poage said. Most of them are rural, many of them elderly. Many senior citizens have never had an education beyond the 8th grade. The only thing a rural elderly woman can do is use her God-given talent. Then in economic terms she is affecting her life and the economic well-being of the community.

"Crafts is something the Appalachian woman can feel good about. If she can sell her quilt for $80 to $200 instead of the $10 or $20 she used to get, she is contributing to her family. And she's not disturbing the status quo of family relationships. Keeping the traditional roles is very important."

Meanwhile 60 women in Stearns, Kentucky, banded together last March to form the Stearns Miners' Wives Club, mainly in support of their striking husbands. But like so many wifely groups before them— including Kentucky's family Brookside Women's Club of the strike-ridden 1930s—the women of Stearns have found additional reasons to stay together, reasons that may have more to do with female unity than with labor solidarity.

"The Brookside group still meets," says Irene Vanover, president of the Stearns organization. "They even sent us a check last month. I expect our group will be going long after the strike is over."

In Rutland, Vermont, the Southern Vermont Women's Health Center is a cooperative dedicated "to working collectively to provide good health care at a price every woman can afford, and to provide it in a supportive atmosphere."

Four-years-old now and still going strong, with no outside funding, the Center provides gynecological checkups and birth control advice. Because the staff serves most rural women, they hope to expand their program to help with problems of transportation and child care that their patients often face.

"There were strong feelings," says Susan Farrow, a member of the collective, "that women wanted to be the decision-makers, to take the power back into their own hands. That's why we organized."

In Wolf Creek, Oregon, Elana Mikels, a retired social worker from San Francisco, has formed with other rural women an organization called "our OWN" (Older Women's Network). Responding to a need for older women to be with others their own age, they are attempting to lessen social isolation through a network of correspondence, newsletters and retreats. They envision the creation of self-sufficient rural women's communities, in the form of land trusts, offering "emotional, spiritual and economic support to women in an environment that is healthful, wholesome and congenial."

Legal problems, relative to land, abound for rural southern blacks as the next article written by an attorney explains. As land passes from generation to generation it is subdivided into smaller holdings. These are not useful for obtaining financing. There is also the problem of the land being lost by its owners. Federal lending agencies impose more demanding requirements for loans than is required by the enabling legislation, thus contributing to lost opportunities for people.

8

C. SCOTT GRABER

Where There's No Will, There's No Way

One-third of the land held by blacks in the rural South cannot be bought, sold or traded away, nor can it be used as collateral for housing or for agriculture. Commonly called "heirs property," it is almost without market value. Tens of thousands of black farm families and millions of acres of farmland are affected.

To understand heirs property one must recall a little southern history. In the rural South, especially among blacks, wills and other testamentary devices were rare. When a man died, his land usually passed by statute to his wife and children. When the wife and children died, the land passed to the grandchildren. Two or three generations later one hundred people could be part owners of one hundred acres.

But what is wrong with shared ownership? After all, the land can be lived on and farmed by any of its owners. Yes, the land can be lived on and farmed, but that's about the extent of it. Because ownership is uncertain or scattered, this land cannot be mortgaged, or put up as collateral to finance farm equipment, or used in any other way to generate credit.

Reprinted from C. Scott Graber, "Where There's No Will, There's No Way," *Rural America*, Vol. 3, No. 8, July 1978, p. 3, by permission of the author and the journal.

But the biggest problem is not the credit; the biggest problem is the likelihood that the property will be lost by those who own it. Any one of the various "heirs" can sell his interest in the land. A person—or developer—bent on acquisition can purchase the interest of any single heir, then demand that "his" interest be partitioned from the tract. If the land cannot be easily subdivided—and very often that is the case—then the court will order a sale of the land and a division of the proceeds. It is not uncommon for the person triggering the sale to purchase the entire tract, which may have been the plan from the beginning.

Land in South Carolina's Sea Islands (a popular coastal resort) and tracts in the Citronelle oil field (north of Mobile, Alabama) were forced on the market by this device. These involuntary sales remain a serious problem in Alabama. The Emergency Land Fund (ELF)—a non-profit organization created to slow black land loss in the South—spends a great deal of time trying to rally heirs, raise enough money to purchase the endangered property and protect those heirs who live on the land. The Alabama office of the ELF participated in at least 70 partition suits last year.

Tax sales can be an equally serious consequence of multiple owner-ship. Usually one heir, the one still living on the land, has been paying the taxes. His death precipitates a crisis. Which heir will assume the tax burden? Who will return home and maintain the land? Sometimes the family discovers that no one is interested in farming or paying the taxes. If the family is small, it may be able to consolidate the interests and sell, but this kind of cooperation is difficult when twenty, forty or more people are involved.

While there are many reasons that black owners lose their land—including voluntary sales—heirs property accelerates the process. With two or three exceptions, every county in the South having sig-nificant minority land ownership "lost" a large part of that ownership between 1969 and 1974. If the attrition continues, one can reasonably assume that black land ownership in the South will virtually vanish by 1985.

Another problem is credit. The Farmers Home Administration (FmHA) has a well-intentioned housing program designed to put lower-income families under a decent roof, but when it comes to security for a loan, the agency is stiff-necked. It wants clear title, and nothing else will do. The Housing Act of 1949 (the measure that created the FmHA's program) does not insist on clear title. The lan-guage of that act requires security "upon the applicant's equity in the farm" that will reasonably assure repayment of the debt. There is even language in the regulations that would allow the use of "a partial interest" to secure a housing loan, when the interest is large enough to cover the value of the loan.

In spite of this language, Farmers Home rarely lends money secured by an interest in heirs property. In most instances, the FmHA county supervisor will advise a person with an interest in heirs property—regardless of the *size* of that interest—to find another piece of land. Or, he might advise the person to buy a mobile home.

Early this year a bill was introduced in Congress that would have helped these black farmers. Senate Bill 1150 would have authorized the secretary of agriculture to make loans on land even when there were "remote outstanding claims."

The distant cousin in Cleveland who will not cooperate or even acknowledge that he has a one-sixty-fourth interest would not be allowed to block the loan; this interest would be identified as "remote."

But it appears that the Congress is going to reject this language. The failure of the Farmers Home Administration to endorse the amendment seems responsible for its deletion from the final bill. This is a tragedy. For the first time we had an opportunity at the federal level to untangle this legal mess and put millions of acres of land back into productive use. For the time being, at least, we have let that chance slip by.

The next item is short but says a great deal. It suggests that contemporary intelligence tests contain an urban bias. A few years ago we began to realize that ethnic and racial minority groups were subjected to testing utilizing instruments designed with a slant that worked to their disadvantage. Now it appears that the same thing may be true for rural dwellers as compared to urbanites. If this is the case, the implications can be profound.

9

I.Q.'s Flunk Rural Test

A college psychology professor says most I.Q. tests are rigged against rural children.

In an interview with *ruralamerica*, George W. Albee, a professor of psychology at the University of Vermont, claimed most tests contain a definite urban bias. This bias, he said, is a result of the sampling techniques used in constructing the tests.

"I think that most tests heavily rely on vocabulary that is part of the urban culture," Albee said. "Simply take a look at the words kids are being asked to define and you will find they are very clearly oriented for city kids."

He gave as examples words like subway, delicatessen and smog, which he said would be more familiar to urban than to rural children.

Albee, a past president of the American Psychological Association, said urban-oriented words are likely to be used on tests because most tests rely largely on city samples. Before I.Q. tests are used on the general public, they are tried on a random sample of children, who then become the standard by which other children are judged.

These samples are heavily weighted with urban children, Albee said,

Reprinted from "I.Q.'s Flunk Rural Test," *Rural America*, Vol. 3, No.7, June 1978, p. 11, by permission of the journal.

because of the ease with which responses can be collected. "They are all right there in one place," he explained.

Albee cited one of the most popular tests, the Wechsler Intelligence Scale for Children, as a typical example. "Wechsler (developer of the test) spent most of his professional life at Bellevue hospital in New York," Albee said. "His test was standardized on a group from New York City."

The final article in this section reinforces the point with which we started, change. Beale describes the dramatic changes that are occurring in rural America and speculates about the future, including wondering what impact gasoline prices and shortages may have on movement of people to the country. In May 1979 gasoline had reached one dollar a gallon, amidst predictions that it was headed for double that price and for severe shortages and rationing. We may indeed soon learn just how far rural development can and will go.

10

CALVIN BEALE

Renewal of Population Growth in Rural and Small-Town America

Twenty years ago in the Department of Agriculture, a colleague and I put out an annual report on trends in the farm population. Each year we would have to say that there had been an out-migration of about a million and a half people leaving the farms. We were the bearers of bad news and we were unpopular because no one wanted the farm population to decline. When we put the report out, congressmen of the opposition party felt obliged to comment on it. Now this was in the Benson administration, so Democrats in Congress would immediately issue a statement noting this huge decline, deploring it and blaming it all on the Republican administration. In the 1960's, during the Freeman agricultural administration, we were still having about a million people a year leaving the farm. So Republicans in Congress would issue statements condemning this change and blaming it on the administration in power. What it really illustrated was the fact that the

Reprinted from Calvin Beale, "Renewal of Population Growth in Rural and Small-Town America," *Conference on Rural America: Proceedings*, July 1976, pp. 30–31, by permission of the author and the Minnesota Humanities Commission.

set of forces causing the out-migration was extremely powerful. There was a complex of issues reflecting a profound technological revolution. The out-migration was inevitable. It did not really result from agricultural policies, except that they certainly affected the timing of it. When I would hear a politician making a speech of this type, I would find myself asking rhetorically, "If that's the explanation here, what's causing the out-migration of farm people in the Soviet Union, Sweden, England, Canada, France, Germany, Italy, and Australia, and in every other even semi-advanced nation of the world?" The movement is something that has transcended political systems and national boundaries.

We couldn't keep taking a million people out of the farm population every year. We weren't going to abandon farming, so the end had to come sometime. The widespread turnaround in rural and small town population that is observed nationally since 1970 had begun in some areas before that and was a little more delayed in others. It's of major significance and it's happening much faster than I thought it would. In the 1960's we had a net loss of about three million people from the non-metropolitan counties of the U.S. In the '50's it was more like six or seven million in the decade. Since 1970, however, an average of about 400,000 more people each year have moved into the non-metropolitan counties of the U.S. than have moved out of them. I want to stress that it is dramatic, multifaceted change. Few movements are simple. It can be shown to affect 48 of the 50 states, and those two exceptions are small, basically metropolitan New England states. It is not just a sprawling out from metropolitan areas. That is taking place, yes, but the larger trend is much more than that. It's not just people coming out to new suburbs. Since the late '60's, there has been a near end to the displacement out of agriculture and an absolute end to the displacement of people out of mining, which is a major rural industry. The drop in coal mining in Appalachia, for example, ended in 1969. Since 1970 we've had more rapid growth of employment in trade, services, communication, transportation, construction, in fact every major industry category in the non-metropolitan areas, than we have had in the metro area—with the exception of government. Government employment is still growing more rapidly in the metropolitan areas, but that is mostly state and local government expansion rather than federal.

There are also non-economic aspects to this movement. The ecological and environmental movements and the youth revolution have all effected a change in attitudes of people as to where they would like to live, and what scale, what size of community they would like to live in. In addition we've had a major increase in the number of retired people. The number of people who as retired workers receive benefits under the social security system has been increasing about five per cent a year each year since 1970; whereas, the total population has been growing only by about one per cent a year. Millions of these people have a comparable private pension plan which when added to social security gives them not just a survival income, but a good, decent retirement income. Most of them don't move when they retire, but those who do, move disproportionately to rural and small town areas.

Many people have become discouraged with life in the major cities. Problems of crime, drugs, pollution, congestion and racial conflicts have all been factors in motivating people either not to migrate to such areas or to move away if they already live there. The small metropolitan areas—the Rochester, Fargo, Sioux Falls types—have been behaving demographically more like the rural areas and very small towns. They are attracting more migrants into them now than before. The cutting point seems to be up around the level of three quarters of a million population. Above that, areas are either having out-migration or attracting, on the average, fewer migrants than before. Below that, they are increasing the trend of in movement or reversing from decline to growth.

Not every county is now growing. We still have about 600 rural counties that are declining in population. But that's only half the number that were declining in the '60's and their rate of decline is typically just a fraction of what it used to be. Some of the growth is going into very small towns. Some of it is going into the open country. It is not simply a growth inside places such as Crookston or Thief River Falls. Ten years ago you could hardly read an article on the small town without the term "dying small town." A stereotype like this is usually based on a kernel of truth, but that stereotype has colored in a pernicious way our public thinking on small towns. Most of them under 2,500 population were not declining, and of those that were, only a minority were having major declines. But it's true that in Minnesota and the Dakotas, there were many little places with two, three, four hundred people that were declining in population. Most rural towns of less than 2,500 people in the U.S. have had a decline in the number of retail, consumer-oriented business establishments. I think this has misled us into thinking that they were all having declines in population. The dying in the small towns has mostly been a death of business functions, but in a majority of them the residential function has remained. Today this residential function is increasing. People are increasingly living out in the open country, building homes, occupying the abandoned farm homes, living in small villages.

I don't know what the future will hold for this trend. There is a combination of forces now acting here that has built up a momentum that will last at least through this decade and take us into the next. The trend seems to place more people in the kind of community in which they would like to live, with respect to size and scale of settlement. It is not an energy conservative form of settlement. What would happen if we had another oil embargo or if the price of gasoline got up to where it is in Europe at $1.25 or $1.30 a gallon? Rural people do have a greater dependence on private transportation and gasoline than the urban people. Data show that they consume more gasoline per capita. If we had a true energy crisis, this could affect the movement we see.

The trend does change the age composition of the local population. There are more retirement areas, but also many counties that are being buttressed by younger people. The trend does create a demand for new services or expanded services. It creates water and sewage demands and problems if the growth takes place too quickly. So often social movements don't happen at the pace that would be most desirable even if the overall trend itself is desirable. What is happening is of a nationally significant character and, like that earlier movement from the farm, it is international in its character too. We're leading the way, but reports of decentralization are beginning to come in from other highly urbanized nations in the world, that, in fact, have all the urbanization they need.

II.   Rural Human Services

One of the most frequently encountered observations about the nonurban scene is that there is a dearth of human services. This clearly is an accurate portrayal, but more is involved. In part what appears to be an absence of resources is instead a difference in resources. General, or what Ginsberg calls basic, resources such as county public social service agencies ("welfare departments") are present. It is the more specialized kinds of provisions that are lacking. A medical illustration may make the point; depending upon size many rural communities have doctors who are general practitioners or family physicians but few have neurosurgeons or cardiovascular specialists.

The presence of a social agency in a county is only one of the considerations; some rural counties are geographically large and a client or potential client may reside many miles from the county seat town or population centers where an agency is located. In such instances distance and lack of proximity are the obstacles to the availability of services rather than actual absence. One response to this problem is to operate a system of one or more satellite offices in outlying sections of a county. Obtaining a feasible site can be difficult, and in some communities churches, schools, or other public facilities are utilized. This exemplifies the kind of resourcefulness and flexibility required to provide needed services in some rural areas.

One means for expanding the accessibility of services to rural dwellers is to make the programs mobile and bring them to the consumer. This has been done with libraries, certain health programs, and other provisions as described in one of the following articles. Mobility of services is not a panacea, of course, but it can greatly increase utilization.

Another aspect of programming for human needs in areas of towns and farms is to add to the basic services other narrower or more specialized measures. A family life education program might be added to a mental health center. A planned parenthood clinic could be opened in an unused section of an existent small hospital operated by a town or county. Or some other program may be appended to a public welfare agency. In other words rural communities typically are not able to afford or support an array of separate special programs characteristic of the city but may be able to provide some of these measures, even many, through multipurpose organizations.

In addition to the need for multipurpose approaches in planning for social services, another possible answer in providing required resources is to plan in larger geographical units, for example, multicounty. In Iowa at the present time training and education for handicapped and developmentally disabled children is afforded by multicounty area education agencies (AEAs). Many school social workers are employed in these multidiscipline systems, which now cover the entire state and bring services to widely scattered children, families, schools, and other agency personnel. A county mental health center in a rural area has entered into agreements with two neighboring smaller counties through which a member of the center staff spends one day a week in each of the other two counties seeing clients, doing advocacy, providing consultation, and engaging in various forms of intervention and planning. Antipoverty community action programs serve regions through multipurpose neighborhood centers in scattered locations in multiple counties. Antiquated county jails may be replaced by regional correctional facilities. There is an impressive list of actual provisions and potential possibilities for providing human services on a broader geographic scale than has often been done.

A caveat is necessary, however, in that small towns often take great civic pride and boast of their local organizations. There may be competition between neighboring communities and long-standing rivalries that impede cooperative efforts. When school or church closings are proposed through consolidations and mergers with the idea of a more economic and efficient operation, there is often immense local opposition and expression of the community's investment in its own organizations. The "loss" of a school, for example, may be equated in local minds with the demise of the town.

A noteworthy characteristic of the means by which nonmetropolitan communities meet human needs is informality. This informality is one reason it is sometimes concluded that services do not exist in small communities when in fact they do, but not in the usual urban mode. Clergy often provide considerable direct service such as counseling, and local law enforcement persons such as county sheriff, town police, constable, or marshal also offer assistance in crises situations and other problems. School personnel, physicians, and public health persons are among the informal helpers.

An illustration of how programs develop and operate in some small communities may be useful. Some years ago just outside the town limits of the county seat in one rural county was the most popular night spot in the community. In a dry state mixed drinks are hard to find and illegal liquor was always available there. The proprietor had moved easily from rum-running during prohibition to liquor by the drink when only beer was legal. In addition to these activities, he was active in community affairs and could be counted on to initiate a fund drive for any distressed family. He was especially active in a local club and was dedicated to its program of eye donations. Anyone patronizing his bar very long would find him or herself with a donor's card and involved in a discussion of the importance of organ donations. It can be assumed that this small town had an inordinate number of eye donors, thanks to the bar "over the line."

An aspect of rural informality is the propensity for using volunteers rather than professionals. Manpower developments in the 1960s and 1970s were such that now more is known about optimum training and utilization of personnel. There is an attendant receptiveness to diversity in staffing and a willingness to more extensively tap indigenous workers and paraprofessionals. While the relative absence of rural professionals may be seen as a weakness, the possibilities for using volunteers should be recognized as a strength. Professional helpers in rural areas may be used somewhat differently than in the city, for example, to recruit, organize and train volunteers to carry out defined activities about which there is community agreement and priority setting.

Recently two different rural midwestern communities engaged in fund raising for the benefit of families in which catastrophic illnesses had struck. A council of church women instigated the activity in one community in which a youngster suffered from leukemia. An evening benefit including a basketball game, a lunch, and a raffle raised $7,800. In another rural community forty miles away, a wife struggled with cancer. Thousands of dollars were raised to assist with her horrendous medical expenses. The means utilized for the fund raising there included an auction of donated goods and services. These gatherings often become major social events in the community. Many of us in the helping professions decry the need for such activities, preferring social policies that provide adequate income maintenance and health insurances. But in the absence of such institutionalized societal protections the needs are often critical and rural communities frequently rise to the challenge. Each community will have its own traditions and patterns in such matters and the action taken will typically be informal but that some help is made available is the crucial point.

The self-help movement is particularly relevant for the rural way of life. On farms it is common for neighbors to combine their efforts in the planting or harvesting of crops for a farmer who is incapacitated by illness or injury. A force that may work in the opposite direction, however, is the decline of the farm segment of rural America. As increasing numbers of rural dwellers are commuters to towns and cities for employment, the countryside takes on some of the characteristics of the suburban "bedroom" communities. When this happens the cooperative and self-help activities may decline accordingly. There is a great deal of inventiveness and self-sufficiency in many nonmetropolitan neighborhoods that may go a long way toward the meeting of human needs even in the apparent absence of organized social welfare programs.

It has often been noted that religion plays a larger role generally in rural communities than in cities. This is an important feature of the rural way of life even if it does not necessarily follow that churches are involved in outreach of a social welfare nature. Often congregations are more than willing to be helpful to persons from their own group in times of need, but this tendency runs against still another rural value, personal and family independence and self-reliance. Some rural dwellers are unwilling to admit that a problem exists or to accept help. Their resistance on an individual basis can be greater to offers of assistance from within their own group, perhaps because of the embarrassment and the threat to pride felt. Other individuals and families are more willing to receive help from, say, their church than from a social agency. At any rate an established resource in nonmetropolitan communities is the church.

Another resource characteristic of hundreds of small towns is the service club, an established helper. Any and all groups in a community are noteworthy from a human service perspective (for example, PTA, women's clubs, lodges, commercial and farm organizations), but the service clubs are especially so because by definition and commitment they have a service focus. Lions, Kiwanis, Rotary and others are widespread. A social worker in a small community may want to consider the pros and cons of affiliating him or herself with a service club. In spite of that decision, however, these organizations as resources should always be kept in mind by the rural worker.

Any consideration of rural social services must take into account the makeup of the population and its needs. Racial and ethnic minorities are part of the rural scene that is often thought of as homogeneous. Three disadvantaged groups that are found to a significant degree in nonurban America are the Chicano, American Indian, and Negro. Serious social problems for all of these groups are poverty and the related concerns of housing, health, and education. A problem for Chicanos is their involvement in migratory farm labor with its constant mobility, deficient housing, poor health care, and inadequate services. In some places at the present time programs are being provided to assist the migratory farm families in leaving the migrant stream and settling into a more stable community situation. This means a change of employment and putting down roots in a community. The language barrier is a complicating factor in serving Chicanos. Assuming a social worker does not speak Spanish, one of the most important services may be finding someone who does to serve as interpreter. As a result it may be possible to better utilize existent services and to develop needed but nonexistent ones.

Perhaps half or more of American Indians are rural, some living on reservations and others in other small communities.[1] A frequently encountered phenomenon is repeated movement of Indians between reservations and other communities, which is related to family ties and attempts to improve themselves economically. Severe health problems, shortened life spans, and high suicide rates are among the hazards of life for this group. Services for American Indians are complex and confusing because various governmental levels and organizations are involved and there are tribal differences. Social workers are found in the Bureau of Indian Affairs and Indian Health Service. A human service worker in a community with Native Americans will need to be cognizant of programs specifically for Indians, which are usually governmental, and other avenues for serving this group, both actual and potential. For example, in some parts of the country church denominational activities are significant resources for Indians. But again existence and utilization are two different things, and the challenge for the worker may be how to help people take advantage of such services. Cultural differences are noteworthy in working with Indians and must be assessed in planning and implementing programs as one of the articles in this section suggests.

Change characterizes the picture for blacks in that most are now urban. Yet millions are still in rural communities, and poverty and its accompanying problems persist, perhaps more so in the South than anywhere else. As Ginsberg notes, many of the efforts of organizations to improve the situation for blacks have been directed more to the urban world, leaving the rural black deprived and unserved.[2] There has probably been less militancy and activism relative to social issues and discrimination in sparsely populated areas than in the urban centers. An unknown element for the future is what impact the return of blacks to the rural South will have. These are persons who moved to northern cities from the rural South and now are returning. According to Ginsberg one of every twenty-five black migrants had done so by 1970.[3] One can speculate that such returnees may have undergone significant changes attitudinally and in other ways over the years and that helping programs will need to deal with these changing aspirations.

Various rural social welfare programs are presented in the readings in this section. These measures are a response to the numerous problems characterizing nonmetropolitan America such as those discussed in the first section. The article by the Grabers deals with a basic human need, health, and programming for this need in one part of the nation. Delivery of social services in rural areas is the subject of Louise Johnson's article. Rural school social work is addressed in the next selection by Mooers and Powe. Norris discusses ways of serving the elderly in small communities. Rural crime and corrections is the subject of the Wayne Johnson article. Different aspects of programs aimed at the problem of child abuse are considered in the next two readings by Leistyna and Sefcik/Ormsby. Day-care for rural children is the subject of Barbara Brown's article. The importance of considering cultural differences is stressed in the Ishisaka contribution on working with American Indians. A method of providing help for handicapped rural children is presented by Hutinger and McKee. The Kelleys describe an innovative way of maximizing manpower in the human services by training natural helpers. Finally, an item of historical interest by Phil Brown reminds us of the tremendous impact that social policy decisions can have when there is commitment and implementation accompanying the decision. All America, rural and urban, could be transformed to greater human dignity and justice if we had today the commitment to such needs as health and housing that was made decades ago to electrifying the farms.

NOTES

1. *Statistical Abstract of the United States* (Washington, D.C.: U.S. Government Printing Office, 1978), p. 35.
2. Leon H. Ginsberg, "Rural Social Work," *Encyclopedia of Social Work* (Washington, D.C.: National Association of Social Workers, 1977), p. 1230.
3. Ibid., p. 1229.

The federal "war on poverty" had significant successes as demonstrated in this article, although there were and are problems. One group of problems has to do with the passage of programs from one governmental bureaucracy (OEO) to another (HEW). Assuming a program survives, which is an unsafe assumption in these times of austerity for human services, there is a question whether its comprehensive preventive nature will be preserved, as in this case, or whether it will take a narrower focus. That services make a difference is clear, even in or perhaps especially in rural areas of abject poverty and primitive health conditions. One result, perhaps unintended, of the described programs is the emergence of a whole new class of better paid, better skilled, upwardly mobile local citizens employed to staff the various health services.

11

SCOTT AND SUSAN GRABER

Health Care in the Rural South

In the lower part of South Carolina there is a remnant of Lyndon Johnson's Great Society, a health program that serves the 20,000 poor people who live in the marshes, mud flats and pine forests of heavily black Beaufort and Jasper Counties. Beaufort-Jasper Comprehensive Health Services is unlike any other such program in the United States. Not a part of a medical school nor associated with a large hospital, it is isolated and rural in every sense. The leadership is black, nonprofessional and native to the salt marsh. While the program means doctors, it also means false teeth, potable water and screen doors. By any standard of measurement, the program is a success.

Back in 1965, the infant mortality rate in Beaufort County was 62 per 1,000 births; today, sixteen infants per 1,000 die at birth. In 1965, one-third of the homes in Beaufort County lacked indoor plumbing; today, 16 percent are without a tub and toilet. In a period of six years, Comprehensive Health has made a tangible difference in the quality of life for the black people of the South Carolina "low country."

But the program may starve to death. It faces a 24 per cent cut in its operating budget this year, and the Department of Health, Education, and Welfare threatens another slice next year. It is obvious that neither the state nor the local governments have the inclination or wherewithal to continue the program. The demise of Comprehensive Health will mean the loss of much more than the medical services that have made the program valuable and effective. It will put an end to innovative nutrition, housing, water and transportation projects as well. HEW's concept of "basic ambulatory health care" differs from the "comprehensive" philosophy pioneered by the Office of Economic Opportunity, which funded Beaufort-Jasper Comprehensive Health at the outset. HEW is attempting to retool its approach to public health in the United States, and it means to reshape Comprehensive Health in the process.

OEO backed Beaufort-Jasper Comprehensive Health at a time when we were told we could "lick" poverty and "bring home the bacon" in Vietnam. It was a reflex action when we still believed in our reflexes. Now 20,000 people rely on that action. False teeth, indoor toilets and a job behind a desk are integral parts of the experiment. The poor are coming to look upon Comprehensive Health as a kind of subgovernment; one that employs 264 doctors, nurses, plumbers, security officers and human resource specialists. And like almost every modern government, it has grown so fast that few seem to appreciate its size or influence.

The story of the Beaufort-Jasper Center began in the spring of 1968 when a South Carolina doctor, Donald Gatch, published an article in *Esquire.* Gatch detailed the hunger, malnutrition and poverty that are indigenous to the low country. Gatch spoke of worms, hunger and feces in the back yard; of swollen bellies and tumble-down shanties. The story was picked up and retold in every major city in the United States.

The choice of Beaufort County was a remarkably good one for the media representatives who came bounding into South Carolina. Not only was there hunger, there was also wealth; Hilton Head Island and its affluent escapist population provided a nice contrast. Not only were there tapeworms, there were politicians like L. Mendel Rivers and Strom Thurmond, who could be relied upon for wonderfully insensitive remarks: "You had them [the poor] back in the days of Jesus Christ, you have got some now, and you will have some in the future." Not to be outdone, Mendel Rivers engaged in Churchillian rhetoric: "I have no intention of immortalizing poverty or dishing out food stamps."

The Beaufort-Jasper experiment was intended to see if such a program could function in isolation. It had every right to fail, if for no other reason than the lay of the land, or the lack of land. Beaufort County is actually a group of islands, a place the sea will not relinquish. But these are strange islands surrounded by water and marsh and miles of "pluff mud." Causeways link the larger islands of St. Helena and Hilton Head; but others like Daufuskie—the setting for the movie *Conrack*—remain isolated. The low country poor are not containerized. They are spread throughout the two counties. There are no obvious ghettos, no "projects," no logical place to begin.

The Marine Corps, which has two bases in Beaufort County, generates $7 out of every $10 that flow into the county's economy—thanks in part to the legendary Rivers, who was chairman of the House Armed Services Committee. The average per capita income of the military personnel—and of the civilian employees who work at Parris Island and the Marine Corps Air Station—is $4,383. The average per capita of those not affiliated with the Marines is estimated to be $2,319. In Jasper, per capita income is estimated at a dismal $1,515. These figures can be made even more depressing if the extremely affluent—living in and about Hilton Head Island—are removed from the equation.

Jasper County is doggedly making its way back to the 19th century. There has been a slow decline in population in the last ten years, and in 1974 one of the county's two "industries" (a small furniture factory) closed shop. Almost half the land mass is owned by paper companies —Continental Can, Westvaco—and private hunting clubs. These lands, mostly pine forest, produce little tax revenue. In fact, an average acre of trees in Jasper County generates 68¢ in real estate taxes.

Before OEO gave the Beaufort-Jasper Comprehensive Health Services its first money, $654,373, it had operated out of a single decrepit station wagon. In 1971, the program got $1,776,991; it also got several new vehicles, as well as its first dentists and an environmental health section. By the end of 1971, there were four satellite clinics. By 1975, Comprehensive Health was building homes, digging wells, counseling the unemployed, repairing furniture, and organizing a store on Daufuskie Island.

Medical care is now rendered at five clinics, three in Beaufort County, two in Jasper. Each clinic has at least one doctor, as well as nurses, paramedicals and family health workers. The Central Facility at Chelsea includes a dental clinic, a pharmacy, a mental health unit and a laboratory; it also employs a full complement of insurance clerks, "manpower specialists," planners, grant getters and memo writers.

Patients are linked to the facilities by a fleet of two dozen vans and mini-buses and one surplus landing craft. People are shuttled from obscure places like Big Estate, Low Bottom and Little Snooks to the nearest clinic. The vans and buses hold the system together. They carry the program across the bridges, down the dirt roads and into the lives of people who otherwise would have little or no access to medical care.

Every morning the waiting rooms swell with black people, sitting on orange and blue plastic chairs or standing along the walls. They usually remain silent. They are processed through a receptionist, an insurance clerk, a paramedical (stethoscope around the neck), perhaps an X-ray or lab technician and, finally, a doctor. A visit usually consumes an entire morning.

That is the traditional, clinic-oriented part of Comprehensive Health. There is an essential "outreach" service as well. Evelena Glover is a typical outreach worker. She spends her days bouncing in a mini-van over the back roads that connect the small settlements on St. Helena Island. She takes blood pressure, runs urinalysis tests, changes dressings, gives children ringworm treatments. There are about five Evelena Glovers at each clinic, and each of the five sees about forty families a week.

The Community Services Department is located at a faded crossroads called Coosawhatchie. Plumbers, carpenters, back-hoes and bushhogs operate here. A large black man named Emory Campbell heads the department. "You are never going to have healthy people until they are living in a healthy environment." Campbell says. "Treating a patient for the symptoms of an illness, and not for the causes, is only prolonging an unhealthy situation."

Many people in the low country have never seen a septic tank or know what one does. Emory Campbell is on intimate terms with septic tanks—and with drain fields, "cluster wells" and asbestos shingles. He and his people are responsible for thirty-three cluster wells, serving ninety-five families who formerly carried their water home in Clorox bottles. Campbell has rebuilt roofs, toilets and screens.

With money from the federally funded National Demonstration Water Project, the program is completing a water system for the Levy-Limehouse-Bellinger Hill communities in Jasper. And with help from Clemson University, it has built three "basic home" prototypes; it plans to build fourteen of these low-cost homes in 1976.

Nutrition has always been a problem in this region. Low country people eat and drink the wrong things—rice, grits, R.C. Cola. And this diet has, by necessity, been stitched into the local landscape. Diabetes, hypertension and obesity are a common part of the setting. In April 1976, Comprehensive Health opened a nutrition center featuring a demonstration kitchen and demonstration diets. It remains to be seen if the nutrition center can persuade the people to abandon their grits and R.C., as well as their fried chicken, pigs feet and sweet potato pie.

Thomas C. Barnwell Jr., a former shrimp fisherman, is Comprehensive Health's project director. Barnwell spreads his message with evangelical intensity, and there are no Philistines in his camp. You are born again to the concept of comprehensive health care, or Barnwell shows you the door. He was born on Hilton Head Island, where for years his father owned the only truck and did a modest cartage business to and from the ferry. He left the island before developer Charles Fraser made it a symbol of the New South, with condominiums, tennis courts and pastel cabanas. Says Mary King, formerly a consultant with OEO, "We knew we had something special in Tom Barnwell. With a lot of our local people we had a 'push-me pull-you' relationship, but not with Tom. It was only a question of supporting his decisions."

Barnwell has been a controversial director. At the outset of his directorship, he screwed up his courage and bellowed at "Fritz" Hollings (the junior Senator from South Carolina): "There has been too much talking and not enough action. If you have come down here just to talk, you might just as well forget it." Later, sensing that publicity from the Gatch article had wounded local pride, Barnwell began to forge relationships with anyone who would listen to his story. John West, former Governor of South Carolina, came to Beaufort. So did Jimmy Carter, then Governor of Georgia. "Tom has an incredible intensity," says Mary King. "And he was smart enough to understand that he needed people like Strom Thurmond."

In 1969, Barnwell fell in love with a white VISTA volunteer from Iowa. While the romance was not easy for the white community to swallow, for many blacks it was totally incomprehensible. "They gonna hang you, son," said Hannah Barnwell. "No black man is goin' to marry no white woman in this county."

While this debate was in progress, Barnwell was sucked into a power struggle. Another local black, William Grant, saw the opportunities inherent in becoming the medical messiah to the poor in the two counties. As chairman of the Comprehensive Health Board, he practiced a day-to-day supervision that made Barnwell extremely uncomfortable. They fought over policy, over money, and ultimately over Barnwell's infatuation with the VISTA volunteer, Susan Carter.

Grant and his board would argue over such matters as the distance between Barnwell's desk and Ms. Carter's desk. The board changed Ms. Carter's title, then transferred her to the Coosawhatchie satellite clinic. Barnwell counterattacked, publicly questioning Grant's frequent trips and his personal use of agency vehicles. He went on to question Grant's competence and his right to run the agency.

In the end William Grant was forced out. Thomas Barnwell and Susan Carter were married in 1970 before the apprehensive probate judge in Beaufort County's picturesque courthouse. Despite Hannah Barnwell's warning, the marriage took hold, and the Iowa farm girl has given stability and foundation to Barnwell's frenetic existence.

One of Barnwell's headaches has been his inability to hold on to his doctors. Part of the problem is the long hours; sometimes a physician will see thirty-five or forty patients in a day. Lack of administrative support is also a factor. Nearly every doctor who has left Comprehensive Health has complained that he could not get a letter typed or an X-ray forwarded to Charleston. One doctor, who had repeatedly requested a key to the records room without getting any results, finally kicked the door apart. Whatever the reasons, none of the doctors has remained with the program any longer than his obligation demanded.

It is a difficult situation. The doctors are isolated in small communities that offer little, if anything, in the way of diversion. No colleagues to talk with; no Wednesday golf; no participation in the fine arts; only an endless round of sick people. A doctor may arrive with enthusiasm and goodness in his heart, but he knows he could be making $15,000 to $20,000 a year more in private practice somewhere else. Comprehensive Health's official position does not help. As Wallace Brown, the project's administrator, puts it, "Doctors are purely technicians. They are not expected to become involved in the agency's policy making."

Often overlooked, in evaluating a program like Comprehensive Health, is the extent to which it has given local blacks both the desire and the skills with which to perform managerial functions. (In the generations before the program, blacks held almost no jobs above the blue-collar level in Beaufort and Jasper Counties.) For example, Comprehensive Health removed Evelena Glover, the St. Helena outreach worker, from a tedious, unproductive life and kept her in South Carolina. At least in this one area, the program has helped to combat the tendency of poor blacks to get the hell out of the South.

Blacks began to leave Beaufort County in 1890. At first only a few left the "islands," restless people who wanted a little excitement. But word that one could make $5 or $6 a day in New York City spread quickly and the race to Harlem was on. Between 1920 and 1930 more than 70,000 blacks pulled out of South Carolina, migrating up the eastern seaboard to Philadelphia, New York and Boston. This exodus stripped the South of much of its prospective black leadership. Many blacks who wanted to be managers—who would eventually succeed in "the system"—left home.

When OEO started Comprehensive Health, it wanted local blacks to run it. Of course, there were no Harvard Business School graduates among the black population. There were shrimpers (like Barnwell) and farmers and teachers and folders of laundry at Parris Island. Few of these people had more than a high school diploma. Although he has taken numerous college courses, Barnwell has no degree; nor does Wally Brown or Hyland Davis, who is head of the water project. There is very little management experience.

Yet the nature of the work has inevitably created a small middle class in the Beaufort-Jasper black communities. No longer is a black man limited to the cotton field or the Parris Island laundry. No longer is the black funeral director the top of the line. The agency pays its insurance director $13,000. It pays the data processing director $10,-000. A personnel resource specialist makes $13,000, and its director of finance, $16,000. These middle-management jobs have, by and large, been held by blacks, and some of the "managers" are now moving from Comprehensive Health into the local economy. The program's black attorney was recently hired by a white law firm in Beaufort.

The blacks who run Comprehensive Health seem to understand that this is their main chance and that they themselves must find the solutions to the project's problems. They must deal with the prevailing HEW policy that would strike "comprehensive" from the project's title, give ambulatory health care, and leave all the rest—screen doors, septic tanks, furniture repair—to somebody else, or to nobody at all.

Bob Williams, an official at HEW's regional office in Atlanta, is soft-spoken and articulate. He serves as liaison between three health programs in South Carolina and the regional office. "Congress cut our budget by $45 million," Williams begins. "We decided ... this office decided to make a 24 per cent cut across the board. We're not going after Barnwell, or Barnwell's program. We cut everybody in the region.

"I think most of the programs will make it. They may have to trim a little administrative fat, but they'll survive. Most of the programs will still be able to deliver basic ambulatory health care."

What about the other, less basic items that Comprehensive Health provides? Williams picks his words with obvious care. "We are in the business of providing doctors, nurses, dentists and outreach people. We do not hire . . . we don't fund carpenters, electricians or people like that. We believe that there are other agencies that are more logical places to pick up this kind of money."

But the people in Beaufort-Jasper wonder about the future. Does this mean that HEW won't fund the transportation program in the future?

"I didn't say that. We are suggesting . . . we actually began suggesting three years ago that Comprehensive Health look around for other means of support." Williams is especially careful here. "HEW cannot fund this agency forever."

HEW is not happy funding "in-hospital care." Nor does it like funding the buses and vans that shuttle the poor to and from the clinics. Although HEW has agreed to pay the salaries of the program's environmental health staff, it will not pay for any of the materials that they use. HEW will not buy boards or pipe or toilet bowls. The hush-puppied and seersuckered folk at HEW are suggesting alternative sources of funds, such as the Environmental Protection Agency.

"We went over to the EPA," notes Emory Campbell, "and they tossed this funding literature at us. I couldn't find the words *septic tank* anywhere. Those guys [EPA officials] must assume that everyone has a sewage line at his disposal."

Neither Beaufort nor Jasper will finance the digging of a well, although the health departments will tell you the required distance between the "contemplated well" and the "contemplated septic tank." Neither county can provide money for home repairs or help untangle the complex local title problems that make home improvement loans very difficult to obtain.

"The Farmers Home [Department of Agriculture] won't lend you money unless you make $3,600 a year," Campbell continues. "My God, most of the people we need to reach make $2,300 or less."

It is not any easy job explaining HEW's "back-to-basics" philosophy to St. Helena farmer John Boles. He knows only that his tap water is no longer salty. Neither is it easy to explain the 24 per cent cut in the budget to Lymus Green, also a farmer, who has a roof that no longer leaks when a thunderhead blows off St. Helena Sound. Wally Brown, project administrator, is not happy with HEW. "They cannot dictate our goals and objectives," Brown declares. "They are hired to carry out the intent of Congress. They do not have the final word; the people have the final word."

If "the people" are to have the final word, then Barnwell and Brown must prevail upon Strom Thurmond to level his senatorial sights on HEW's Atlanta hierarchy. Improbable as it may seem, Thurmond, the Dixiecrat, has come to Barnwell's rescue at least twice. He kept the agency funded when it was making difficult passage from the crumbling auspices of OEO to a reluctant HEW; Thurmond also kept the agency's transportation system intact when the General Services Administration tried to disperse the fleet of vans. Senator Hollings has been equally generous with his influence. He restored thousands of dollars that had been cut from the 1974 budget. Even the local politicians—the same who were mortified by the Gatch revelations—have helped in recent years. Political realities probably explain this phenomenon; the black vote is now something to be reckoned with in the South. Thurmond, after all, has a politician's sense of loyalty, an undiluted sense of obligation to his constituency. Barnwell and Comprehensive Health are now perceived as constituency. Mendel Davis, the successor to Mendel Rivers in the U.S. House, says he admires Barnwell. "The most persistent man I have ever met," Davis calls him. "He is constantly calling me or my staff. Constantly writing, keeping us abreast of legislation. Persistence is the word that keeps coming to mind."

Like Donald Gatch, Tom Barnwell knows the market value of guilt. When Barnwell testified before McGovern's Select Committee on Nutrition, he discovered what guilt would buy. In 1968 it bought him the basic tools with which to build Comprehensive Health. Today, when Nixon, Lockheed, Gulf and the CIA have diluted our capacity for guilt, Barnwell must be more subtle when trading in this commodity. But as an advocate of the poor he understands that it is an important tool.

If Barnwell is to keep Comprehensive Health truly comprehensive, he must also become a capitalist. . . . Specifically, the program must collect every dollar it can collect from the patients themselves. In requiring Comprehensive Health to offer its services to the entire community, HEW ordered it to adopt a "sliding fee scale" determined by an individual's ability to pay. But determining income was easier in theory than in practice. The current method is simply to ask the patient what he or she earns (no verification is required). Wally Brown admits there are difficulties. "The fee scale is not working. We are not even making 50 per cent of the money we thought we would make."

Because of Thomas Barnwell and his team of secular evangelists, Beaufort and Jasper are no longer on the bottom of every statistical list. In fact, Beaufort County now has the lowest rate of infant mortality in South Carolina, and Jasper has the third lowest. In 1970, mental patients from Beaufort were being returned to the state hospital in

Columbia for further treatment at the rate of fifteen per month; that rate has been reduced by one-third.

Despite the economic threats, some officials at Comprehensive Health are optimistic. "I think that a moderate or liberal President could change the picture," says Louis Dore, director of personnel. "I think someone like a Udall or even a Carter would restore funds to the agency. We'll just have to wait and see."

Meanwhile, Tom Barnwell camps in the halls of Congress. He tells his story, the only story he knows or cares about, to Thurmond and Hollings and anyone else he can find in the Rayburn or Dirksen Office Buildings. He doesn't bellow any longer. The new Barnwell is quiet and intense, and he is no longer limited to guilt. He now has another product that is equally salable. He can sell success.

In the next article the delivery of social services in rural communities is discussed in terms of the kinds of resources typically present. Size is delineated as a significant variable, and four types of communities are identified in relation to size. Although these classes of towns overlap, as the author acknowledges, each is examined relative to its distinctive features. The distinctions are useful in considering actual and needed services. One kind of community, the reservation, is particularly interesting and important for social work.

12

LOUISE C. JOHNSON

Human Service Delivery Patterns in Nonmetropolitan Communities

When considering the distinctive attributes of social work in nonmetropolitan America, the major difference seems to be in the service delivery system. There is a growing body of literature relative to "rural social work." Careful consideration of that literature[1] leads to the observation that the practice of social work in rural areas is different because of the service delivery system, rather than because the principles of "good" social work are different. "Good" social work calls for differing responses to cultural diversity; for "starting where the client is"; for "understanding the situation." To work in rural settings a worker must understand not only rural culture but must also understand and work both within and with the rural service delivery system.

While the literature usually uses the term "rural social work," the author prefers the concept social work in nonmetropolitan areas. This term seems to more accurately describe the phenomenon being con-

From Louise C. Johnson, "Human Service Delivery Patterns in Nonmetropolitan Communities," an original article, by permission of the author.

sidered. Not only does it imply that the carrying out of social work tasks is different; it also is a misnomer in relation to "rural." Rural is a concept that is defined in many ways; "a state of mind," and "all communities with a population under 2,500," to specify two. It is a term understood in different ways by different persons; it is nonspecific. Nonmetropolitan refers specifically to those communities with a population under 50,000, the minimum size of a metropolitan community. Social work in nonmetropolitan settings is a more accurate expression of the phenomenon being considered.

The information base used in developing this article is broad and varied. Initially, the source was personal observation of rural practice from the vantage point of a faculty position in two states with large rural populations. Reading of the growing but illusive body of social work literature about social work in rural communities was another important source, as was attendance at a number of conferences on "rural social work." A very important source has been community surveys done by student groups in small communities of varying size, composition, and cultural background. Finally, an extensive literature search has been conducted, making heavy use of materials available on ERIC.[2] This search considered materials not only from social services, but also materials dealing with mental health, health, education, and rural extension programs. From this base two models have been developed: (1) a schema that describes the components of a service delivery system, and (2) a four-part model that describes four types of service delivery systems in nonmetropolitan America. Each type seems to make differing use of the various system components. These models are helpful in identifying important concepts useful in understanding nonmetropolitan practice. In addition, gaps in knowledge and issues that need consideration begin to emerge.

When identifying components of a service delivery system workers usually identify the various social agencies and sometimes consider services provided by other professionals. In the nonmetropolitan situation a far broader view must be considered. One frequent component referred to in the literature is the "natural helper." Another way of looking at the service delivery system is to look at resources. By using this approach, a schema can be developed that moves from personal through natural to formal resources.

Personal.   While usually not thought of as a part of the service delivery system, this resource is never the less a resource that most rural cultures expect persons to use. Personal resources are the personal strengths all persons have (though to differing degrees) within themselves. The concept of "rugged individualism" places high expectation on individuals to care for themselves. While this expectation is often unrealistic, this resource should not be overlooked and should be included in the resource schema.

Natural. Resources or helpers to be considered in this area include immediate family, friends, co-workers, "extended family," "natural helpers," volunteers, "benefits," and self-help groups.

In communities where the informal systems are strong, and where people are aware of each other's concerns and problems, these systems are most important. Social workers need to respect and maximize the concern people have for one another, the help they give in the context of family, friendships, and the work place.

The *"extended family"* has traditionally been strong in the small community. In ethnic communities, such as among the American Indian, it has special significance. "Extended families" have their peculiar ways of helping and taking care of one another. Social workers have not focused on maximizing this resource or found ways to link it with other parts of the resource network. The work of Speck and Attneave on *Family Network*[3] could be useful in developing practice in this area.

Natural helpers are persons who possess certain helping skills and exercise them in the context of mutual relationships. These persons are usually people who make helping a part of their everyday life. They are hardworking and optimistic about people being able to change. They are mature, friendly people who often have had past experiences with the same problem as the people they are helping. They are trustworthy and able to keep confidences. They usually have had common life experiences and values as the persons they are helping. They are available and share a sense of mutuality with others. Residents of small communities know who these persons are, though it is very difficult for the professional to identify them without help. Collins and Pancoast have begun to identify strategies for working with these "natural helpers."[4]

The concept of "volunteering" is often foreign to the rural context. Rural persons see helping as a part of their life-style or their "Christian duty." They may give hours of time in visiting the shut-in, in working on a benefit dinner, or in various kinds of organizational work. Yet they will resist efforts to organize or train volunteers. Traditional ways of working with "volunteers" seem inappropriate for nonmetropolitan settings. Ways need to be found to maximize and work with community helping systems.

An important component of the small community helping system is the *"benefit."* If an individual or family has a catastrophic illness or accident, the community will very quickly mobilize to raise money for this family. Large sums of money are raised very quickly. To be eligible for this kind of help, the individuals must be accepted members of the community and have had little control of the catastrophe situation. Long-term residents who are considered "upstanding" and hardworking are most apt to be "acceptable." Recognition and understanding of this resource is important in understanding the breadth of the natural helping system.

Another component of the helping system, while undeveloped in nonmetropolitan communities, is the "self-help" group. These groups capture the spirit of mutual aid, which is so congruent with rural values. They also are useful in overcoming social isolation, a feeling far too often present when persons living in small communities have problems. These groups are useful for persons who are dealing with their own problems, such as alcoholism (AA), child abuse (Parents Anonymous), or for persons who are living with people who have problems such as children with developmental disabilities and for persons who are in life transition stages, such as the Widow to Widow program.[5]

This natural helping network often has no linkage with the more formal services. There is a need to develop understanding of and practice principles and techniques for working with and developing linkages with this important and overlooked portion of the service delivery system.

Formal.   The formal service delivery system is one social workers are more familiar with and are more comfortable in working with. However, because of the limited resources in small communities, it too must be conceptualized broadly. Other professionals need to be not only identified but their areas of expertise also must be utilized. This would include ministers, educators, extension service personnel, law enforcement and court personnel, and medical resource persons to name those most often found in nonmetropolitan communities.

Organizations are another resource. Many small community organizations have resources for the use of their members or others in the community in times of need. Examples of this are the American Legion with services for veterans or the interest of Lions Clubs in visual problems. Sometimes organizations can be developed to aid with specific problems in a community on a short-term basis. A community group formed to obtain a playground would be an example. There are also community service organizations that are set up to provide specific services, such as to operate used clothing stores or information and referral services. These services usually function without direct involvement of professional workers.

The formal service delivery system also includes the *formal agen-*

cies. Service delivery by these agencies takes many different forms. Not only is the professional worker often a baccalaureate social worker, but many nonprofessional workers and paraprofessionals are also used. Often the paraprofessionals are longtime residents of the community, which makes service more acceptable to some persons. They are particularly effective as outreach workers. Agencies with the primary administration base in another community use several service patterns when delivering service to small communities. These include the *out-station* model. In this model a worker is stationed in the small community on a full-time basis but receives administrative services from outside the community. Another model is the *circuit-riding* model. Here a worker or group of workers move from small community to small community providing service on a one-day basis, weekly, biweekly, or monthly. Last, but never the less important, are services available to individuals but for which they must leave the community to receive the service.

The social worker in the small community must develop a wide repertoire of techniques and skills in order to develop the resource potential of this system. The role of broker and advocate, as well as mobilizer, is important. The concepts of "linkage" and "networking" become important.

"Linkage" refers to the process whereby a person or family with specific needs is connected with a resource in a manner that enables the development of a helping system. This concept of linkage becomes especially important when persons needing resources in small communities are different or are seen by the majority of the community as "unworthy."

"Networking" has two distinct usages. First is the notion "that each person has a wide array of relationships"; the label "network" ordinarily suggests that with a portion of these people we have a relationship permitting us to "approach them."[6] The other usage refers to a "community network." In this usage there seems to be a central person or organization with the "network" being formed around a specific interest or service concern. This interest could be very narrow, such as services for the aging, or it could be very broad, such as a "community helping network."[7]

The concepts of linkage and networking give indications as to ways the various resources in a community can be brought together so as to form a functional service delivery system. A dysfunctional aspect of the present nonmetropolitan service delivery system is that often various resources operate without awareness of understanding of or communication with one another.

TYPES OF SERVICE DELIVERY

Four types of service delivery in nonmetropolitan communities have been identified. The observations from which this model has been developed have been made over a period of seven years in two midwestern Great Plains states. The survey of the literature seems to support these findings if allowances are made for regional variations. Three kinds of observations have been used: (1) direct observation by the author in discussions with social workers in many communities; (2) student projects that involved a social systems study of a small community; and (3) student observation about their home communities on written assignments.

The *small city* is a community with a population of between 15,000 to 50,000. In some instances communities of 15,000 to 20,000 may not have these characteristics, particularly if they are geographically near a larger community. The service delivery system resembles that of a small metropolitan community with a variety of formal services, public and private. These services will probably include a public social services office with several service divisions, a mental health center, one or perhaps more private family agencies, social workers in secondary settings, such as health care facilities and schools, other human service professionals (nonsocial work), a community action program, and one or more community service agencies. These communities usually have a senior citizens program, one or more self-help groups, and a United Community Fund. Usually this service system includes one or more workers with a master's degree in social work. They are very often county seat towns with a county extension service and court service workers. While this service system may resemble that of a small metropolitan area it has some differences. First, the agencies are smaller. There may be only one or two social workers in all agencies except the public agency. Even this will be a smaller agency. Second, there seems to be more working together among the agencies, at least in some communities. There is an informal system that enables workers to know each other, work together, and avoid duplication of effort. The informal network also includes other kinds of community helpers. It is a service system that relies heavily on the formal system; however, linkages with the natural system could enhance its effectiveness.

The *small town* is a community of between 8,000 and 20,000 population. Communities on both the upper and lower end of this range may not fit into this classification. This community will often have a small public social services office. It is usually a county seat community. Sometimes it will have a mental health center, but usually not.

It may have a United Community Fund, but this group is often in-effective. This community may have out-posted or circuit-riding workers from agencies administratively housed outside of the commu-nity. There may be a social worker in a nursing home and occasionally in a hospital. There are fewer other professional helpers though the other professional helpers are important parts of the service delivery systems. These communities usually have a senior citizens program and often have community service agencies. At best, one or two of the workers may have a master's degree in social work.

Services provided by a variety of organizations to their members and a natural helping system become more evident. The coordination of the service delivery system is often problematic unless one commu-nity individual takes responsibility for "getting people together." This situation probably exists because so many of the components of the service delivery system have strong linkages outside the community or because the formal systems and the informal/natural systems do not know how to work together. The natural system is strong. Linkage between the formal and natural systems with each playing comple-mentary roles would greatly strengthen the service delivery. The con-cept of "networking" is relevant as a means of strengthening the helping system in this type of community.

The *rural community* is under 10,000 in population. Formal social services in this community are usually not present. However, if the community is geographically remote from larger communities and is a county seat a few may be present. These would usually consist of a small public social services office and circuit-riding workers. Usually community residents must leave the community for most formal ser-vices. Although the natural helping network is very strong, it is often hidden from the "outside" professional worker. One means of pro-viding services to this type of community is to develop ways of work-ing with the natural system.

The *reservation community* has a different service delivery system. There is a formal system consisting of the BIA services, the Indian Public Health Services, and the Public Social Services Agency. Then there is a growing tribal system of services. The CAP programs usually are a part of this system. On some reservations some of the formal social services are under tribal control. All of these formal services have considerable difficulty in working together, and there are often problems in knowing which agency is the appropriate one. In addition, there are very strong natural helping systems. These systems are based in extended families or small settlements. The traditional elders or medicine men are important components of these systems. Most reservation workers have little knowledge of these systems and even less knowledge of how to work with them. "Networking" could be an effective means of service coordination. This coordination must include the natural systems.

ISSUES

Consideration of the nature of service delivery systems raises many issues that can only be addressed by further observation and discussion. Among them are:

1. How to develop a cooperative and complementary service network that meets the needs of nonmetropolitan peoples in a manner that is congruent with their culture. This would include such questions as: What is the role of the social worker with the natural helping network? How are existing resources made more responsive to those who are different and those who are deemed "undeserving"? It includes questions of efficiency, effectiveness, and accessibility.
2. How to develop social workers who are sensitive to this nonmetropolitan service delivery system. Included in this issue are questions about how social workers can develop skill in working with a wide variety of persons who are neither other social workers or clients. Also questions about the nature of the natural helping system are important.
3. Concepts, such as case management, coordination, linkage, and networking, must be operationalized in nonmetropolitan communities. The skills involved in these processes need to be identified and refined. Understandings developed by the operationalism need to be conceptualized and disseminated.
4. The concept of regionalization must be considered carefully. Regionalization has been a concept often given considerable emphasis in the delivery of nonmetropolitan service. However, it also is not congruent with the concerns about local control that exist in many small communities. To regionalize small communities with large communities often leads not to better service but to less service than is acceptable and accessible in the small community. Workers "out-posted" or "circuit-riding" in small communities must be enabled to work with communities in creative ways that enable helping networks to form.

The key to efficient, accessible, and effective service lies in the service delivery system. A broad view of this system and understanding of how to work with and link its component parts is essential for the nonmetropolitan social worker if nonmetropolitan persons are to have a useful service delivery system.

NOTES

1. Especially useful are Leon H. Ginsberg, *Social Work in Rural Communities* (New York: Council on Social Work Education, 1976); *Human Services in the Rural Environment Reader* (formerly published by University of Wisconsin Extension); and readers from a number of conferences on rural social work.
2. Educational Resources Information Center.
3. Rose V. Speck and Carolyn L. Attneave, *Family Networks: A New Approach to Family Problems* (New York: Pantheon, 1973).
4. Alice H. Collins and Diane L. Pancoast, *Natural Helping Networks: A Strategy for Prevention* (New York: Natural Association of Social Workers, 1976).
5. Alan Gartner and Frank Riessman, *Self Help in the Human Services* (San Francisco: Jossey-Bass, 1977).
6. Seymour B. Sarson et al., *Human Services and Resource Networks* (San Francisco: Jossey-Bass, 1977), p. 3.
7. Ibid.; for further discussion of this idea see the complete book.

SELECTED BIBLIOGRAPHY

Austin, Michael. "A Network of Help for England's Elderly." *Social Work*, 21, 2 (March 1976): 114–119.

Bast, Dave. *Human Services in the Rural Environment Reader.* Madison: Center for Social Service, University of Wisconsin Extension, 1977.

Buxton, Edward B. *Social Work in Rural Areas.* Madison: University of Wisconsin Extension, 1977.

Collins, Alice H., and Pancoast, Diane L. *Natural Helping Networks: A Strategy for Prevention.* New York: National Association of Social Workers, 1976.

Gartner, Alan, and Riessman, Frank. *Self Help in the Human Services.* San Francisco: Jossey-Bass, 1977.

Ginsberg, Leon H. *Social Work in Rural Communities.* New York: Council on Social Work Education, 1976.

Green, Ronald K., and Webster, Stephan A., eds. *Social Work in*

Rural Areas. Knoxville: University of Tennessee School of Social Work, 1976.

Grunebaun, Henry, ed. *The Practice of Community Mental Health.* Boston: Little Brown, 1970.

Hassinger, Edward W., and Whiting, Larry R. *Rural Health Service: Organization, Delivery and Use.* Ames: Iowa State University Press, 1976.

Katz, Alfred H., and Bender, Eugene I. *The Strength In Us: Self Help in the Modern World.* New York: New View Points, 1976.

Muhlberger, Esther. "Collaboration for Community Mental Health." *Social Work,* 20, 6 (November 1975): 445–447.

Sarson, Seymour B., et al. *Human Services and Resource Networks.* San Francisco: Jossey-Bass, 1977, p. 3.

Speck, Rose V., and Attneave, Carolyn L. *Family Networks: A New Approach to Family Problems.* New York: Pantheon, 1973.

Surdoch, Pete W., Jr. *Montana's Rural Social Service Delivery System* —Final Report. Helena: Montana Department of Social and Rehabilitation Services, 1974.

Wagenfeld, Morton O., and Robin, Stanley. *The Social Worker in the Rural Community Mental Health Center.* Paper presented at Rural Sociological Society Annual Meeting, San Francisco, 1975, ED111583.

Williams, Ann S.; Youmans, Russel C.; and Sorensen, Donald M. *Providing Rural Public Services: Leadership and Organizational Considerations.* Western Rural Development Center, Oregon State University, Special Report, No. 449, December 1975, ED 122977.

The dimensions of overwhelming poverty and basic deprivation in the rural deep South are vividly traced in this article. When school social work was introduced it was aimed at fundamental problems—attendance and dropouts. Successes in combatting such problems are described as well as the expansion of social work service from the elementary to the secondary levels and to broader concerns.

13

GARY R. MOOERS AND DAVID POWE

School Social Work in a Rural Southern Setting

The public school system, perhaps more than any other social institution, offers the most beneficial setting for the effective use of social work in preventing and ameliorating the problems of school age children. Parents and children alike are often more receptive to social work services provided by the familiar setting of the school than they are through non-educationally oriented social service agencies. Although school social work services are not yet universally provided by all school systems, it is increasingly recognized by professional educators and social workers that social services can benefit children, parents, teachers, and administrative personnel as they strive to make schools instruments which produce knowledgeable and well adjusted graduates.

Although the need for social services within the public school system is desirable in all circumstances—it seems particularly crucial in a rural setting that lacks many of the social services resources customarily found in urbanized areas. If a large percentage of the students come from home situations characterized by extreme poverty, inade-

Reprinted from Gary R. Mooers and David Powe, "School Social Work in a Rural Southern Setting," *Human Services in the Rural Environment*, Vol. 3, No. 3, March 1978, pp. 1–5, by permission of the authors and the journal.

quate housing, parental illiteracy, and both geographic and cultural isolation, then these services become even more critically needed by the school system. If this school system is located in Mississippi which has no compulsory education law requiring children to attend school until a certain chronological age is achieved, a strong social service component seems mandatory if the generational bonds of illiteracy and economic stagnation are to be overcome. Such a situation exists in LeFlore County, Mississippi.

The LeFlore County School District contains 583 square miles, consisting of the entire area of LeFlore County, Mississippi with the exception of the City of Greenwood which has its own school district. The largest town in the district is extremely rural with only a few hamlets such as Money (population 200) interrupting the agrarian landscape. On a superficial basis, a casual observer might conclude that this area remains unchanged from earlier times, but he would be missing a dramatic process which is permanently changing the way of life in this part of rural Mississippi.

The area covered by the LeFlore County School District is rapidly converting from a traditional plantation based society with a need for a large unskilled labor force to a modern agri-business economy which requires specialized skilled labor. Some of the largest cotton-planting companies in the world are located in this county but the mechanization of agricultural tasks has resulted in a situation where a small number of skilled employees are needed rather than a large number of unskilled workers. For example, one person operating a mechanical cotton picker replaces 249 individuals picking cotton by hand.

This use of machines to till the soil and harvest the crops has greatly changed the lives of those who were manual laborers in the plantation economy. At one time it was profitable for the plantation owner to have a reserve of people who were in a state of complete dependence and it was to his advantage to keep them so. This need no longer exists, but the people still exist. There has been considerable outward migration to nearby cities and northern industrial centers, but many individuals are left possessing yesterday's job skills in today's labor market. A large proportion of these people continue to live in tenant houses on plantations even though they are not employed by the owner.

A graphic picture of the population served by this school district was provided by an extensive study in 1969. The average family had eight children and almost half of the first born children were born when the mother was seventeen years of age or younger. Ninety-six percent of the parents did not graduate from high school, seventy-five percent did not graduate from elementary school and thirty-three percent of the parents were completely illiterate. Approximately two-thirds of the parents lived in small houses on the plantations where they used to work and almost half of the houses had no toilet facilities inside or outside of the home. A great majority of the homes were neither owned nor rented and were generally in great need of repair. Very few of the homes contained reading materials and almost ninety percent of the homes were without a television set. Approximately one-half of the heads of the household were unemployed. Figures obtained from the Mississippi Department of Public Welfare indicated that approximately thirty-eight percent of LeFlore County's residents receive some form of public welfare assistance.

The logistics of education in LeFlore County have undergone a remarkable transition. Twenty years ago there were 140 small isolated all black schools in the county. The great majority were located on individual plantations and consisted of one room. The inadequacy of the physical plants was usually matched by the poor academic preparation of the teachers. These schools were characterized by poor attendance and an almost universal drop-out rate. In 1959, only three black students in the county had stayed until the twelfth grade. In 1960 the plantation schools were closed and the school district was consolidated into ten schools including two high schools.

The consolidated schools were a vast improvement over the previous one-room school houses but problems which had previously remained hidden surfaced when the isolated plantation children were placed in schools with children from more affluent homes. The extreme poverty, the existing educational gaps, and the social isolation that the students brought with them to school presented problems which the school system was ill prepared to handle. Perhaps the most serious tangible problem was the extremely high rate of students dropping out before graduation. Since Mississippi had no compulsory school attendance law, the students could not be forced to come to school so another answer had to be found.

In 1966, a Visiting Teacher Program was initiated to encourage children to remain in school and to persuade children who had never attended to begin. Even though this program met with little success, the dimensions of the problem were vividly revealed to the administration. In 1968, the program was redesigned into an Attendance Counseling Program and a full time person with a degree in social work was employed. By 1969, three social workers were hired to provide a comprehensive program of social services. This approach was common to school social work throughout the country, but was a major innovation in Mississippi as this was the first such program established in the state. It was felt that in order to provide the services which were required by the children in LeFlore County, a completely new approach had to be taken.

The LeFlore County School Social Work/Attendance Counseling Program presently employs seven social workers. Each worker is responsible for one or more schools, depending on the size of the caseload. The workers receive referrals from faculty members, administrators, community agencies, and individuals concerning problems and needs of students enrolled in the LeFlore County Schools. Special attention is given to attendance problems which may be the first step in identifying more deeply rooted problems. The ' workers investigate and follow through on these cases in order to implement corrective steps so that regular attendance results.

In a time of accountability where programs must justify their existence, it seems apparent that the Social Work personnel have been instrumental in alleviating many attendance problems. Prior to the inception of the social work program to the present time, the average daily attendance (ADA) has risen from 83.8% to 94.1%, a gain of 10.3%. This represents an average of 530 children attending school each day who otherwise would have stayed home. In a year's time, this means an additional 95,400 cumulative school days of attendance.

The State of Mississippi presently provides $1,000 for supportive services for each teacher unit. A teacher unit is calculated as the state's base salary for one teacher for every 27 students in average daily attendance. Concentrated social work in the area of attendance has enabled the district to increase its teacher units, based on an increase from 93% to 97% Mean Percentage Present—1968 to 1975, at a time when enrollment has decreased more than 15%. The increased attendance is an obvious advantage to a school district operating with limited facilities and financial resources.

Another area of concern was the high dropout rate, on both the elementary and secondary levels. During the early sixties each child entering the first grade in LeFlore County School District had only a 50-50 chance of reaching the third grade. In the three school years from 1969 through 1971, the dropout rate for grades one through six was reduced by more than 50%, while the total dropout rate was reduced by almost 25%. From 1972 through 1975, the dropout rate for the same grades was reduced by 18%, while the total dropout rate was reduced by 21%.

Originally set up to deal with only potential dropouts in elementary school, the program was expanded during the 1971–72 school year to include high school students. During this first year of operation the number of high school dropouts was reduced by 26%. In the school years from 1972–73 through 1974–75, the dropout rate decreased by 27%.

The above figures appear to demonstrate that the Social Work Program has been quite successful in achieving its goal of increasing the average daily attendance and reducing the rate of student dropouts in the LeFlore County School System. Since excessive absenteeism and dropping out of school are often only symptoms of other problems, it would seem that this program has also been successful in areas outside the narrow range of attendance. One such example of an apparent mushrooming effect that this program has is shown in the reports on vandalism.

Although all school vandalism is rising at an alarming rate on a national level, the LeFlore County School District has found itself in a position of diminishing school vandalism. In the school years from 1972 through 1975, the school district has noted a decrease in vandalism of 7%, 9% and nearly 12%.

It seems appropriate to examine this program in terms of its philosophy, priorities, and methods to determine why this program has proved to be beneficial and worthwhile. The Social Work Program is centered on the belief that the main purpose of any educational system is to provide educational opportunities for all children that will enable them to maximize their potential creatively and usefully. For this purpose to be achieved, the social workers work closely and continuously with students, parents, teachers, and other school personnel.

The social workers attempt to make school a place where children want to come rather than a place where they are forced to come. Like teachers, they are concerned that children make good beginnings in the school setting and are there to help with problems throughout a child's career in the school system. Obviously, they are involved in cases involving sporadic attendance or withdrawal from school, but they also work closely in situations where children are exhibiting poor emotional or academic adjustment, where children clash with teachers or dislike aspects of school life, and where lack of suitable clothing or other family problems seem to be interfering with the educational process. Individual counseling, group sessions, and referral to appropriate social agencies, are all preventive methods which seek to help the child better utilize the educational resources of the school.

Parental attitudes and circumstances are often crucial factors in determining whether a child is successful in school or not. The social workers act as liaisons between the school and the parents and actively seek parents' assistance in resolving problems which occur at school. This "problem solving partnership" between the school and the parents can develop a positive attitude toward the school and often changes educational attitudes of parents. The parents are encouraged to take an active interest in the education of their children and are shown how to assist their children at home even if the help only consists of expressing an interest and taking time to let the children relate their day's experience at school.

The LeFlore County Social Work Program also deals closely with teachers and other individuals within the school system. Besides accepting referrals and working with specific problems, the social workers conduct an ongoing in-service training program for educational personnel instructing them on the role of the school social worker and helping them understand the problems of children attending this school district. Social workers play a number of roles as they interact with other employees of the school system. They may explain the needs and home situation of an individual child, they may interpret the behavior of a withdrawn or destructive youngster so that his classroom needs may be better met. They may act as an advocate for a child they feel has been dealt with unfairly by a school employee. In all of these roles the goal is the same: to enable the school to better meet the educational needs of the students.

It seems apparent that this program has been a success in increasing attendance rates and reducing the number of students who drop out before graduation. There are other intangible benefits that, while perhaps impossible to adequately measure, exist nonetheless. School has probably become a more beneficial experience for many children because of the work of this program. Parents have taken an increased pride in the academic accomplishments of their children as they have been brought into the decision-making process. The school has become a more relevant and responsive institution which responds more appropriately to the needs of its students.

It is important to bear in mind that these accomplishments have been made without the customary legal sanctions that are part of a compulsory school law. Coercion and legal threats have not been a part of this program. What has made this program successful has been a strong belief in people and a conviction that a viable social work program could make a beneficial impact on the lives of students, parents and school employees. Social workers have worked as "enablers" with the groups above so that each student can go as far as his innate potential can carry him in a harmonious educational environment. Obviously, there is much left to be done, but the success of this program indicates that professionally trained social workers functioning within a rural school system can certainly contribute to the breaking of the cycle of poverty, illiteracy, apathy, and despair which have existed so long in the rural South.

When one thinks of rural areas New York State probably does not come to mind because we associate New York with bigness, the giant metropolis. But vast sections of this state and its urban neighbors are extremely rural. This article describes a variety of services for the rural elderly, persons often scattered and isolated in such communities. Diverse needs are met through multifaceted centers distributed about the county. Some of the possibilities of programming for this age group can be perceived through the experience of one county.

14

JEAN NORRIS

Multipurpose Centers in a Rural County

Long, severe winters and winding country roads often force older people in rural areas to be isolated, but in Franklin County, New York, older people are taking part in a variety of activities sponsored through the county's network of senior centers.

Franklin County which boasts a population of 40,000 is predominately rural, with nearly half of its land area within the massive Adirondack Park. The 1,674 square miles comprising its land area are bounded on the north by Canada's Quebec province. Although there are population centers at each end of the county, the nearest large city is Montreal, with the mid-section of the county mountainous and sparsely populated.

Franklin's residents are not only isolated from major population centers but have the lowest per capita income of any county in the State and the highest unemployment rate. There is a serious shortage of doctors and medical services which compounds problems for the 14 percent of the population who are over 60.

Reprinted from Jean Norris, "Multipurpose Centers in a Rural County," *Aging*, May–June 1978, pp. 18–20, by permission of the author.

Although the county's population is just 40,000, Franklin received nearly 40 percent of State funds under Title V of the Older Americans Act for the acquisition, alteration, and renovation of facilities as multipurpose senior centers.

William O'Reilly, Director of the Franklin County Office for the Aging, says that the centers received the large funding grant because the county was already operating a number of centers and because the senior citizens took the initiative in applying for government assistance. He feels it is easier to insure that all of the county's elderly are assisted than it is in a larger urban area, because of the close-knit nature of the small communities and an on-going outreach program conducted by each adult center director.

TRANSPORTATION PROVIDES THE KEY

The initiative of the senior citizens who are described as both proud and independent also enabled the centers to acquire new buses for their transportation programs. New 20-passenger buses are now on the road at three centers as well as two 12-passenger vehicles obtained under the Capital Assistance Grant Program of the Urban Mass Transportation Administration. Each month the adult centers provide over 9,000 rides and cover over 11,000 miles throughout the county.

Since the county lacks public transportation, the program is vital to both the elderly and handicapped who use the free service for visits to doctors and social service agencies, as well as for errands and shopping on a regular weekly basis. Despite severe road conditions the buses were only kept from making rounds on one day last winter. Most of the drivers are retired school bus employees who take pride in their ability to reach their destination no matter what the road conditions are. Many of the secondary roads outside the towns are unpaved, but are kept accessible through a well-equipped plowing system designed to prevent any Franklin County resident from being isolated during the long winters.

Countywide services offer a variety of programs. The nutrition program, which operates through the senior centers, serves over 9,000 meals per month, including meals-on-wheels and doctor-prescribed special diets for those who require them.

The North Country Center of Gerontology offers educational opportunities through the community college and is setting up a project to bring entertainment and information to the homes of those elderly who are visually or physically handicapped. The Emeritus Studies

Program offers college level courses in adult centers and any senior citizen can audit courses.

For those who need supportive services, the Senior Citizens Council has instituted a Home Care Program which brings public health nurses and home health aides as well as housekeepers to the homes of the elderly.

The Franklin County Office for the Aging coordinates services and ensures that the elderly receive assistance through Food Stamps, Medicaid, and other social services. The RSVP program is also run through the Office for the Aging and has over 500 volunteers at work throughout the county—half of whom are employed at the adult centers. Low income people over 55 are given community jobs under Title IX of the Older Americans Act. Through the Pastoral Outreach Service, sponsored by the North Franklin Ministerial Association, volunteers regularly visit an isolated or lonely elderly person on a one-to-one basis.

ADULT CENTERS AND SENIOR CLUBS

There are eight full-time Multipurpose Adult Centers in the county with full-time nutrition and transportation programs. Other services include educational, physical fitness, and craft programs. Assistance is also available in applying for Medicaid, Medicare, Food Stamps, Supplemental Security Income, and Senior Citizen Discount Cards. Counseling on life insurance and tax filing is also offered, as well as blood pressure clinics. The centers also provide referrals and transportation for health screening services.

In smaller communities with populations under 500 there are senior citizen clubs which meet monthly for social events and dinners. Cooperative events and trips offer the elderly from the centers and clubs throughout the county an opportunity to mix together. The highlight of the year is the Seniorama, held each May during Older Americans Month. It is a large fair-picnic-convention held by and for older citizens. A formal dinner, during which the Senior Citizen of the Year is announced, is the finale of this one day spectacular. Last year over 1,500 people attended.

Franklin County's elderly participate in many self-help activities to raise money for the centers and their programs. A fiddlers' contest, square dances, and ice cream festivals were held along with traditional fund raisers such as bingo and card games, rummage sales, craft and bake sales, and auctions. Raffle tickets were sold on everything from handmade quilts to a trip to the Bahamas. During the latter part of

1976 and 1977, the adult centers, senior citizen clubs, and their advisory boards raised a total of $100,000 to initiate various projects, including $51,000 which was used to provide heat, lights, and transportation for the nutrition programs.

The Multipurpose Centers are used by the communities at large for a variety of activities. In December the Harvard Glee Club performed at the Malone Golden Age Club where they were served dinner by the senior citizens and entertained by the Kitchen Band.

Throughout the year the facilities at each center are used by young people for parties and dances, for bingo games and craft lessons. The general public is encouraged to use the blood pressure clinics and many young adults work at the centers as volunteers and as Title VI Manpower employees.

Each center has its own unique history and services to offer the seniors in their individual locations.

The Akwesasne Office for the Aging provides services for the approximately 300 senior Mohawk Indians at the St. Regis Mohawk Indian Reservation. Their senior citizen center is located in the Akwesasne Community Building and offers assistance to any Indian over 55. They also encourage the re-affirmation of old ideals by being a strong vocal group within their community.

Since 1971 the senior citizens of the Brushton-Moira area have been meeting and have expanded their services to encompass many small rural communities. They have recently completed a survey in cooperation with other senior citizen clubs, which has shown a need for senior housing and will soon result in the establishment of Franklin County's first senior run housing. In the five rural communities surveyed there is a total elderly population of 562. Of the 177 persons who responded, 92 said they would move into senior housing and 68 indicated they might be interested in the future. A typical profile of an elderly person residing in the area is that of a single woman over 62, living in a one member household, with an income of less than $3,000 a year from social security. They own houses in small towns, which are not modern but adequate, but they would prefer a one bedroom apartment and could pay $60-$70 a month rent.

The Burke Adult Center serves four rural villages. The membership owns its own building, a beautifully renovated Grange Hall, and runs a store from which handcrafted items made at the center are sold.

A more urban facility is the Malone Adult Center in downtown Malone, the county seat. In addition to the regular nutrition and transportation services, Malone has the Kitchen Band, made up of seniors with a flair for making music with pots, pans, and kitchen utensils. The eldest band member is 80 and the group is popular with local citizens of all ages.

The Five Town Adult Center at St. Regis Falls was first formally organized in 1970. As its name implies, the center serves the senior citizens in five towns with a full nutrition, recreation, and transportation program. The Sarana Lake Multipurpose Adult Center publishes a biweekly newspaper written and edited by the members of the center. They also have a store stocked with donated goods, with proceeds going toward their fund raising programs. The seniors are planning on moving into a facility of their own in the near future.

The Adirondack Adult Center in Tupper Lake began as a senior citizen club in 1969. It is also a full service center. They sponsor monthly bingo games at the Geriatrics Ward of the hospital and provide prizes and refreshments. Other community services performed by this civic minded group include the running of the annual heart fund drive, setting up a blood donor clinic, and the establishment of a midtown community garden.

Fort Covington is the newest multipurpose center and the farthest North. There are about 143 elderly households in the town which directly borders Canada and the St. Regis Mohawk Indian Reservation. At present meals are served in a school basement where other programs are also held. An abandoned church will soon become a modern multipurpose center there and the senior citizens of this tiny town are working hard to create a facility equal to the others in the county.

"North Country pride and perseverance distinguish the Franklin County Senior Citizens, who go ahead and help themselves, needing only encouragement from us to begin new, innovative programs. These people are not used to having anything done for them and resent accepting handouts. Our job is to present programs to them and assist with paperwork. They can then willingly and eagerly raise funds and keep the programs going," concluded Mr. O'Reilly.

*Crime and delinquency in nonmetropolitan America are largely
neglected concerns, both in the criminology literature and in that
on rural social services as is pointed out in the following article.
It is not surprising, therefore, that program innovations in the
areas of law enforcement, adjudication, and corrections are little
known. The article describes several promising provisions and
new developments in these contexts within rural communities.
These constitute some hopeful signs in a generally bleak field.*

15

H. WAYNE JOHNSON

Crime, Delinquency and Criminal Justice
Services in Rural America

Conspicuous by its absence in the emerging rural social services literature is examination of the problems of crime and delinquency and
correctional programs. . . .

This absence of attention to these social problems and programs on
the rural scene perhaps should not be surprising. There is the image
of clean air, green countryside, crime-free rural America in contrast
to corrupt, wicked, crime-ridden urban centers.

Any rural dweller can testify to the inaccuracy of this picture in
view of rising rates of crime and delinquency in these sections of the
nation. Rustling of livestock, theft of equipment, burglary of farm and
small town homes, and vandalism are only some of the acts confronting rural residents.

What do the statistics show? While record keeping in the crime and
delinquency field leaves much to be desired in the United States, the
best information available makes it quite clear that there is reason for

Reprinted from H. Wayne Johnson, "Crime, Delinquency and Criminal Justice Services in Rural America," *Human Services in the Rural Environment*, Vol. 3, No. 4,
April 1978, pp. 1–5, by permission of the author and the journal.

concern rather than complacency relative to such deviancy in the rural community. Although there continues to be more crime and a higher rate of illegal activity in the cities, the growth of crime is greater in the non-metropolitan sections. For example, FBI *Uniform Crime Reports* (for the year 1976) compares the arrest rate for cities, suburban, and rural areas for each year from 1972 through 1976. While the urban rate remained fairly constant with a slight drop over this period, the rate for rural areas showed a marked and steady increase every year except for 1975–76 when it was almost constant. The suburban arrest rate, higher than the rural but lower than the urban, was more erratic over these five years with an overall modest increase.[1]

Youth and young adults play a large part in the nation's crime. However, according to the FBI report, the distributions of arrests were lower for the younger age groups in the rural areas.[2] *Juvenile Court Statistics*, another federal source of information, indicates that in 1974 urban court cases of juveniles (in contrast to arrests) increased by 11 percent over the previous year and semi-urban cases increased by 3 percent whereas rural cases of juveniles in court increased by 15 percent.[3] The increase of juvenile cases in rural courts is associated more with male than female delinquency.[4] It is seen then that whichever measure is used, arrests or juvenile court cases, rural America is not free of offenses and offenders. It does enjoy a comparatively favorable situation in contrast to the cities and suburbs in this regard, but change is present and crime may be increasing more rapidly in the rural parts of the nation.

RURAL CRIMINAL JUSTICE SERVICES

Three major subsystems constitute the criminal justice system regardless of community size—law enforcement, judicial, and corrections. In each of these groups of activities existent as rural entities, the usual characterizations apply along such lines as lack of resources, relative isolation and small size with the attendant limitations.

There are problems and potentialities in each of these three subsystems. The intent here is to be suggestive rather than exhaustive relative to some of the possibilities for program and policy development. In the case of law enforcement in the rural community, the major lines of defense are municipal police, constables, and marshals on one hand and the county sheriff system on the other. Various kinds of strengthening of rural law enforcement have occurred over the past decade due to a number of developments, but particularly resulting from efforts of the Law Enforcement Assistance Administration (LEAA). As a result, rural law enforcement, too, is more sophisticated and advanced than ever before.

One of the recent innovations has been police social work due principally to the pioneering efforts of Professor Harvey Treger at the University of Illinois, Chicago Circle. The idea is to team social workers with police personnel toward the solution of problems frequently encountered by police such as domestic disputes and youth difficulties.

What is noteworthy from the perspective of the present discussion is that almost all of the social work/police activity thus far has been in small cities. Illinois has been the site of most of this development in the nation so far, beginning in such communities as Wheaton and Niles, each about 31,000 population.[5] While these are suburbs of Chicago, in Iowa a social worker is already employed in the police department in a community of 20,000 and consideration of implementing such a program is currently underway in other communities.

The possibilities of strengthening the human service system would appear to be considerable through the addition of social work to law enforcement and blending these two endeavors. In general, the kind of social worker called for in this context in the rural area would appear to be a competent generalist with strong clinical skills.

One of the major developments particularly prevalent in the judicial arena today is diversion, the idea being to provide alternative programming for the accused or convicted offender to route him or her away from the sequence of consequences traditionally flowing from deviancy. Through diversion it is hoped to avoid the all too often damaging results of incarceration or other destructive aspects of processing in the usual court, probation, incarceration, parole experience. By nature, diversion can be designed for nonpopulous communities. An Iowa county of 72,000 population instituted a juvenile diversion program which aims at early diversion, i.e., prior to the filing of a delinquency petition by the county attorney's office. This model is such that it is readily adaptable to much smaller counties. Two or more adjacent counties could jointly carry out this program effectively.

Thirdly, corrections present perhaps the greatest number of challenges and opportunities within the overall criminal justice spectrum. Every rural area is served by both juvenile and adult probation and parole in some way, even if this is one overworked agent serving several counties officed at considerable distance. The need is for qualified and adequately paid staff to serve a geographical area that is of reasonable size and caseloads that are not excessive. While this seems utopian in some parts of the country, progress is being made in many areas.

The institutional aspect of corrections deserves special comment. A traditional part of our societal response to criminality has been and continues to be the county jail and town lock-up. Some of these structures are among the most obsolete and deplorable relative to inadequacy of physical plant and dearth of any meaningful programming for inmates. Each facility needs to be assessed individually to ascertain whether it should be razed, modernized or whatever. Such decisions should be made within the context of a total integrated state plan for detention and short term incarceration, the role of the jail. Most states will find that they have more jails than are needed as we move toward the twenty-first century. Regional facilities may be at least a partial answer. Whatever directions are ultimately taken, it is a bit paradoxical to contemplate the most local of all correctional (penal) facilities in an era in which community based corrections has become a popular phrase in some professional circles.

Juveniles present a serious problem in that, based on the standards of such organizations as the National Council on Crime and Delinquency, very few should be detained in jail. Most specialized separate juvenile detention centers are in metropolitan communities. It is not surprising that a considerable number of rural youths find themselves detained in such places as the county jail. The inappropriateness of such placements is testified to by all too frequent suicides and other tragedies accompanying the jailing of youth. Detention is overused for juveniles, both rural and urban. Part of the answer, then, is a reduction in the amount of detention. Other partial solutions in rural areas are multicounty regional detention facilities, greater use of temporary foster care on a highly individualized basis, and group shelter care homes. With the latter, extra consideration may need to be given to security features without converting a home to a bastille. This has been done in some communities and can be done in others.

State training schools for juveniles and penitentiaries and reformatories for adults are longer term institutions. Interestingly many, if not most, of these facilities are located in rural areas although today they are populated by largely urban offenders. Not only are they typically not in a city, they are not even within the boundaries of a small community. Rather they are often on the edge of a town or located entirely in the country. Like many state mental hospitals historically, their remote locations put the "client" group out of sight and out of mind of the general populace. Often these facilities included a farm or were situated on a farm. Therefore employees of such institutions including social workers and counselors are often rural dwellers.

The need today is for diversity in programming and for deinstitutionalization. The nation is experiencing a building boom in prisons at the very time that it should be developing genuinely community based non-institutional programs. For example, in Iowa, a rural state, a recent plan recommended the expenditure of $55 million over five years to "up-grade the corrections system." The question is what form this upgrading will take. If most of it goes for brick, mortar and steel to construct institutions that are exorbitantly expensive to erect and maintain and destructive to the persons to be "served," it is money poorly spent. Legislators should very carefully consider what these sums of money could purchase in community based programs such as a system of smaller, less architecturally secure institutions with a diversity of objectives, release centers and half-way houses with an emphasis on education, training, and employment, programs of partial confinement, restitution, and community service to name a few. The focus should be, then, on deinstitutionalization and the provision of alternatives.

Returning to juvenile delinquency again, there are many possibilities for developing services in the rural community. Group homes are one promising resource that can be established even in very small communities. A variety of structural and administrative arrangements are available for such programming.

In 1976 another program was created in Iowa to fill the human services gap for rural youth. It was entitled the "Career Development Program" (CDP). As of 1977, 75 percent of the 500 youths in this self-help program were from communities of under 8,000. Almost all were drop-outs and about half had been in trouble with the law. The program is for youth aged 16 to 21 and aims at promoting career exploration development, academic opportunity and job training.[6]

A Washington, D.C., consultant to the program observed, "Generally rural areas are a wasteland as far as resources for youth with special needs are concerned. The small town kids I met in Iowa were among the most emotionally battered I've seen anywhere in the country.

"In cities, youngsters usually have a peer group—if only a street gang—to identify with. It's not so easy in small towns." A successful product of the program said, "Once a small town kid gets a bad reputation, it's almost impossible to shake it no matter what you do...the county sheriff was one of the few who tried to help me."[7]

The last program innovation that will be mentioned here which is compatible with the rural scene is also flourishing in rural Iowa. In-home or family-based care is being used by the State Department of

Social Services as well as some private organizations having contracts with the state. Families, Inc. is an example. Located in a small town of 1,300 it serves nine counties, two of which are urban, two semi-urban and the remainder quite rural. In fact, four have county populations of under 20,000. Workers carrying small case loads invest heavily in families in which at least one child is headed toward institutionalization in the absence of substantial intervention. Much of the work is in the client's home, often during the afternoons and evenings when the entire family is present. The intensity and continuity of highly individualized service appear to have paid off well in this program.

To conclude, contrary to the image, there is crime and delinquency in rural America. Perhaps contrary to another image there are also services for families and individuals involved in such deviancy. Opportunities for additional rural programs abound and a few possible directions have been indicated here.

NOTES

1. Federal Bureau of Investigation, *Uniform Crime Reports* (Washington, D.C., 1977), p. 171.
2. Ibid., p. 172.
3. U.S. Department of Justice, *Juvenile Court Statistics*, 1974 (Washington, D.C., 1977), p. 5.
4. Ibid., p. 6.
5. Harvey Treger, "Wheaton-Niles and Maywood Police-Social Service Projects," *Federal Probation*, September, 1976, pp. 33–39.
6. *Des Moines Register*, March 13, 1977.
7. Ibid.

The next two articles are concerned with problems of child abuse and neglect and efforts at remedying them. The first by Leistyna addresses the need for multidisciplinary advocacy and for involved team members who will work actively for the well-being of rural youngsters.

16

JOSEPH A. LEISTYNA

Advocacy for the Abused Rural Child

Much of what we have learned about child abuse and neglect in the United States stems from studies of lower-class, urban families. Little information has been available on the needs of many of our rural children, especially those from impoverished and developmentally crippling environments. However, several newly established child abuse programs are focusing on the needs of rural communities and more information on these activities should become available in the near future.

Joann Davies recently described some of the specialized skills that rural child protection professionals need in order to provide an effective program.[1] She also described such difficulties as the loneliness of decision making, the geographic distances involved, the isolation of the rural child protection worker and the lack of specialized resources, all handicaps which must be overcome in order to assure a successful program.

As the only practicing pediatrician in a rural county in Virginia during the years 1972 to 1975, I had an opportunity to work with a group of local professionals who served as volunteers in establishing, with the guidance of Anthony Shaw, professor of pediatrics and sur-

Reprinted from Joseph A. Leistyna, "Advocacy for the Abused Rural Child," *Children Today*, May–June 1978, pp. 26–27, 39, by permission of the author.

gery, and his co-workers at the University of Virginia, one of the original community-based child protection teams in the state. This project later resulted in revision of Virginia's child abuse and neglect laws to include provision for the establishment of a network of hospital and community-based child protection teams throughout the state.[2]

Our multidisciplinary team consisted of two nurses, two social workers, three physicians (a surgeon, an obstetrician and a pediatrician), a mental health worker, a schoolteacher and a local attorney. Between 1974 and 1975, during the first full year of operation, the team investigated 47 cases of child abuse and neglect in a county of 18,000 people. These 47 cases, along with several others that the child protection team was not able to fully investigate by the end of the year, gave the county an overall incidence rate of 300 cases per 100,000 population. This rate exceeded C. Henry Kempe's original estimates of 25 to 30 cases per 100,000 population by tenfold[3] and closely approximated the current estimate of the National Center on Child Abuse and Neglect, Children's Bureau, ACYF, that a million children in the United States may fall victim to abuse and neglect each year.

Of the 47 cases evaluated by our child protection team, 29 involved physical abuse, including two deaths from severe trauma. The remainder included 10 cases of neglect, two cases of emotional abuse and six cases of sexual molestation. Forty-two of the children came from low-income families that were stressed by a number of environmental and social factors: poverty, deprivation, ignorance, apathy, social isolation (many of the families were without telephones or reliable automobiles) and inaccessibility to supportive health care systems. Home visits by the team's social workers often revealed the same desolate, non-nurturing, often violent lifestyle that Elizabeth Elmer found so lethal to normal psycho-social development in children of poor, inner-city families.[4]

A notable weakness in our child abuse program was the routine follow-up of active cases. In the entire county, there were only three social workers, four public health nurses and four mental health workers, three of whom worked part time. There were no parent aides, day care centers, crisis nurseries, hotlines or Parents Anonymous groups. Any therapeutic approach to working with abusive families was difficult—the county was large, entirely rural and without public transportation, and salaried personnel were too few to accomplish the tasks necessary to maintain an effective child abuse program. It was obvious that a cadre of child protective workers would have to be recruited and trained to supplement our inadequate staff. Since local funds were not available, the child protection team members evolved a comprehensive grant proposal which was submitted to HEW, without success.

Urban study groups continued to attract most of the nation's research and demonstration funds.

It is of vital importance that attention be directed to increase the delivery of supportive services to rural children and their distressed families. Personnel capable of functioning in remote areas, far from the variety of resources found in the city, must be recruited and trained; the delivery of appropriate services demands a keen awareness of social and environmental factors unique to small towns and isolated farming communities. Supportive services require funding. Funding in turn requires an interested sponsor—a political figure seeking a large return at the polls, for example, or a demanding child advocacy group, neither of which abounds in rural areas.

Who, then, is to assume responsibility for advocacy for abused and neglected rural children? Local and regional governments bemoan their financial incapabilities and react slowly to public pressure and opinion. Rural politicians often fail to identify community needs; they may be suspicious of "big government" intervention through funded programs and fear a loss of local autonomy. Rural physicians are too few in number and fully occupied in providing care for those families who are motivated to seek help, capable of transporting themselves to the provider and able and willing to pay for necessary services.

Effective advocacy for abused and neglected children requires professional education and training so that symptoms of abuse, neglect and deprivation are identified and reported. It also requires professional ability to evaluate the special needs and problems of abused children and the effect of treatment programs for them, including any harmful effects. It is also necessary to make sure that children will receive continuing treatment until their homes are safe, the parents' problems are under control and the child's physical, psychological and developmental disorders are successfully treated.[5]

Who is to provide the special education and training to achieve these goals, especially in rural communities? Can medical centers provide such a resource? If so, medical institutions must first become more deeply involved in the broad concepts of child and family health, including the evolvement of interdisciplinary, community-oriented patient care models. The components of such outreach programs would address the social, educational, psychological, economic and ecologic exigencies that impact on healthy family function; the effect on the prevention, early identification and treatment of child abuse and neglect is obvious.

In order to generate institutional commitment to such programs, child service providers at every level (physicians, nurses, teachers, nursery and day care workers, advocacy groups, private and public agencies) must agitate and advocate that medical centers across the nation be induced to regionalize and organize their catchment areas. Effective agitation and advocacy demands concerted provider and interagency cooperation and a unified, interdisciplinary "assault" on the nearest medical institution.

Coordinated, direct contact by advocacy groups should be made with the following:

- Regional and state public health officials who can be useful allies when presenting statistics and community needs assessments to a medical center faculty.
- State legislators who have special interest in health issues and input into the policies of state medical schools.
- Representatives of private industry in the community (especially newly relocated complexes that have moved from urban areas) who recognize the need for outreach services for their employees.
- Department chairmen of medical schools, who are often very receptive to community needs once they have been systematically informed of the needs and community interest in meeting them has been demonstrated.
- Any local citizens who are associated with the nearest medical center, especially physicians and other professionals who are alumni of that institution.

A willingness to cooperate with any outreach programs that the medical schools may attempt is of utmost importance. This includes cooperation in providing a usable facility within the community; one successful program often leads to another. Advocates should also be willing to attend meetings and functions of local organizations and to speak about the needs of the community. Public awareness and an aroused community interest facilitate initiation and implementation of program proposals among legislators, health department personnel and medical school administrators. Medical institutions can thus be motivated to seek adequate funding to develop outreach units, mini-clinics and a corps of resource personnel to serve those rural areas which lack essential facilities.

Such program commitment would facilitate the establishment of workable child abuse programs, on-going health and special therapeutic services for distressed rural families, expansion of rural school curricula to include family life and child development courses and the promotion of adult education programs to include courses in parenting and childrearing. It would also encourage the design and implementation of efficient patient transport systems.

It is crucial to the future well-being of many of America's rural children and their multi-problem families that all disciplines in the allied child health services advocate for the development, implementation and coordination of comprehensive and accessible supportive services, services presently non-existent in large areas of our nation.

NOTES

1. J. Davies, "The Specialized Skills of Rural Child Protection Professionals." National Child Protection *Newsletter*, V (No. 1), 1977.
2. Virginia Child Protection *Newsletter*, IV (No. 2), 1977.
3. C. H. Kempe and R. E. Helfer, *Helping the Battered Child and His Family*. Philadelphia and Toronto, J. B. Lippincott, 1972.
4. E. Elmer, "A Follow-Up Study of Traumatized Children," *Pediatrics*, 59:273, 1977.
5. B. Fraser and H. P. Martin, "An Advocate for the Abused Child," in H. P. Martin (ed.), *The Abused Child*. Cambridge, Ballinger Publishing Co., 1976.

In recent years abuse and neglect of children has been in the national spotlight. As with many social problems, it tends to receive less attention in the country than in the city, often leaving the impression that it does not exist in nonmetropolitan communities. The authors of the following article discuss some of the reasons for this unawareness or denial. Clearly larger communities have no monopoly on child abuse. One multicounty rural region's experience with developing programs aimed at dealing with the neglect and abuse of children is traced. Various considerations are explored, including the use of volunteers, a team approach, education, and prevention.

17

THOMAS R. SEFCIK AND NANCY J. ORMSBY

Establishing a Rural Child Abuse/Neglect Treatment Program

That children are abused, neglected and sexually exploited in rural as well as urban areas has been documented, recognized and accepted in all research into child abuse and neglect. Individuals, agencies and professionals in nonurban communities are also aware of local instances of child maltreatment. Yet historically child abuse prevention and treatment programs have been extremely difficult to organize, fund and implement in the rural setting. This paper examines some of the factors that may account for this difficulty, and describes the development of a rural program.

Rural community attitudes, based largely on misconceptions regarding child abuse/neglect and maltreating parents, are a significant

Reprinted from Thomas R. Sefcik and Nancy J. Ormsby, "Establishing a Rural Child Abuse/Neglect Treatment Program," *Child Welfare*, March 1978, Vol. 57, No. 3, pp. 187–195, by permission of the authors and the publisher, Child Welfare League of America.

factor. A lack of awareness of and education about the incidence and impact of child abuse/neglect and its "spin-off" problems in the community (truancy, juvenile delinquency, crime, etc.) contributes to a lack of concern and, therefore, a lack of involvement and support. Small-town conservatism, the perceived threat to parental rights and family privacy, fear of becoming involved through reporting, lack of knowledge regarding the law and reporting procedures, small-town politics and power structures, the geographic scattering of the population, and scarce or inaccessible resources—all play a part in impeding the development of a rural child protection program. Common to both rural and urban areas is the existence of a combination of "turfism" and "tunnel-vision" among professionals that interferes with communication, cooperation and the professional respect necessary to a multidisciplinary approach to the problem. The lack of funding necessary for a coordinated program is also a vital factor and one that is usually dependent upon community attitudes and priorities.

The following description of the development of Project Children relates the methods employed to address these various issues. However, the most significant factor was learning to work with people, both professional and lay, in a manner nonthreatening to the small community.

INITIAL DEVELOPMENT

Project Children is a rural child abuse/neglect program serving a five-county area in southcentral Indiana. The region has a population of about 142,000, the center being Columbus, with about 37,000. According to 1970 census data, the region is 61.6% rural.

The program was conceived in the fall of 1971 in Columbus as a result of the involvement of a volunteer with an abused child and her family. The involvement persisted for months and exposed a lack of services dealing with child abuse and neglect. After becoming knowledgeable about child abuse, speaking to organizations and groups and creating community concern, this volunteer convened a group of agency and independent professionals who, in March 1974, formed the Bartholomew County Child Abuse Council. This initial effort fostered additional child abuse councils in Brown, Decatur, Jackson and Jennings counties. Because of the regional scope that the program was taking, the Quinco Consulting Center assumed responsibility for coordination and funding of the child abuse program by adding the position of program coordinator to a children's services federal grant application. (Quinco Consulting Center is a comprehensive mental health facility serving the five counties.) Selection of the coordinator in November 1974 was a five-county cooperative effort.

The cooperative selection process was important in program implementation. Involvement of various representatives of the "system," particularly the directors of the five county Departments of Public Welfare, assured their acceptance of and cooperation with the program coordinator. "Foreigners" are not always readily accepted by small-town citizens, and particularly a "foreigner" whose job may necessitate exposing faults within local agencies.

The coordinator's job, whether in a rural or urban area, is to develop an effective system for identifying and serving families in which abuse and neglect occur. The purpose is 1) to develop a service network in which the various agencies' roles and relationships are clear, and 2) to provide the best system for helping families by avoiding overlapping functions and ensuring that essential services are available in the community [1].

After a program has identified the existence of child abuse and neglect in the region, and the lack of a coordinated and effective system to deal with the problem, the focus should be on a needs assessment. Questions that should be asked are: Is there a need for a child abuse program? Is a coordinator needed? Should there be a new program or could an existing program be altered to achieve the required results? In Project Children the needs assessment was conducted by individuals of the five counties, who concluded that a program and a coordinator were necessary to meet the needs.

In the early stages of the program the objectives were 1) to become visible in the community, 2) to become acquainted with influential persons within the community who might later be recruited to aid in the program, and 3) to determine community attitudes toward child abuse and neglect, program innovation and reporting responsibility.

Visibility was achieved quickly through the child abuse councils in the five counties. The councils are linkages between the local communities and Project Children. They are composed of representatives of various agencies and disciplines and are organized toward the remediation and prevention of child abuse and neglect. The councils serve as a forum to discuss faults in the "system" and program needs and directions. They also serve as a vehicle for bringing together the "system" representatives, allowing for improved relationships, communication and cooperation. Also, local council members are usually familiar with local power structures and influential persons, i.e., agents for change.

Determining community attitudes deserves special consideration. It is easy for professionals and so-called "experts" in child abuse to be trapped into telling a community what is needed. Forcing programs upon communities will result in little payoff and usually in failure. Groundwork to develop community awareness and concern is a necessity.

A preliminary step in establishing Project Children was to meet with the directors of the five county Departments of Public Welfare to discuss their needs and identify problems. The meeting resulted in a 2-day training session for DPW child protection service staff. The objectives were 1) to increase these professionals' expertise in child abuse, and 2) to determine the various approaches to investigation and treatment being used in the five counties. The training areas included: investigation, use of authority, problem identification, developing a service/treatment plan, and use of community resources.

From this training began the individual county child abuse case consultation contracts. Currently Project Children is providing up to 56 hours of consultation monthly to five county DPWs.

HOSPITAL CHILD PROTECTION TEAM

After the January 1975 training of child protective service staff and initiation of the consultation service, an effort was made to develop a multidisciplinary team approach to child abuse. The rationale was that the individual child protection worker could not be an expert in medicine and psychology as well as social work, but could be an expert in his/her own area, child welfare. The development of a child protection team began in February 1975.

Each member of the team is important to team functioning. The key member is a physician, preferably a pediatrician. The physician lends credibility to the team with other members of the medical community; functions as a liaison between the team, the medical staff, and the hospital; and, finally, adds his medical expertise to the abuse investigation.

The DPW worker gives legal authority to the team and may ultimately assume coordination of the treatment plan for the family. The psychologist and/or psychiatric social worker provide expertise in identifying any emotional problems of the child and his/her parents.

The police officer, the emergency room nurse, the pediatric nurse, and the public health nurse may also provide vital information. The team attorney counsels the team as to a client's legal rights and the legal practicality of a treatment plan.

After it was decided that a child protection team was needed, a hospital protocol for reporting suspected child abuse cases was devised. Various committees within the hospital (emergency room, pediatrics, medical staff and the hospital board) were required to approve this format, along with the DPW. The team physician was invaluable in directing the protocol through the hospital committees.

While the protocol was being discussed by the hospital committees, the team set about developing a procedure for handling hospital child abuse cases. The child protection team is authorized by the county welfare department to investigate hospital-referred cases of child, abuse and neglect. In an investigation, the following evaluations are completed: a family study/social history; a medical evaluation of the child; and a psychological evaluation of the parents/child. These evaluations are usually made by four persons, and completed within 2 to 3 days after admission of the child.

The conclusion of the team process is a team meeting to discuss information obtained in the interviews. There are four questions to be answered: 1) Is this a case of child abuse/neglect? 2) Is wardship/guardianship necessary to protect the child? 3) Does the child have to be removed from the home? 4) What is the treatment plan, that is, what services must be provided and by whom? The most important question after abuse/neglect has been confirmed concerns the treatment plan. What is essentially being asked is, "How do we try to help the family?"

After a treatment plan is formulated, the team's recommendations are forwarded to the welfare department and the case is assigned to a coordinator, who is usually DPW staff. The team meets every 6 to 8 weeks to review the status of the case.

The Bartholomew County Child Protection Team was formed in March 1975, and staffs about 30 hospital cases a year. Of the 60 or more cases seen by the team, only in five did the team recommend temporary removal of the child from the home. Since March 1975, two additional teams have been formed in other hospitals within the five counties.

PARENT AIDE PROGRAM

In the five-county area, as in many other rural areas, the lack of available staff, the lack of time to devote to the abusive family, and the threat imposed by the DPW in regard to removal of the child, all indicated the need for an alternate method of servicing the abusive parent. Therefore, volunteers were recruited to meet the needs of abusing families.

The Parent Aide Volunteers are individuals who work with abusing parents on a one-to-one basis. They give the parents—who may be hurt, suspicious, isolated and damaged—possibly their first experience of a supportive, nonjudgmental friend. The aim is to nurture the parents, not provide substitute mothering for the child [3].

How are volunteers recruited? The easiest way to obtain volunteers is from a community-awareness program. As one speaks to groups, clubs and other organizations, members of the audience inevitably ask what they can do to help. Also, a newspaper article is invaluable in recruitment. In this manner 17 volunteers were recruited, and the first parent aide training began in July 1975.

After being periodically revised over the last 2 years, the Project Children training program, based on five sessions, covers the following areas: role of the parent aide; dynamics of child abuse; high-risk indicators; crisis intervention; child abuse from the child's perspective; working with the parent; legal aspects; and confidentiality.

After the training and case assignment, periodic group meetings are held with the volunteers. The volunteers discuss the progress of the parents and the problems encountered, with the possibility of obtaining a solution from other group members. The meetings also serve as ongoing training sessions. Speakers discuss Goal Attainment Scaling (a research method used to evaluate the progress of the client), "the helping relationship," child management approaches, Parent Effectiveness Training, communication skills, etc.

Parent Aides are assigned cases from the welfare department, mental health center, Head Start Program and family service agency. In each case, the volunteer is supervised by the referring case worker. Additional supervision and coordination are provided by the program's volunteer coordinator.

Forty-two parent aide volunteers have been trained since July 1975, and have worked with 78 families. The average involvement with a family lasts 14.6 hours a month, for 5.9 months. There has been noticeable positive change in most of the families involved.

COMMUNITY EDUCATION

A significant part of the program development was that of informing and educating the community. A community education and awareness campaign in a rural area must be sensitive to local norms and attitudes regarding child abuse/neglect. In our region, we encountered complacency, along with an initial reluctance of both lay and professional people to acknowledge its existence. Therefore, an outreach effort was begun, to educate citizens regarding child abuse/neglect etiology, identification, Indiana child abuse law and reporting procedures, child and family advocacy, etc. Letters offering a program on child abuse/neglect were sent to organizations throughout the five-county area.

Requests for programs came in slowly at first, but within a year had increased tremendously. Since December 1, 1974, 392 presentations have been made to civic and community groups, and junior and senior high school classes. Pamphlets and posters were developed and distributed to increase public awareness of child abuse/neglect, Indiana law and reporting procedures. Audiovisual materials were acquired and news media were contacted. They responded with sensitive reporting on child abuse/neglect and local efforts to combat it.

Concurrently, training for professionals began in anticipation of an increase in reports of child abuse/neglect. This was important in guaranteeing an appropriate response to the reporter, and effective delivery of service to the child and family. Failure to have the "system" ready generally results in "turning off" the reporting public, particularly the physician, nurse, teacher, etc.

Policies and guidelines were developed for and adopted by the professional community (schools, hospitals, law enforcement agencies) on handling suspected cases of abuse/neglect. Policy development involved representatives from each agency or discipline. Policy statements, in themselves, can do little to ensure an appropriate response from a person or agency. It is the implementation of that policy by the agency that provides for a standardized and effective approach to carrying out individual and collective responsibilities. Implementation is achieved through firm directives from the agency head and specialized training to all staff. Training designs specific to each profession were developed for the training programs.

PREVENTION

In the area of prevention, the initial focus was on two identified needs: 1) a child care facility that would serve children 0–6 years of age, since existing programs accepted only children 3–6 years of age; and 2) a parenthood course as part of a junior and senior high school curriculum. Community support was mobilized for development of a comprehensive child care facility, Columbus Child Care Center, scheduled to open in the autumn of 1978. The center will accommodate 240 children, 0–6 years of age, providing 24-hour care (crisis) and drop-in (respite) care. The development of programs to strengthen family life will also be a part of the center's services.

A parenthood course (Exploring Childhood) was added to the curriculum of one junior high school in 1976 and one senior high school in 1977, and is in the planning stages in two other junior and senior high schools in the region [4]. Project Children's role in this effort was to document the need for education for parenthood, help the schools to obtain information and materials, and promote the course as a requirement for all students.

Another prevention activity was to institute a program based on Systematic Training for Effective Parenting [2]. The nine-session program meets weekly and discusses the following topics: the child's goals of misbehavior; encouragement; effective listening; exploring alternatives; natural and logical consequences; I-messages; reflective listening; and a family meeting. The program was started in January 1977 with a group of families having problems in abuse, neglect and child management. All members of the initial group were clients of the county welfare department. The model program has been slightly altered to fit the needs of these clients.

CONCLUSION

Project Children has been in operation since November 1974, initiating 10 new services within five counties. Although this program may not be unusual for an urban area, it may be rare for a rural area. It has tried to put limited resources to their best use, and is fortunate to have a group of professionals and lay persons who, while active in other areas, are dedicated to the cause of preventing child abuse and neglect. Project Children is not an ideal program, but the effort has been worthwhile, has had a positive effect upon the community, and has had a significant effect upon child abuse and neglect in the region.

REFERENCES

1. *Handbook for Implementing Child Abuse and Neglect Service Programs.* Berkeley, Calif.: Berkeley Planning Associates, 1975.
2. Dinkemeyer, Don, and McKay, Gary. *Systematic Training for Effective Parenting.* Circle Pines, N.M.: American Guidance Service.
3. Adapted from "Child Abuse and Neglect Coordinating Organization: Parent Surrogate Program." South Bend, Ind.
4. "Exploring Childhood," developed by the Education Development Center, Social Studies Program, 15 Mifflin Pl., Cambridge, Mass. 02138.

There can be little doubt as to the need for day-care services for children in modern America with about half of all mothers employed outside the home. How to meet this need, particularly in rural areas, is a large question. In the next article Barbara Brown addresses this issue based on experience in a midwestern state. A multipronged approach is suggested as having potential with family day-care being at the core.

18

BARBARA J. BROWN

Rural Day Care: A Social Service Delivery Problem

Child care is a primary social service to the child and to the family. An increasingly important component of child care is day care—that is, "care for children away from their home for less than twenty-four hours a day." Day care is an integral part of the State of Wisconsin's Title XX plan and is a primary service in helping keep families intact.

The problems of developing, delivering and stabilizing day care services in a rural area are unique. The same factors that influence the delivery of other social services in this environment, shape day care services—population, geographic area, climate, distance, economics and the traditional individualistic structure of society.

In exploring the day care picture in Northern Wisconsin and identifying problems and solutions of the delivery of these services, the first need is to survey the environmental and historical factors of the region.

Northern Wisconsin is a sparsely populated, rural area. (Northern Wisconsin, for our purposes, includes the counties of Ashland, Bay-

Reprinted from Barbara J. Brown, "Rural Day Care: A Social Service Delivery Problem," *Human Services in the Rural Environment*, Vol.3, No. 2, February 1978, pp. 19–24, by permission of the author and journal.

field, Burnett, Douglas, Florence, Forest, Iron Langlade, Lincoln, Marathon, Oneida, Price, Rusk, Sawyer, Taylor, Vilas and Washburn.) Even urban centers are "rural" in flavor. They range in size from the largest cities of Wausau (population 33,000) and Superior (population 31,000) to towns and villages of 200 to 300 population. The area has only three cities of 15,000 or over population.[1] *Population* is a factor in developing day care sources.

The "rural" designation in this area does not mean that the main economic base is meat, dairy and grain products. Statistically, most Northern counties have less than 5 million dollars annual income from these sources.[2] In this largely forested area, lumber and its products and tourism are the main industries. This economic base determines the family income for the region. The median family income ranges from $4,705.00 of Forest County to $7,731.00 of Oneida County. This median income range compares to a figure of $10,509.00 of Dane County (Madison).[3] *Economy* is a determining factor in day care services.

Northern counties are vast in area with thinly spread population. The number of people per square mile in the Region—1 person per 138 square miles in Florence County and 1 person per 93 square miles in Forest County—reflects the people/land ratio. Compare these figures to Dane County which has a ratio of 1 person per 2.5 square miles.[4] Long distance travel is the way of life in Northern Wisconsin. *Distance* structures the type of service and is a factor in delivering day care in Northern Wisconsin.

Traditionally, and shaped by the rugged environment, the Northern Wisconsinite has vestiges of pioneerism. As in many isolated rural areas, the people have not been current with the major events of politics, economics and changing idea structures. Such elements tend to shape a highly individualistic person, who has deep family and community roots. *Tradition* is a factor in the development of day care services.

Historically, home-centered child care in Wisconsin is the type of child care used by 80 percent of the families. A number of factors enter into this choice: 1) providing care for children in a home is generic to their life style; 2) a widely scattered living pattern makes access to large child care centers inconvenient; 3) small population bases do not support the large, centrally-based center; 4) there has been little experience with center-based programs, and there is a reluctance to entrust child care to a "public" program.

Woven into this background of tradition and environment are two factors which color the picture of day care service delivery. Traditionally, the extended family was a major factor in this culture. What we

now define as social services were "family" services in the extended
family situation—child care was a major service performed by the
extended family or the near neighbor. As elsewhere, the family structure is changing to the nuclear unit—often far distant and isolated
from any family ties. With this radical change, parents must look
elsewhere for the services once provided by the large family unit.

Along with change in family structure is the change in wage earners
in the family. Nationally, the number of working parents with children
under 6 years of age is now 4.4 million, with a prediction of 32 percent
increase by 1985.[5] Further, the old family structure of a couple—
father working, mother at home caring for the children—has drastically changed. The number of single parents with pre-school children is
significant and is sharply increasing.[6]

These factors are pressuring parents to use day care of an unknown
quality and quantity. Evaluation and searching for day care is a new
problem for many parents. There are few sources to help with assessment. Lack of day care resources does affect participation in the job
market. Decreased income encourages family breakdown and welfare
roles increase. The need of day care resources then becomes a community problem—a delivery of social services problem.

Northern Wisconsin parents still, most frequently, use the home-
centered day care. Hit and miss, they try to choose a child care service
from this invisible system of day care operators. Most family day care
is privately operated. These providers are isolated from the community by environmental factors, by long working hours and by little or
no communication with any existing social services agencies.

What are the problems that face the parent, the community, the
county and the state in maintaining and developing this most widely
used type of child care—family-centered day care? How can a structure of child care be built that is indigenous and useful to this area?
The problem can be outlined as three-fold: 1) need of viable communications with family day care providers; 2) development of a support
system by the providers and the existing agencies; and 3) community
visibility. The problems are not unique, but the system developed must
be unique.

In the past ten years, nationally, a variety of experimental programs
have been initiated to improve the family day care experience. These
programs range from informal individual efforts loosely connected by
an information system, as in the Portland, Oregon, Day Care Neighborhood System, to highly structured day care systems in New York
City and Milwaukee.[7]

Concerned with the quality of day care provided in the home center,
the Colorado Department of Education, the Community College of

Denver and the Mile High Child Care Association of Denver worked together to develop a training program for the home-centered day care provider, which went beyond the minimal requirements of licensing. The training was a combination of group sessions and home visits by field workers. Perhaps one of the most important and lasting results of this project was the organization of the strong, influential family day care association in Denver, Boulder and other areas.[8]

A most interesting and effective project supporting the home-centered day care program has been initiated in Wisconsin. The Coordinated Child Care Services, Inc. is a tri-county organization that provides basic support for a three-fold group—the family day care provider, the Racine County Department of Social Services, and the parent. The Coordinated Child Care Services, Inc. supports Racine County Department of Social Services by recruiting and administering family day care homes for use by the Department. The Racine County Department of Social Services provides comprehensive support to the child caretaker by supplying training, administrative services, equipment, and by arranging for FDA food subsidies. The parents benefit by having stable and supervised care for their children.[9]

The principal effort of all of these projects is the support of the family day care provider in an effort to bring stabilization and improved quality to family day care.

In this Northern region, as in nationwide statistics, family-centered day care is used by the majority of children in out-of-home care. Several innovative programs have been developed by agencies, by counties, by communities, and by individuals to support the home-centered day care provider and the parents and children that use this service. Correlated with these supportive services, there has been a marked increase in the number of licensed home-centered day care centers within the last five years.

Projects that have been developed to support home-centered day care programs are:

1. *1973 Federal Child Welfare Grant—Development of Small Group Day Care in the Family Home Setting*
   The object of this project was to identify and to develop licensed day care centers, for eight or less children, located in the family home. Four agencies (a day care center, an incorporated child care board, a social service agency, and a CAP agency) participated in the project. Each agency recruited a specified number of day care providers. Direct monies were given to the day care providers for start-up costs—i.e., meeting building code requirements in the home and purchase of equipment and supplies for programming.

Training was supplied by the agencies and by the Division of Community Services. Ten centers were developed, five centers are still operating. A significant result of this project was community visibility for the home-centered day care. The project proved to be a model and a change agent for several areas where home-centered day care has increased in numbers. A second part of the project was the development of Toy Kits, based on cognitive and stimulation skills for use in the home-centered program. The kits serve as a learning tool for: 1) the day care provider; and 2) the child enrolled at the center. Materials in the kits are keyed to using the home environment as a learning device. The kits are left in the center for six to eight weeks and then passed to another center. The kits are enthusiastically endorsed by child care providers as excellent supporting material. Use of the kits is continuing.

2. *Day Care Start-Up Grant—1975—Support System for Family Care*
   Oneida County Department of Social Services developed a support system for their isolated family day care providers including the following components:
   A. A series of toy kits were developed to be used in the home center. The County Homemaker took the kit into the home. She then spent time working with the day care provider and the children in the use of the toys in the kit.
   B. A child development library is available at the social service department for the day care provider.
   C. Two training meetings were held for the day care provider. There was expertise and information from Early Childhood professionals. Not surprisingly, the strength of these meetings was the participants' exchange of ideas and discussion of problems. It is reassuring to realize that you are not the only child care provider who has unanswered questions.

3. *Federal Child Welfare Grant—1976—Development of Skill Kits*
   A second series of skill kits, patterned after the 1973 project, was developed to: 1) meet the needs of the increased number of home-centered day care centers, and 2) to respond to the popularity of the original set of skill kits.

4. *Day Care Start-Up Grant—1976—Parent Training for Prevention of Child Abuse/Neglect*
   Oneida County developed a training program to be used as preventive agent for child abuse/neglect. Selected parents spend time helping in a home-centered day care program, learning parenting skills and techniques.

5. *Day Care Start-Up Grants*
   Start-up grants for day care centers during the past four years

have provided support for fourteen home-centered programs. The grants were awarded directly to the day care provider for use in start-up costs in developing a day care center program.

6. *Division of Community Services Training Funds*

A film strip—"It's Like Home"—was developed by the Rhinelander Division of Community Services for use with community groups and prospective day care providers. The film presents the exploratory and unique learning environment of the home-centered program, and is used as a training component for the child care provider in this kind of day care.

With the disappearance of the extended family and the increased number of employed women with children under six years of age, the familiar family structure is fragmenting. It is a suitable time to ask questions about the care of our children.

1. What conditions need to be present to enable a family to care for children?
2. What social services must be provided to replace the extended family?
3. How can the factors in a rural setting, with the inherent traditions and environment that prevent child day care from being a viable social service, be ameliorated?
4. Designing a support system for the home-centered day care program is a two-way communication—what support does the home-centered day care provider want?
5. What does "community visibility" do for social services?

NOTES

1. *State of Wisconsin Blue Book*, Wisconsin Legislative Bureau, "Local Government," Wisconsin Document Sales and Distribution, Madison, Wisconsin.
2. Ibid., "Farm Income."
3. Ibid., "Household Incomes."
4. Ibid., "Geography."
5. *Day Care Facts*, Women's Bureau, U.S. Department of Labor, Pamphlet 16 (Rev.), Washington, D.C., 1973.
6. *Toward a National Policy for Children and Families*, Advisory Committee on Child Development, DHEW, UCD, National Academy of Sciences, Washington, D.C.
7. Urich, Heide, Director, *A Study of Family Day Care Systems in*

Massachusetts, Child Care Resource Center, 123 Mt. Auburn Street, Cambridge, Mass., 1972.

8. *Developing Training Support Systems for Home Day Care*, E.P.D.A. Project 1010, Colorado Department of Education, Denver, Colorado 80203.

9. Consultation with Marlene Mura, Director, Coordinated Child Services, Inc., 815 Silver Street, Racine, Wisconsin.

Perhaps nowhere in the United States are cultural differences more relevant for social services than in a comparison of white middle-class society with some American Indian practices. As the next article indicates this is important with regard to whether certain conditions become defined as problems, specifically neglect and abuse of children. Family and child behaviors have differing meanings in varied cultural contexts. Often there is too much of a tendency to pass judgment on situations involving persons of ethnic minority groups by coming at these conditions from reference points external to the group and not understanding what they mean within it.

About half of the Indian population in this country is rural although many of those in the program discussed were in the process of adjusting to urban settings. Most, however, saw themselves as "reservation families." Flowing from various concerns it is too easy to build a case for the removal of children from families and particularly so with minorities. The program described is an effort to keep families intact. Elements of this program could be applicable in either rural or urban environments.

19

HIDEKI ISHISAKA

American Indians and Foster Care: Cultural Factors and Separation

Concern regarding the child welfare system in the U.S., specifically in the area of foster care, has been growing [7:340–341; 18:321–333;

Reprinted from Hideki Ishisaka, "American Indians and Foster Care: Cultural Factors and Separation," *Child Welfare*, Vol. LVII, No. 5, May 1978, pp. 299–308, by permission of the author and the publisher, Child Welfare League of America.

19:132–142]. It has been estimated that there are 220,000 children living in foster care homes that receive state funds [6:219–223]. Although this is a national problem involving children and families from all sectors of the population, the threat of child separation may be disproportionately greater for families of underprivileged ethnic-minority groups [24;23:15–17, 22].

Neave and Matheson surveyed families involved in child separation in British Columbia, Canada, to ascertain patterns of child separation and factors associated with those patterns [23]. The authors used a two-part typology to analyze causes: norm-violative separations were due to physical abuse, neglect, desertion/abandonment of children and sexual deviation or imprisonment of parents; non-norm-violative separations were due to family problems or needs that could be helped or met by placement of the child outside of the home.

Neave and Matheson suggest that for families involved in non-norm-violative separations, existing services may be adequate, but for families involved in norm-violative separations, additional services may be necessary. Families involved in norm-violative separations tended to evidence characteristics that resulted in social marginality.

The information regarding American Indian families involved with foster care presented in this paper supports Neave and Matheson's general finding. Additional information from this study suggests that life-style patterns and/or cultural differences in behavior play a critical role in the separation of Indian children from their parents. The data are derived from a 2½-year research and demonstration project funded by the Office of Child Development, Department of Health, Education and Welfare. The project had as its major goal the development of procedures by which American Indian families could be assisted to avert child separation. A residential facility was located. American Indian program staff were hired and trained, and families were admitted into the project. The project, called the Alternative to Foster Care Program (ATFCP), was the first program of its kind in the United States. The ATFCP provided families with apartment units in its residential facility. Services available through project staff included child care, child management counseling, dietary counseling, employment and social service advocacy and other case management services. When indicated, referrals were made to treatment services available in the locale for difficulties with alcohol and other problems in personal functioning.

Data contained in this study represent a majority of the 26 families

TABLE 1
Reason for Referral

Norm-Violative		Non-Norm-Violative	
Abandonment	11 cases	Escape from abusive	
Abandonment and		partner	4
physical abuse	1	Illness of parent	1
Abandonment/neglect	1	Psychiatric problem	
Physical abuse	2	of parent	1
Neglect		Extreme youth and indigent	
Parental sexual	2	status of mother	2
deviation	1		
	18 (69%)		8 (31%)

who have been in residence. The families were admitted to the ATFCP program on the basis of need for service, with no attempt to select a representative sample. Following the typology developed by Neave and Matheson, the families were sorted according to the reason for separation or the threat of separation. The results are shown in Table 1.

SUMMARY OF DESCRIPTIVE DATA

The families had varied child placement histories, ranging from no previous child separations to 16 individual child separations for one family. Nineteen families (73%) had had prior separations. The majority of the families were headed by women (85%), with only four couples intact. Family heads were economically marginal (92%) and were largely dependent on public welfare. Family heads' formal education ranged from 3 to 13 years, with 10 years as both a mean and median. In only five families was the head of the household a skilled worker. The rest reported little, if any, employment history. The majority were making the rural-urban move. Seventeen defined themselves as reservation families. Yet even among those heads of household who identified their families as urban, ignorance of available social programs, transportation systems and medical services, to name but a few examples, indicated that there was an urban adjustment problem for all families. This problem may be related to the large number of family heads ($N = 23$) who requested assistance with alcohol management. The most common alcohol use pattern among the family heads was so-called "binge" drinking. In only one instance was there evidence of chronic alcohol abuse. In the majority of cases of alcohol use, it was part of the rationale for child separation provided

by referring caseworkers or other agency personnel. The most frequent complaint about the families was abandonment associated with
alcohol abuse by the parent(s). Abuse-neglect as separate categories
were sometimes confounded, due to problems of definition. Neglect
resulting from abandonment is an example of the overlapping of norm-
violative categories used by referring personnel. Because of the large
number of recidivist families, including many who had children separated at the time of admission to the ATFCP, reconstitution of the
family unit was a goal for 65% of all families in residence. In most cases
the ATFCP staff were able to help family heads regain custody of their
children.

Criticism of Practices

Reexamination of child welfare policies and agency procedures in
regard to Indians may be necessary. Criticism of existing foster care
practices is made on two levels, one general, the other specific to
cultural minorities.

First, the foster care system fails to make adequate efforts to avoid
initial placement [25:3–9; 3:499–503]. In the absence of established
and standardized definitions that inform caseworkers as to when children should be removed or returned to their parents, decision making
tends to be highly subjective [21: 13–17].

Another problem is the use of the family pathology model for decision making in regard to separation. Maas has suggested that the use
of questionable indicators of family pathology be deemphasized, in the
absence of validated associations between family pathology and subsequent childhood disorders [19:132–142]. Mech has pointed to the
problem of decision making in foster care placement [20: 26–51].
Procedures for making decisions do not always include all available
options, nor is there adequate documentation after separation that
placement was the best choice. A final general problem is the ubiquitous use of the terms abandonment, neglect and abuse as proffered
reasons for the separation of children from their parents. There is a
great need for more precise definitions of such widely used terms [21:
13–17; 5: 432–443]. Distinctions must be made between cases in
which documented parental behaviors can be related to harm or potential harm to children and cases in which the decision to separate
is based on inferred potential threat, given subjective indicators.

These issues are relevant to all groups in the child care system; for
ethnic minority groups, other considerations play a role in the placement decision. The characteristics of families involved in the ATFCP
were consistent with the concept of a multiproblem family. The

ATFCP families were highly vulnerable to child separations involving alleged norm-violative conduct by the parents. As mentioned, abandonment accounted for a majority of the separations, and in many cases assumed norm-violative conduct was associated with alcohol problems. But over the course of the ATFCP operation, staff noted few instances of neglectful or abusive behavior on the part of parents toward their children. The most frequent pattern among the family heads who did drink and for whom drinking was a self-defined problem was the tendency to leave children in the care of older siblings or on their own when parents were drinking. Through interviews with the parents, it became clear that for the majority, such behavior was not seen as faulty parenting or as grounds for child separation.

Among Indian cultures, different conceptions of childhood competence may be related to presumed norm-violative conduct by parents [22:165]. Cultures vary in regard to the responsibilities deemed appropriate to children of different ages. That younger children are sometimes left under the care of older children does not necessarily constitute grounds for child separation. Adequate care is an empirical issue that must be addressed case by case. In several instances over the course of the ATFCP operation, young children were left under the care of older brothers and sisters who were also young (for example, 8 years old). Yet, the younger children appeared to be well cared for, and there were other adults in the vicinity in case of emergencies. A source of misunderstanding may be related to differences in norms of parental conduct. Parenting customs may be brought to the urban environment from cultural settings in which they are common practice, but in the city such practices are viewed by social agents as deviant and evidence of faulty parenting. Jayaratne has raised serious issues relevant to sociocultural differences and their potential role in the misperception of parenting behaviors on the part of social agents [15:5–9].

SILENCE AS A RESPONSE

An example of a cultural difference reported in the literature on American Indians is a case in point. Among the Western Apache, silence plays an important role in cultural functioning [2:213 ff.] Silence is considered an appropriate response at times of role ambiguity. A child returning from a boarding school may be greeted with silence on the part of the parents because it is unknown what changes in the child may have occurred in the child's absence from home. With time, silence is broken as parents and child become reacquainted through nonverbal signs. Such a cultural pattern invites cultural misunder-standing. An outsider witnessing what would be an occasion for em-braces and verbal intimacy among Anglo people might misperceive the Western Apache cultural pattern as an indication of coldness of parents toward their child, or make other culturally biased inferences.

Another example has been described by Good Tracks—a pattern of noninterference among certain Indian groups [11:30–34]. Noninter-ference is a standard of conduct derived from the traditional value placed on individual rights and prerogatives that extend to children as well as adults. The rights of a child include the expectation that his or her autonomy will be respected by others. The child learns early not to interfere with others. The parents may ignore intrusive or interfering youngsters, and may be seen as uncaring or uninvolved, rather than evidencing a pattern of parenting different from that of the majority society.

Among the families at the ATFCP there were few examples of inadequate parenting judged by their own cultural standards. The common perception of family functioning by staff members was of harmonious and warm relationships between parents and children. Parents tended to be permissive, seldom insisting that the children comply with parental wishes. But where children violated standards of behavior consistent with their Indian cultural backgrounds, the parents assumed a direct and forceful role in guidance. As Locklear contends, the role of the parent in traditional Indian cultures as an authority figure must be understood [17:202–207]. The role can in-clude corporal punishment when deemed necessary. In a time of in-creasing disapproval of corporal punishment, such punishment can be misinterpreted as abuse or evidence of potential abuse.

Misperceptions of behavior and unfounded inferences regarding motives can play a significant role in the decision to separate Indian children from their parents. The experiences of the ATFCP staff indi-cate either an unwillingness or an inability of some caseworkers and other agency personnel involved with Indian families to consider cul-tural factors in regard to problem identification and in service provi-sion.

CULTURAL GENOCIDE?

Yet, problems associated with the placement decision are only a small part of the general dilemma of Indians in the foster care system. Incalculable damage to many Indian children may be the result of repeated or permanent separation from parents. The potential deculturative effect of such dispositions lends support to Farris and Farris' accusation that such policies amount to cultural genocide [9:386–389]. Some data suggest that removal of Indian children from their homes with relocation to culturally alien environments has serious implications for identity development. Identity confusion has been demonstrated to be a result of the removal of children from their natural parents and cultural contexts for educational purposes [14:7–17; 16:94–103; 10:85–92].

For the ATFCP families, use of alcohol was not necessarily seen as the cause of parenting deficiencies. The high rate of alcohol use may be associated with the pressures of urban adjustment. In addition to the stress engendered by leaving family and other social supports, adults had to deal with unemployment, social marginality, discrimination and prejudice [4:359–369]. Value conflicts, loneliness and unfamiliarity with aspects of life in a heavily populated area may all increase stress and the likelihood of use of alcohol [26:398–403; 13:35–38; 1:199–205].

As mentioned, the pattern most evident in the ATFCP group was "binge drinking." There was only one case of chronic alcohol use. In that sense the ATFCP sample's use of alcohol supports Price's observation that physical addiction to alcohol may be low among Indians and alcohol use could be lessened if the predisposing conditions for binge drinking were remediated [24:17–26]. Among the ATFCP clients, drinking patterns suggested that for some, drinking was a means of escape from a punishing day-to-day life, and to relieve a sense of personal failure and inadequacy [12:306–321; 8:72–87]. But drinking also appeared to serve a social purpose. Deprived of close friends and relatives by the relocation to the urban environment, many of the clients seemed to use drinking as a means of socializing with other Indians. It is unlikely that any one explanation covers the variety of drinking patterns in this heterogeneous population [24:17–26].

In view of the possible cultural biases influencing the decision to separate, every attempt should be made to keep Indian children in their homes. Neave and Matheson suggest that new types of service delivery be made available to the societally marginal families frequently associated with norm-violative child separations [23]. Alcohol use should be treated when parents request treatment, but assumed alcohol abuse should not be construed as grounds for child separation unless there is clear evidence that alcohol use creates a situation dangerous to the child.

Day care centers would permit parents time out from parenting. An opportunity to engage in other activities would benefit many, especially single-parent families lacking resources for child care. Classes to familiarize new arrivals from reservation areas with urban resources and services would help them to cope in an alien environment.

Finally, in those cases in which separation is unavoidable, work with parents toward early return of children to their homes should be an integral part of the initial treatment plan. Every attempt should be made to strengthen the Indian family through resources and supports. Only in this way can progress be made toward preventing many Indian children from becoming drifters in the child welfare system.

In the long run, the focus on individual difficulties, e.g., alcohol, may be dysfunctional. For the majority of the ATFCP clients, the obstacles to personal achievement and adjustment were external. There is a great need to make new opportunities available to Indians. The removal of children from their parents due to family poverty or misperceptions of parenting behavior because of differing cultural standards is not an adequate response. Chronic unemployment, educational underachievement and residence in substandard housing all constitute social problems of enormous consequence to American Indians. Educational programs agreeable to Indians, job training and increased availability of adequate housing are basic changes that must occur if Indian families in both rural and urban areas are to be freed from problems arising from poverty. These problems are all too often seen as originating from within the Indian community itself, and not as the legacy of centuries of restricted opportunities, genocide and forced assimilation.

REFERENCES

1. Ablon, J. "Cultural Conflict in Urban Indians," *Mental Hygiene*, LV (1971).

2. Basso, K. H. "To Give Up on Words: Silence in Western Apache Culture," *Southwestern Journal of Anthropology*, XXVI, 3 (autumn 1970).

3. Bryce, M. E., and Ehlert, R. C. "144 Foster Children," *Child Welfare*, L, 9 (November 1971).

4. Chadwick, B. A., and Stauss, J. H. "The Assimilation of American Indians into Urban Society: The Seattle Case." *Human Organization*, XXXIV, 4 (winter 1975).

5. Cohen, S. J., and Sussman, A. "The Incidence of Child Abuse in the U.S.," *Child Welfare*, LIV, 6 (June 1975).

6. Culley, J. E., et al. "Public Payments for Foster Care," *Social Work*, XXII, 3 (May 1977).

7. Donadello, G. "Commentary," *Child Welfare*, XLVIII, 6 (June 1969).

8. Dozier, E. O. "Problem Drinking Among American Indians," *Quarterly Journal of Studies on Alcohol*, XXVII (March 1966).

9. Farris, C. E., and Farris, L. S. "Indian Children: The Struggle for Survival," *Social Work*, XXI, 5 (September 1976).

10. Goldstein, G. S. "The Model Dormitory," *Psychiatric Annals*, IV, 9 (November 1974).

11. Good Tracks, J. G. "Native American Non-Interference," *Social Work*, XVIII, 6 (November 1973).

12. Graves, T. D. "Acculturation, Access and Alcohol in a Tri-Ethnic Community," *American Anthropology*, LXIX (April 1967).

13. Hamer, J. "Acculturation Stress and the Function of Alcohol Among the Forest Potawatomi," *Quarterly Journal of Studies on Alcohol*, XXX (1969).

14. Hobart, C. W. "Some Consequences of Residential Schooling," *Journal of American Indian Education*, VII, 2 (January 1968).

15. Jayaratne, S. "Child Abusers as Parents and Children: A Review," *Social Work*, XXII, 1 (January 1977).

16. Krush, T., and Bjork, J. "Mental Health Factors in an Indian Boarding School," *Mental Hygiene*, XL (1963).

17. Locklear, H. H. "American Indian Alcoholism: Program for Treatment," *Social Work*, XXII, 3 (May 1977).

18. Maas, H. S. "Children in Long-Term Foster Care," *Child Welfare*, XLVIII, 6 (June 1969).

19. ____ "Children's Environments and Child Welfare," *Child Welfare*, L, 3 (March 1971).

20. Mech, E. V. "Decision Analysis in Foster Care Practice," in H. D. Stone, ed., *Foster Care in Question*. New York Child Welfare League of America, 1970.

21. Nagi, S. Z. "Child Abuse and Neglect Programs: A National Overview," *Children Today*, IV 3 (May-June 1975).

22. National Action for Foster Children; A Survey of Activities Based on Reports Submitted by States and Communities, October 1973–October 1974, U.S. Department of Health, Education and Welfare, Office of Human Development, Office of Child Development, Washington, D.C.

23. Neave, D. C., and Matheson, D. K. "Directions in Research Questions About Policies and Practice in Parent-Child Separation," *Canadian Welfare*, XLVI, 6 (November-December 1970).

24. Price, J. A. "An Applied Analysis of North American Indian Drinking Patterns," *Human Organization*, XXXIV, 1 (spring 1975).

25. Shapiro, D. "Agency Investment in Foster Care: A Followup," *Social Work*, XVII, 6 (November 1973).

26. Westermeyer, J. "Opinions Regarding Alcohol Use Among the Chippewa," *American Journal of Orthopsychiatry*, XLI (1972).

The first years of life are crucial in the development of children and especially so for handicapped youngsters who require professional attention. When an infant living in the country has a handicapping condition, meeting the child's needs is often a greater problem for the parents than for similar parents in an urban location. The special resources required may not be accessible or the travel required for the parents to make them available may be prohibitive. The following article describes how needed services, including professional personnel and special equipment, have been incorporated into a mobile unit that travels a rural area encompassing three counties. A substantial number of children and families are served through this approach, which in the process involves the parents and communities.

20

PATRICIA L. HUTINGER AND NANCY MC KEE

The Baby Buggy: Bringing Services to Handicapped Rural Children

A familiar sight in the farmlands and small towns of west-central Illinois is the "Baby Buggy," a mobile unit operated by the Macomb 0-3 Regional Project to bring a variety of early intervention services to high risk and handicapped infants and their families. The arrival of the Baby Buggy—the name refers to the van's CB radio "handle"—has become an expected and anticipated event in the lives of many families who live in a 3-county rural area within a 50-mile radius of Macomb, Illinois.

The Macomb Project was funded in 1975 as a 3-year demonstration project in the Handicapped Children's Early Education Program, Bu-

Reprinted from Patricia L. Hutinger and Nancy McKee, "The Baby Buggy: Bringing Services to Handicapped Rural Children," *Children Today*, Jan–Feb. 1979, pp. 2–6, by permission of the authors.

reau of Education for the Handicapped (BEH), U.S. Office of Education. Located in the College of Education at Western Illinois University in Macomb, it is a model home-based program for the education/remediation of handicapped, high risk and/or developmentally delayed infants, from birth to age three, and their families.

Parents of handicapped infants in rural areas sometimes find that the extra burden of transporting children to a central location is more troublesome and tiresome than staying home with the child. Travel is also tiring for the child. Thus, rather than attempting to gather children and families together in a central location, the staff decided to develop a "room on wheels" to bring services to the scattered families.

The four project staff members, called Child Development Specialists (CDSs), have experience in both early childhood and special education. They provide a variety of services to handicapped and high risk children whose needs cover a wide spectrum. Some infants are considered at high risk because of maternal diabetes, premature delivery or low birth weight, among other conditions. Others are environmentally deprived and developmentally delayed. Their mental and/or physical handicapping conditions range from mild or moderate to severe and profound. Over 100 children have been served during the past three years.

HOME VISITS

Service delivery centers around weekly home visits to the 47 families in the project. During the first few visits, informal assessments are made, based on observations of the child and parent and the interaction between the CDS and the parent and child. Formal assessment scales are administered to evaluate the child's motor abilities, language, cognitive and sensory development and social and self-help skills. The assessment also helps parents gain a general idea of the child's developmental levels. A final step is determining, through discussion with parents, their primary concerns about their child.

Specific activities for each child are then planned and carried out during the home visit. The CDS sets goals for the child, in agreement with the parents, to be accomplished in 6-month periods.

The curriculum, developed by project staff members, is based upon Piagetian assumptions about child development, and procedures and activities for achieving goals are developed within this framework. A specific activity is assigned for the parent and child to work on each day. Many activities can be used for a variety of learnings. A barn with farm animals, for example, can be used for eliciting language, for developing classification and matching skills, for concept development and for dramatic play. When an objective is too difficult for a child, the CDS helps the parent break the task down into a series of simpler activities for the child. Parents are taught to record the child's progress between visits.

An occupational therapist, who is a consultant to the project, visits families once a month to demonstrate techniques to help enhance a child's motor development.

PARENT INVOLVEMENT

In the Macomb project emphasis is placed on the parent's role as primary teacher of the child. Parents' cooperation is sought in scheduling, planning and carrying out home visits, and the Child Development Specialists work side by side with parents.

Parents' emotional needs are also of concern to the CDS, who listens, offers suggestions and provides encouragement and support. If counseling or other services are indicated, she arranges for these through local community mental health centers and other appropriate agencies.

Parents receive a bimonthly "Baby Buggy" newsletter from the project, which contains information on project happenings, staff news and features on such topics as safety and nutrition. Three parents also serve on the advisory council, which meets every six weeks to review project plans and activities and advises the director on community involvement and suggested courses of action.

SHARING CENTERS

All parents are invited to come to sharing center meetings every two weeks, together with their children, including those in the project and their siblings. Here parents have an opportunity to share their experiences, learn new activities, develop effective ways of dealing with their children and observe other adults and children. For the children, the sharing center is a place where they can either watch other children or participate in a variety of activities. The 1½-hour sessions, held in churches, community centers, the mobile unit or homes, are scheduled and planned with the help of parents, who often contribute many materials used in the sessions.

Activities are planned for children of varying developmental levels and ages, and a curriculum based on a Piagetian approach has been developed for use at the sharing centers. Snack time is an important part of each session, as is a short parent study meeting devoted to such topics as nutrition, behavioral problems, child management and language development.

Another type of sharing center, WADE, is available to families who live in or near Macomb. WADE is held weekly in conjunction with the YMCA Mom 'n' Tot Swim Program. Parents attend with their children, getting into the water along with the CDS to work on various techniques of stimulation, relaxation and body control of children in the water.

PLACEMENT AT AGE THREE

When children reach age three, they are eligible for the public school system's preschool program for handicapped children. Depending upon a child's needs, other placement is also considered and often used. Several children, for example, have been placed in nursery school programs, some have moved into a day care center in a local community, and sometimes a parent elects to work at home with a child, with some assistance from project staff, until the child is ready for kindergarten.

Appropriate placement is determined after consultation among project staff members, parents and all others involved—for example, the school psychologist, classroom preschool teacher, school principal, speech therapist, school nurse and, when indicated, a social worker.

COMMUNITY COORDINATION

Many families are referred to the project by public health nurses, physicians, physical therapists and other hospital workers, and the project maintains a close relationship with staff members of hospitals and community agencies, such as Homemakers and others in the Illinois Department of Children and Family Services. A pediatrician is a member of the project advisory council, and the project coordinator is also a member of interagency councils in two rural counties.

In addition, project staff members also work closely with public school and day care teachers, and a preschool teacher of the handicapped is a member of the advisory council.

Since resources are limited in rural communities, the project helps disseminate information to parents and the community—through the

"Baby Buggy" newsletter, articles in newspapers and presentations to community organizations—on handicapping conditions in general and the importance of early intervention.

Project staff members serve as consultants to other organizations and hold workshops and conferences for professional workers. This past summer the project sponsored a 2-week workshop, in conjunction with the Illinois Consortium of BEH First Chance (Handicapped Children's Early Education Program) projects, on strategies for working with young handicapped children.

THE MOBILE UNIT

The use of mobile units to deliver services is not new. The Red Cross (bloodmobile), the American Tuberculosis Association and the American Lung Association (chest x-rays) have used mobile units for medical/laboratory services. Bookmobiles have long been an effective means of bringing reading materials to rural populations, while "traveling classrooms" have been used in Appalachia and other areas of the country. Mobile units have also been used to transport senior citizens, handicapped individuals and those in need of special services.

The uses of the mobile unit in the Macomb project are varied. One of the first steps in the project is the medical stabilization of each child, and the van is sometimes used to take children and parents to physicians' offices, public health clinics and medical centers for diagnostic work and inoculations. It is particularly useful when there are several children from the same area scheduled for a clinic appointment.

Screening and evaluation may also be done in the mobile unit. Perhaps the simplest form of screening which can be accomplished there is the basic audiological evaluation, which can be conducted by a Child Development Specialist trained or assisted by an audiologist. A portable audio-meter may be easily installed in the mobile unit.

The occupational therapist, accompanied by a CDS, travels and works with children in the mobile unit.

Some "home" visits are conducted in the unit. Often parents have rather negative feelings about agencies; they do not trust the schools and they do not want their children labeled "handicapped." In addition, they do not want to become involved with "the University." For these parents, the Baby Buggy offers a safe, neutral territory.

Sometimes a parent is uncomfortable inviting the staff member into her home—she may feel that her house is not as orderly as it should be, or that there is not adequate space. (Some of the families live in trailers with less floor space than is in the van.) Or another adult may have to sleep in the living room during the daytime because he or she works nights. In these cases, the mobile unit offers an ideal alternative. It can be used as a model, helping the mother to see ways of child-proofing her home. Also, when a mother is home alone day after day, without transportation, a visit to the mobile unit provides a change of pace—she "gets out" for a while.

The mobile unit also provides a model demonstration area for work with children and parents. When weather is above freezing, the small bathtub can become the site for various gross and fine motor activities —and vocalization. The tub can also be used for soap suds painting and water play, and as a substitute for the WADE program for children who cannot come to the one held at the YMCA. Techniques for positioning and bathing children can easily be demonstrated in the tub.

The unit's small kitchen can be used to teach special food preparation techniques and ways to help children learn to feed themselves or to use adaptive feeding aids.

Both fathers and mothers are interested in the unit and its equipment, while the children are attracted by the stimulating materials it contains. Practical use is made of equipment like the CB radio. One staff member uses the radio as a motivational device to elicit spontaneous language from children. (Lest CB enthusiasts become alarmed, the radio is not turned on while the child is talking into it.) When the CB is turned on for the child to listen to, it becomes a tool for auditory training. Some children who are just beginning to climb manage to get up into the driver's seat and, under close supervision, pretend to drive. This ability will not necessarily be present on one home visit (the child is unable to get into the seat), but on the next visit, he or she crawls into the bucket seat and sits there radiating confidence and delight.

If two families in the project live relatively close to each other, the Baby Buggy is used for small sharing centers. It can also transport several sets of children and parents to sharing centers in centrally located churches or community buildings. Sometimes it is used to take families to the weekly water activities program at the YMCA. Afterwards, parents and staff members meet in it for snacks and discussion of the morning's activities.

Sometimes staff members use the mobile unit to travel to nearby conferences, workshops and in-service training sessions. In this way they can plan programs, discuss ideas or work on budget during their travel time. The unit also serves as the site of periodic staff retreats, enabling the entire staff to confer away from the interruptions of jangling telephones, drop-in visitors and students in need of help.

The mobile home used in the project was chosen, after careful consideration, partly because of the competitiveness of its price ($12,-000 in 1975), and because the company was willing to make special modifications, including the installation of a small bathtub, a diaper/laundry receptacle, a full-length mirror, and special child-proof screen door and ignitor switches on the gas/electric refrigerator and heater.

After the mobile unit was in use for five months, remodeling was undertaken. The original brown shag rug was removed and lighter colored indoor-outdoor carpeting, donated by a wholesale dealer, was installed. One of the built-in bench seats was removed to make more floor space, and a child-sized bean bag chair was added, along with an unbreakable mirror which can be attached to the wall at child height. Colorful, stimulating pictures help brighten the dark wood-toned paneling. Cost of the remodeling, accomplished by project staff and one additional person was minimal—$116.45.

Other adaptations after the unit was purchased included lettering on the side of the vehicle, which was done by a local high school student for $10.00. An 8-track tape deck was adapted for cassette tapes through the installation of a converter. During the second year of the project, the CB radio was purchased and installed.

MAINTENANCE AND COST

Supplies necessary for efficient day-to-day operation include liquid propane gas, paint, a fire extinguisher and a space heater. (Since the mobile unit is too tall to be housed in the university garage, it sits outside all year, plugged into an electrical outlet especially erected for it.) Other items needed include sets of keys for all project staff members, pans, towel racks, a plexiglas mirror, deodorizer, paper products and the small bean bag chair. Normal maintenance requires regular lubrication and oil changes, periodic tune-ups and necessary waste dumping. Water tanks must also be filled from time to time.

The van averages 8.45 miles per gallon in highway and country road driving. During the first two years of the project, it traveled a total of 13,220 miles. (Other vehicles, such as university-owned cars, were also used during the second year.) Usually a staff member scheduled for home visits takes the van for a day at a time. In the third year of operation it was in use almost every day. The direct operating costs for the first two years were $2,167.51; when other costs, such as installation of the electrical outlet and various supplies, were added, the total cost was $2,607.76.

CONCLUSION

A home-based program aimed at serving children and families in a rural area offers a unique challenge. By providing an easily accessible place for screening and evaluation, "home" visits and sharing centers —as well as transportation for staff members and families in the project—the Baby Buggy has proved to be an effective means of meeting the challenge.

Human services are multifaceted matters as the next article by the Kelleys demonstrates. On one hand, training natural helpers to provide assistance in nonmetropolitan areas is itself to provide a service. On the other, the contributions that these recently trained people may then make tend to have a ripple effect far beyond the core activity of their preparation by professionals. It is an exciting way of working in small communities.

21

PATRICIA KELLEY AND VERNE KELLEY

Training Natural Helpers in Rural Communities

The seventies was a decade of interest and innovation in rural community mental health programs. The community emphasis of the Community Mental Health Centers Act of 1963 and the social movements of the later sixties gave impetus to the innovations carried out in the seventies. Several studies had demonstrated an extreme shortage of mental health services in rural areas,[1] and the social climate grew favorable for reform and change. There has been growing recognition that specialized clinical techniques that must be appropriate in urban areas might not be as helpful with rural clients and that the small primary community in rural areas might mitigate against persons seeking services from "outsiders." The lack of anonymity in rural areas has also suggested the need for alternative service delivery in mental health programs.

Iowa is a good state for experimentation with new ideas in rural community mental health delivery. It is a rural state; half of the population lives on farms or in communities with less than 5,000

From Patricia Kelley and Verne Kelley, "Training Natural Helpers in Rural Communities," an original article, by permission of the authors.

A different version of this article was presented at the Psychiatric Outpatient Clinics of America Conference in Chicago, May 1978, and is being published in the proceedings of that meeting.

persons.[2] Community mental health centers cover much of Iowa: 87 of the 99 counties and 94 percent of the population. There is a strong involvement of rural citizens in policy formulation because the centers are locally controlled. The Iowa pattern can facilitate innovation, an example of which will be discussed in this article: the development of training programs for rural natural helpers by the Mid-Eastern Iowa Community Mental Health Center and the University of Iowa.

The Mid-Eastern Iowa Community Mental Health Center was established in 1969. Like other Iowa community mental health centers, it is an Iowa nonprofit corporation with its policies established by a board of directors representing the area served. The board of directors has formal contracts with three counties that provide all funds except patient fees. The board uses these funds to employ a staff to carry out the contracted services.

The staff of seven professional and two clerical persons serves about 900 persons a year in outpatient clinical services and provides about 1,200 hours a year in community service. The staff also supervises graduate students planning to enter mental health professions.

The stated goals of the center are: (1) to serve the mental health needs of families and individuals through outpatient services; (2) to reduce the utilization of the area state hospital through aftercare; (3) to serve community needs through consultation, joint planning, and training programs with relevant organizations and individuals; (4) to serve the experiential and supervisory needs of graduate students entering mental health professions; and (5) to develop a pattern of services that is accessible and available close to home to provide as little disruption as possible to family life and to employment.

To implement the latter goals the center operates offices in all three of the counties it serves. The central office is located in Iowa City, which is the home of the University of Iowa, and is in Johnson County, population 72,127. Offices are also located in the two rural counties, which are staffed one day a week. Cedar County has a population of 17,489, and the office is in Tipton, population 2,877. Iowa County has a population of 15,419, and the office is in Marengo, population, 2,234. The economics of the rural counties are based on agribusiness, which is also substantially true of Johnson County.

The two rural offices are staffed by the center's director and co-author of this paper who has developed working relationships with many professionals in these communities.

By 1972 the center's board was pressing for more community education and consultation. At the same time the staff was searching for alternative methods of service delivery. Not only was the demand for service exceeding the supply of professional staff time, but also there were people with personal problems who did not need or would not use professional mental health services. This was especially true in the two rural counties in which the satellite offices were quite visible, and where many people knew each other.

One alternative explored was the use of indigenous helpers, paraprofessionals, and volunteers. This model had become popularized in the social welfare field in the sixties because of a manpower lag with the expanding programs and because of the growing recognition that people closest to a situation can often be most helpful.[3] A look at this movement was helpful for recognizing nonprofessionals as a potential resource, but the plan was rejected because of three basic problems. First, these helpers would be officially attached to the agency itself and would thus not alleviate the "stigma" problem. Second, the cost of time and money in recruitment, screening, supervising, insurance, space, and even salary with the paraprofessionals (although not with volunteers) would be prohibitive. Third, the process of training people and making them official arms of an agency might reduce the spontaneity, naturalness, and closeness to the situation, which were the very factors that made these people desirable helpers in the first place.[4]

Although another alternative was chosen, this look at the indigenous helpers, combined with the growing self-help movement of the latter sixties and early seventies, facilitated our receptivity to new ideas. The concept of community control was beginning to proliferate in the community mental health literature, and mental health planning nationally was moving from the institutionally based sickness model to venture into the community. Local control of services and consumer participation were beginning to be taken seriously.[5]

Thus, innovation was a key word in the community mental health movement, and we were looking for patterns appropriate to the catchment area. A psychologist pointed out an article about how community persons were trained to be mental health helpers in rural Susanville, California, where there was a shortage of mental health professionals.[6] A search of the literature suggested that lay counselors could be trained to be effective helpers,[7] and therefore we leaned toward the natural helpers model. We remembered, too, that Frank Kiesler in 1960 had developed a mental health program in rural Grand Rapids, Minnesota, where a large share of the mental health professional staff time went to consulting with the other community professionals (that is, physicians, lawyers, teachers, and clergy) who had been helping naturally before the mental health center had opened.[8] The concept then was expanded beyond lay helpers to include non mental health professionals (physicians, clergy, nurses, teachers, and others) in the natural helping system envisioned. Planning began on the presumption that there was a network of natural helpers at many levels in the community who were already helping people and that assisting them in the helping they were already doing might be the best use of time, energy, and resources. Our project confirmed this belief for us, and research done since our project was completed has backed up this hypothesis. Shirley Patterson of the University of Kansas has studied the natural helper system in rural Kansas and has concluded that natural helpers have unduplicated qualities that should not be drastically changed. She believes that professionals should assist the local helpers rather than the reverse.[9] The Joint Commission on Accreditation of Hospitals has developed and endorsed a conceptual model called the Balanced Service System that includes use of the "folk system" in the natural environment as a basic part of the delivery of mental health services.[10] This concept includes a wide range of mental health services from natural folk systems to institutionalization with the desirable pattern to enter the system as far toward the "most natural" as possible. Edward Buxton of Madison, Wisconsin, has also supported the idea of taking advantage of local systems. He says, "Social workers in rural areas should learn to support existing systems instead of fighting them."[11]

So we had a model and we were ready to try it. The original training projects for natural helpers in rural communities were developed and carried out through a grant from the Office of Child Development and under the auspices of the Community Mental Health Center. The center director (co-author of this article) was project director, and two psychologists and a social work educator from the University (co-author of this article) were trainers. Head trainer was Dr. Eugene Gauron, a university psychologist, who had originally noted the Susanville project and had approached the center about developing a program in Iowa.

The first pilot project was conducted in Cedar County. From October 1972 through April 1973, twenty-four sessions were held for twenty natural helpers; the age range of these helpers was 17 to 58. From October 1973 through May 1974, a similar training program was held in Iowa County for eighteen persons with the age range from 22 to 66. In both communities, the trainees represented "official helpers" (such as persons from public social services, public health, community action programs, and school systems), other professionals not in official public positions (such as a physician and a funeral director), and "invisible helpers" (high school students, beauticians, retired persons, housewives, and business people) who were helping people regularly without any special training or recognition.

Recruitment was done through the project director and his local board members and through ads in the newspaper. Leon Ginsberg has discussed the importance of knowing the community and its systemic networks when working in rural areas, and yet he recognized that outsiders may have more impact because they are not as bound by community patterns.[12] Entry into the community was facilitated by having persons from different levels of involvement. The board persons from each county were actively involved community members and the project director who spent one day a week in the community had working relationships with the professionals in the community and the three trainers who were outsiders. The mix provided the necessary balance for community acceptance. Screening of the trainees was not attempted or necessary since the training was geared toward enhancing their existing natural helping skills, not toward making them assistant mental health workers. The program was explained and there was a request for time commitment. Once these guidelines were understood it was a self-selection process.

After the pilot projects were completed in the two rural counties, the training staff experimented with alternative formats. In July 1974, a two-day workshop was held in Johnson County based on the materials previously developed. This workshop was open to interested persons from any of the three counties served by the center. Twenty persons attended. In a different attempt to reach natural helpers, minisessions on helping skills were conducted with an adult Sunday school class of a local church on two consecutive sessions. There was also a special follow-up session in Cedar County for consultation with the original trainees in 1974.

After the federal grant ran out the community mental health center continued working with natural helpers. The center director continued his weekly visits to the rural counties. About half of the original trainees have moved away, and eight of them are either not visible or their whereabouts are unknown to the director.

Consultation is also being provided to natural helpers who have not received this training. Typically, there are relatives and friends of emotionally disturbed persons who refuse to use professional mental health services. Options are explored and support is given. In addition to providing consultation, the center is also providing new training programs based on the pilot projects, but using its own staff. The board of directors approved an additional half-time staff position so that this training could continue. A second series of helping skills sessions were conducted in Cedar County in 1976 for twelve persons. Assertiveness training programs have been conducted in Iowa County in 1976, in Johnson County in 1977 and in 1978, and at a residential care facility in 1977. A series of helping skills sessions were conducted for Iowa City in 1977 and 1978. Efforts were made to organize a training program for bartenders in both rural counties, but none of the forty-eight persons sent letters of invitation responded. The same is true for bartenders in fifty-six Johnson County taverns and bars. None responded. This illustrates the necessity of thoughtful preparation and community involvement to gain entry into the natural helper network.

Two of the center's staff have collaborated with the School of Social Work faculty (and co-author) to provide summer workshops in helping skills. These workshops are "service courses" offered by the school to nonsocial work professionals. One summer a workshop was conducted for high school students and their guidance counselors to assist them in implementation of peer counseling programs.

The training materials, which were originally developed for the pilot projects and which we have modified and continued to use since, are planned around a competency-based model of education. The skills to be learned were broken into small parts that become separate and sequential learning modules.

Competencies in each skill were outlined and practiced until at least minimal competence was achieved by most persons in the group. Immediate feedback was provided, either verbally or through video-tape. In developing this program we relied heavily on the seven inter-personal variables that Robert Carkhuff suggested were characteristics of good helpers at all levels, from professional therapists to natural peer helpers.[13] These seven variables were communication of empathy, communication of respect, concreteness, genuineness, self-disclosure, confrontation, and immediacy of the relationship. Carkhuff has guidelines with behavioral descriptors for each variable that we used as handouts. He also has a rating scale for each variable describing levels of achievement. Minimal competence in each skill begins at level three on a five-point scale according to Carkhuff. This provided us a convenient checklist for determining minimal competence.

The philosophy of the training program was action oriented, with emphasis on the importance of previous learning in maintaining maladaptive behavior patterns and of new learning in modifying behavior patterns. Some key principles for counseling were adopted from the Susanville, California, project[14] and were given to the trainees to guide their interventions. We also had sessions on special topics, such as interviewing skills, family dynamics, and recognition and management of depression. Throughout the course, emphasis was placed on the importance of knowing when and how to make referrals and of seeking professional consultation. In line with this emphasis, the trainees developed a directory of local community services, including themselves. This emphasis on community control and self-reliance enhanced the natural helping network.

A feature of this pilot project was the inclusion of evaluation techniques to assess the effectiveness of the training program and its impact on the individual trainees. The same evaluation instruments were utilized in both Cedar and Iowa County programs. They included the Personal Orientation Inventory (POI),[15] the discrimination and communication indexes developed by Carkhuff, checklists from a "programmed" patient interview by the trainees, and personal report statements made by the trainees in diaries kept throughout the program. The results of this assessment are reported elsewhere.[16] Significant improvement was shown by both groups in the pilot projects on all measures.

In summary, we endorse the concept of the balanced service system in the delivery of mental health services. We believe that this training program for natural helpers is a step toward implementation of that plan. Iowa has been a good state for a project such as this; the population is dispersed throughout the state, and the mental health centers are locally controlled. Because of these factors, community involvement in planning and implementing mental health services is strong, and there is minimal bureaucracy to interfere with experimentation. Mental health programs in rural areas should support existing folk systems while at the same time provide for professional services to be available to those who need it.

NOTES

1. M. Wagenfeld and S. Robin, "The Social Worker in the Rural Community Mental Health Center," *Social Work in Rural Communities: A Book of Readings*, edited by L. Ginsberg (New York: Council on Social Work Education, 1976), pp. 69–83.

2. U.S. Census, 1970, Iowa (Washington, D.C.: U.S. Government Printing Office, 1971).

3. Shirley Patterson, "Toward a Conceptualization of Natural Helping," *Arete*, 4, 3 (1977): 161–173.

4. David Hardcastle, "The Indigenous Nonprofessional in the Social Service Bureaucracy: A Critical Situation," *Social Work*, 16 (1971): 53–66.

5. J. Mermelstein and P. Sundet, "Community Control and the Determination of Professional Role in Rural Mental Health," in *Human Services in the Rural Environment Reader*, edited by D.

Bast (Madison: Center for Social Service, University of Wisconsin Extension, 1977), pp. 29–45.

6. Ernest Beier, Peter Robinson, and Gino Micheletti, "Susanville: A Community Helps Itself in Mobilization of Community Resources for Self Help in Mental Health," *Journal of Consulting and Clinical Psychology*, 36 (1971): 142–150.

7. Ibid.; Julian Rappaport, Jack M. Chinsky, and Emory L. Cowen, *Innovations in Helping Chronic Patients: College Students in a Mental Institution* (New York: Academic Press, 1971); Robert G. Wahler and Marie Erickson, "Child Behavior Therapy: A Community Program in Appalachia," *Behavior Research and Therapy*, 7 (February 1969): 71–78; E. L. Cowen et al., "Prevention of Emotional Disorders in the School Setting," *Journal of Consulting and Clinical Psychology*, 30 (October 1966): 381–387; Ernest G. Poser, "The Effect of Therapists Training on Group Therapeutic Outcome," *Journal of Consulting Psychology*, 30 (August 1966): 283–289; Robert R. Carkhuff and Charles B. Truax, "Lay Mental Health Counseling: The Effects of Lay Group Counseling," *Journal of Consulting and Clinical Psychology*, 29 (August 1965): 333–336; Margaret J. Rioch et al., "National Institute of Mental Health Pilot Study in Training Mental Health Counselors," *American Journal of Orthopsychiatry*, 33 (July 1963): 678–689.

8. Frank Kiesler, "Is this Psychiatry?" in *Concepts of Community Psychiatry: A Framework for Training*, edited by S. Goldstone (Washington, D.C.: U.S. Government Printing Office, 1965).

9. Shirley Patterson, op. cit., pp. 166–167.

10. "Principles for Accreditation of Community Mental Health Service Programs" (Chicago: Joint Commission of Accreditation of Hospitals, Accreditation Counsel for Psychiatric Facilities, 1976).

11. Edward Buxton, "Delivering Social Services In Rural Areas," in *Social Work In Rural Communities: A Book of Readings*, edited by L. Ginsberg (New York: Council on Social Work Education, 1976), pp. 29–38.

12. Leon Ginsberg, "Observations on Preparing Students for the Practice of Social Work in Rural Communities," in *Educating Social Workers for Practice in Rural Settings: Perspectives and Programs*, edited by L. Levin (Atlanta: Southern Regional Education Board, 1974), pp. 26–35.

13. Robert Carkhuff, *Helping and Human Relations*, 2 vols. (New York: Holt, Rinehart, and Winston, 1969).

14. Beier, Robinson, and Micheletti, op. cit., pp. 142–150.

15. Everett L. Shostrom, *Personal Orientation Inventory: An Inventory for the Measurement of Self Actualization* (San Diego: Educational and Industrial Testing Service, 1966).

16. Verne Kelley, Patricia Kelley, Eugene Gauron, and Edna Rawlings, "Training Helpers in Rural Mental Health Delivery," *Social Work*, 22 (1977): 229–232.

BIBLIOGRAPHY

Beier, E.; Robinson, P.; and Micheletti, G. "Susanville: A Community Helps Itself in Mobilization of Community Resources for Self-Help in Mental Health." *Journal of Consulting and Clinical Psychology*, 36 (1971): 142–150.

Buxton, E. "Delivering Social Services in Rural Areas." In *Social Work in Rural Communities: A Book of Readings*, edited by L. Ginsberg. Council on Social Work Education, 1976, pp. 29–38.

Carkhuff, R., and Truax, C. "Lay Mental Health Counseling: The Effects of Lay Group Counseling." *Journal of Consulting and Clinical Psychology*, 29 (1965): 333–336.

Carkhuff, R. *Helping and Human Relations*, vols. 1 and 2. New York: Holt, Rinehart and Winston, 1969.

Cowen, E.; Zak, M.; Izzo, L.; and Frost, M. "Prevention of Emotional Disorders in the School Setting." *Journal of Consulting and Clinical Psychology*, 30 (1966): 381–387.

Ginsberg, L. "Observations on Preparing Students for the Practice of Social Work in Rural Communities." In *Educating Social Workers for Practice in Rural Settings: Perspectives and Programs*, edited by L. Levin. Atlanta: Southern Regional Education Board, 1975, pp. 26–35.

Hardcastle, D. "The Indigenous Nonprofessional in the Social Service Bureaucracy: A Critical Examination." *Social Work*, 16 (1971): 55–63.

Joint Commission of Accreditation of Hospitals, Accreditation Council for Psychiatric Facilities. "Principals for Accreditation of Community Mental Health Service Programs." Chicago, 1976.

Kelley, V.; Kelley, P.; Gauron, E.; and Rawlings, E. "Training Helpers in Rural Mental Health Delivery." *Social Work*, 22 (1977): 229–232.

Kiesler, F. "Is This Psychiatry?" *Concepts of Community Psychiatry:*

A Framework for Training, edited by S. Goldston. Washington, D.C.: U.S. Government Printing Office, 1965.

Mermelstein, J., and Sundet, P. "Community Control and the Determination of the Professional Role in Rural Mental Health." In *Human Services in the Rural Environment Reader*, edited by Bast. Madison: Center for Social Service, University of Wisconsin Extension, 1977, pp. 29–45.

Patterson, S. "Toward a Conceptualization of Natural Helping." *Arete*, 4, 3 (1977): 161–173.

Poser, E. "The Effect of Therapists' Training on Group Therapeutic Outcome." *Journal of Consulting and Clinical Psychology*, 30 (1966): 283–289.

Rappaport, J.; Chinksy, J.; and Cowen, E. *Innovations in Helping Chronic Patients: College Students in a Mental Institution.* New York: Academic Press, 1971.

Rioch, M.; Elkes, C.; Flint, A.; Usdansky, B.; Newman, R.; and Siber, E. "National Institute of Mental Health Pilot Study in Training Mental Health Counselors." *American Journal of Orthopsychiatry*, 33 (1963), 678–689.

Shostrom, E. *Personal Orientation Inventory: An Inventory for the Measurement of Self-Actualization*, Educational and Industrial Testing Service. San Diego: 1966.

U.S. Census, 1970, *Iowa*. Washington, D.C.: U.S. Government Printing Office, 1971.

Wagengeld, M., and Robin, S. "The Social Worker in the Rural Community Mental Health Center." In *Social Work in Rural Communities: A Book of Readings*, edited by L. Ginsberg. New York: Council on Social Work Education, 1976, pp. 69–83.

Wahler, R., and Erickson, M. "Child Behavior Therapy: A Community Program in Appalachia." *Behavior Research and Therapy*, 7 (1969): 71–78.

Sometimes one may wonder whether all of the existent social welfare programs actually make a difference. Often there is skepticism as to the value of a proposed project. It is useful, therefore, to take a historical perspective, looking back at a particular social innovation and examining its impact. The REA provides an excellent example. It may be alleged that this is a matter of technological rather than social development but that is only partially true. Electricity technology was fully operative long before the 1930s. What was not existent was the national commitment to bring electricity to most rural dwellers.

As is true today in such fields as health, housing, and transportation, many other modern nations were ahead of the United States in rural electrification in the 1930s. And as is true today the cries of socialism, big government, and bureaucracy were hurled by the opposition at proponents of progressive programs such as the REA.

22

PHIL BROWN

Our Rural Past: May 11, 1935, The New Deal Lights Up Seven Million Farms

Franklin Delano Roosevelt signed the executive order that established a Rural Electrification Administration (REA) on May 11, 1935. With a stroke of the pen Roosevelt created an instrument that would provide light and power to benighted rural citizens. The new federal agency was authorized to make low-interest loans to cooperatives and other groups interested in building new rural electrical systems.

The electrification of rural America was going to need all the back-

Reprinted from Phil Brown, "Our Rural Past: May 11, 1935, The New Deal Lights Up Seven Million Farms," *Rural America*, Vol. 3, No. 6, May 1978, p. 5, by permission of the author and the journal.

ing FDR could provide. In 1935 only 744,000 out of the nearly 7 million farms were served by electric power lines. There was opposition to REA in the Congress and outright disbelief in the industry.

When the bill to provide a permanent legislative base for REA was introduced by Senator George Norris of Nebraska and Congressman Sam Rayburn of Texas, the debate ran hot and heavy. Its chief defender in the House proved to be Mississippi's John Rankin, a man remembered more for his racism than his populism. When Connecticut's Representative Schuyler Merritt rose to defend the "progress" private utilities had made in rural America, Rankin took him on:

> *Rankin:* I wonder if the gentleman knows that in New Zealand two-thirds of their farms are electrified, in the United States about ten percent are....
> *Merritt:* ... New Zealand is a socialist state.
> *Rankin:* I wonder if the gentleman knows that in France and Germany 90 percent of their farms are electrified. Those are not socialistic states.
> *Merritt:* No, they are not socialistic but they are imperialistic.
> *Rankin:* I wonder if the gentleman knows that Holland and Switzerland are practically 100 percent electrified.
> *Merritt:* But they are no larger than our New England.
> *Rankin:* I understand that there is no state in New England that has even 25 percent of its rural farms electrified.
> *Merritt:* I do not care to give this gentleman more time.

Utility spokesmen predicted failure. Said W. W. Freeman, vice-president of the Columbia Gas and Electric Corporation, "It is clear that the industry, in its extensive experience in rural and farm service, has found it impossible to realize anything like the estimated results upon which the REA program is based.... The industry (must wait) and realize it will be called upon to pay its share of whatever tax burden is initially and finally assessed."

This was the same Freeman who had been chairman of an industry committee that submitted a report on the rural situation to the first REA Administrator, Morris Cooke. Cooke, who had spent the major portion of his life seeking ways to "electrify" rural America, was amazed to read in the report's conclusion that "there are very few farms requiring electricity for major farm operations that are not now served."

At the outset it was assumed that the private utilities would use REA's funds to expand their systems, but nothing happened until the REA started to build the rural electric systems the cooperative way. At that point the private utilities suddenly became very active; they did almost irreparable harm to the rural electrification program. According to Clyde Ellis, long-time executive director of the National Rural Electric Cooperative Association, in his book *A Great Step:*

"The private companies (though extremely active) were by no means providing area coverage. Instead they waited to learn where farmers were signing up people for a co-op, then sent their crews into those areas to build lines in the most thickly settled sections, neatly cutting the heart out of the proposed co-ops. Often co-op and power company construction crews were building down the same road at the same time. . . .

"Farmers called these power company lines 'spite lines' and 'cream-skimming' and this practice resulted in resentments that persist to this day among rural neighbors, and in the suspicions and mistrust that mark the dealings of many rural people with power companies."

The co-ops had other problems, too. The cost of delivering electricity to scattered farms and rural residents was expensive. The cost had to come down. The utilities said it could not be done—and they represented all the skills and ingenuity of the free enterprise system. But the co-ops, unfettered by tradition, set out to see what they could do.

As Harry Slattery, the third REA administrator, notes in *Rural America Lights Up:* "The REA co-ops set the poles 400 feet apart instead of 200 or 250 feet as had been the practice. They cut the cost of transformers from $60 to $21. They reduced the cost of meters by 40 percent. They speeded up the construction of distribution lines by 60 percent. For years private companies figured on an investment of $1500 to $3000 per mile of rural line. The REA co-ops built equally serviceable lines at $500 to $900 per mile. They built a system that farmers could afford. By 1946 half of all farms were electrified. By 1959 REA had financed 1,000 electric systems providing new or improved service to 4.5 million consumers on 1.4 million miles of line."

The co-ops had won the battle but not the war. Presidents Eisenhower and Nixon both tried to scuttle the program. As recently as last fall an anti-REA memo surfaced in the Office of Management and Budget written by some hold-over bureaucrat who believed the time had come to phase out the whole program.

What George W. Norris wrote in 1940 should have been carved in marble: "We have had to fight hard in the past and there is hard fighting ahead, because selfish and powerful interests are opposed to the economic and social benefits which cheap electric energy is bringing to our farm homes. But nothing can prevent the ultimate success of REA."

III. Working in the Rural Community

To function successfully in nonmetropolitan parts of the nation, it is extremely important for social service workers to understand the nature of such areas in general and their specific communities in particular. Like cities, rural communities differ from each other and possess their own character. They too have strengths and weaknesses. Each has its own history and traditions, and each moves its unique way toward its own future. Some are withering and declining whereas others are booming. Many are experiencing industrialization with the appearance of factories or plants of various kinds. Not only does this affect the local economy but its impact is also totally pervasive in the community. Some rural communities are very much farm and agriculture oriented whereas in others there is little of this type of link to the country. Some are known as mining, lumbering, or fishing towns and such descriptions often accurately reflect the domination of a town by a single economic pursuit. Generally, small communities are becoming more diversified and heterogeneous places. Mining and agriculture no longer monopolize rural life and economy.

There are small communities in which an educational or social welfare institution is located such as a college, mental hospital, prison, training school, or a school for the retarded or other handicapped group. In fact the community may be referred to and thought of as a college town, for example. In such areas it will be necessary to determine local attitudes to see how the facility is perceived and defined by its neighbors. In some places there is still an "asylum" mentality present whereas in others this is far less true. Of course the actual nature of the program in the institution has much to do with how the facility is viewed, but sometimes changes in types of care or treatment take a long time to become incorporated into the thinking and attitudes of even immediate neighbors, some of whom may actually be employed by the institution.

Interestingly, a proposal to establish certain kinds of institutions such as correctional facilities often meets stiff resistance. But to propose closing or reducing an existent institution, perhaps as a manifestation of contemporary trends toward deinstitutionalization and "community-based" programming, is threatening and may meet heavy opposition if the facility is a major employer and a large portion of the town's economy, as it frequently is.

Another feature in college communities may be the "town-gown" phenomenon, and in some places there is considerable division and even conflict between these segments. Some of the same things may happen with other kinds of institutions who import professionals and specialists such as physicians, psychiatrists, psychologists, therapists, researchers, and others for better paying positions and employ local residents for lower echelon jobs as aides, attendants, guards, and custodians. Resentment may be engendered in such situations.

On the other hand, colleges and social welfare facilities should not be thought of as only problematic. In more respects they represent precious resources in localities noted for lack of resources. Institutional personnel may be utilized for consultation at times by other rural workers. Their services may be enlisted and drawn into more distant towns and counties. A social worker may be able to assist an educational agency in relating to local needs through curriculum developments and modifications. Adding appropriate evening and weekend courses and workshops can be responsive to the changing needs of persons in the community. Furthermore, a worker may persuade a local institution to add or expand an outpatient program and in the process better respond to the situations of local and surrounding residents.

In some nonurban areas a particular ethnic or minority group is a significant factor in the life of the neighborhood. In others there may be notable age composition factors such as a disproportionate number of elderly. Influential nationality or religious factors, or both, exist in some communities such as those that may be largely or even entirely Amish, Catholic, Lutheran, Dutch, Czech, or Polish. Other forces unite and hold together certain rural communes. Some rural communities have seasonal components and vary in makeup with the time of the year. Examples are Gatlinburg, Tennessee, Wisconsin Dells, and Estes Park in Colorado. Tourism and lesiure have had powerful ramifications for towns like these with small permanent populations and crowds of transient visitors. Lake communities in many states and retirement centers, particularly in the Sunbelt, provide still other illustrations of the importance of a social worker learning as much as possible about the community.

Communication patterns are another aspect of rural life-styles that to some degree differentiate the country from the city and with which the rural worker needs to be knowledgeable. Informality characterizes rural communication with an established, but informal, network for disseminating rumors and information. Typically, in small towns there are gathering spots where people meet and converse about whatever is uppermost in their concerns and interests at that time. This place may be a cafe, bar, automobile service station, grocery store, or some other business place. Such businesses are often more common for males whereas clubs, churches, and other organizations may provide a comparable avenue for women although this is changing as sex roles change. Schools also play large roles in provision of communication channels.

Many towns have a weekly newspaper that is carefully read by the subscribers. An interesting difference between metropolitan dailies and the rural weekly is the emphasis in the latter on strictly local events in place of national and international news. Often there will be columns devoted exclusively to reporting previous weeks' visits between the homes of families and individuals in the community. Many rural papers carry such columns not only for the town from which the paper emanates but also for other surrounding communities.

In view of these comments on communication it must be noted that a major force in the change permeating the rural environment and in the urbanization of the countryside is the mass media. Rural residents watch the same television programs, read the same daily newspapers, and subscribe to the same magazines as do their city cousins. The impact of the media is profound and has influenced consumer habits, voting activity, and other behaviors.

There is considerable consensus in the growing literature on rural social services that the kind of social worker needed in sparsely settled areas is a generalist. But what does that term mean? It does not mean a person of superficial knowledge or skill but one who represents a breadth of experience and ability. Since there is a need for consciousness raising in small communities and a sensitizing of rural people to existent problems,[1] the generalist should have these kinds of skills. A generalist is one who can provide direct services effectively with individuals and families and can work with all of the other major systems, groups, organizations, and communities. In addition, he or she should be comfortable with all age groups. Knowledge should be possessed about the more extensive and usual social problems such as poverty, mental illness, health difficulties, crime, alcoholism, and family dysfunction along with information on ways of learning more, as required by circumstances, about less common problems. An understanding of broad-based intervention is essential as is knowing how to utilize and expand existent resources and create new ones. A rural human services worker must be a program developer. She or he should be knowledgeable about a variety of fields of service and settings even though these may not be found in the rural community. Being able to mobilize the community to find solutions to its problems is important. In other words, versatility and creativity are qualities particularly useful in the rural sector.

All of this is desired in the rural professional helper when at the same time the social worker ending up in the country often has less formal education. On the other hand, there is some evidence that the number of social workers in nonurban areas holding the master's degree is increasing.[2] Probably the same factors attracting people in general to the country from the city, environmental and others, are also drawing social workers. Formal credentials are not always held in as high esteem by rural dwellers as by urban; what is wanted is someone who can do the job required regardless of diplomas and degrees.

The imaginative nontraditional generalist worker described above at the same time must appreciate the importance of handling oneself in the rural environment in a conventional manner. A new professional in a small town is conspicuous and is on display. There is not the anonymity that exists in cities. In a place where "everybody knows everybody" it is especially important to fit in and be accepted if one is to be able to relate to the local citizens constructively and be effective as a helping agent. This means that a worker may not be able to indulge his or her more idiosyncratic impulses and will have to be mindful of the norms of the community. Kahn makes this point convincingly relative to efforts to do community organizing in rural places.[3]

The process of establishing oneself in a small community takes time and is made easier if one makes a point of meeting and developing relationships with leaders from various sectors: business, churches, schools, farm organizations, government, and others. This activity can contribute to learning a great deal about the community's customs, norms, traditions, and patterns. Who the informal service providers and natural helpers are will begin to emerge. Understanding will be increased on how crises are handled and needs are met and what forms problem solving typically takes.

Just as is true in larger communities, a professional helper in a rural area needs to understand the power structure and decision-making mechanisms. There is a tendency to dismiss such considerations as though they were nonexistent when it comes to small communities. But here, too, decisions are made and action taken and the social worker needs to understand the dynamics.

This necessitates familiarity with both the official and the informal aspects of power wielding. Elected officials are not necessarily the most important decision makers. Sometimes people "behind the scenes" carry a great deal of weight, and if they are supportive of an activity, this can make the difference between the success and failure of a program.

Among the more influential organizations in small towns are churches and service clubs. It is frequently found that power figures in a community have overlapping roles in various groups such as these and therefore they may become crucial to furthering or impeding the attaining of goals. Buxton puts this matter well: ". . . influential people may not do much in opposition to a program, but without their sanction many little people will not take a stand."[4]

Government in sparsely populated sections is also different from in the city. In the country the most significant unit of government for purposes of social services is generally the county and its board of supervisors or commissioners. Town councils and school boards are also part of the picture and can be either facilitative or obstacles relative to social service efforts. A professional needs to learn how to work with these governing bodies. Specialized groups such as the county welfare board are factors with which to deal. Special interest groups of various sorts can provide needed resources. An especially useful person in rural areas is the county extension agent who is the link between the land grant universities and individuals and families living in the country.

The social worker who is going to find working in nonmetropolitan environments satisfying is one who can function independently in relative isolation from other professionals. Generally in small rural agencies there is not the elaborate supervision structure characteristic of larger organizations and consultation may be infrequent and difficult to arrange. Therefore the worker needs to be a "self-starter" who can take initiative and move ahead without much direction from external sources.

Resourcefulness is important in obtaining consultation that may be potentially available in some service systems. For example, some state departments of social services have various resources available to their personnel but these often filter down mainly to the larger units and an agency out of the geographic or population mainstream may operate as if such consultation did not exist. An alert worker can sometimes tap in to this supportive service, perhaps through area or regional offices of the larger system. Self-evaluation is to be encouraged in rural workers since evaluation is so crucial to effective service delivery and to professional development and because it may be extremely limited in the small agency. In this connection it should be noted that in discussing the field experience necessary for the preparation of students for rural practice, Mermelstein and Sundet comment on autonomy as a feature of rural practice.[5] Working in a rural situation can be lonely and the lack of peer stimulation and support is often a concern. This makes journal reading and keeping up with the literature an especially important activity for the worker. Attendance at appropriate conferences, workshops, and institutes is another method of bridging the gap resulting from the absence of peers in the human services. Some such activities are necessary on the worker's part in order to keep abreast of change.

In Section III, the last unit of the book, we examine various considerations necessary to working in the rural community. The articles by Fenby and Schott present some of the basic issues. Osgood presents research findings on a comparison of rural and urban attitudes about welfare. Chambers's comments on rural myths are noteworthy. Mermelstein and Sundet discuss a useful theoretical construct for winning acceptance in a nonmetropolitan context. The merits of using terms such as "client" over "patient" are examined by Hinkle. The Riggs/Kugel article takes up the changes required when a professional helper moves from operating in an urban to a rural setting. A western mountain state is the scene of the Guillaume/Hayes contribution where change is pervasive, though recent. In the next article Jacobsen argues for a locality development model of rural community practice, and in the last selection Weber discusses educating people for professional practice in rural contexts.

NOTES

1. Marvin Kaiser of Kansas State University made this point at the University of Wyoming on March 29, 1979.
2. Leon Ginsberg, *Social Work in Rural Communities* (New York: Council on Social Work Education, 1976), p. 9.
3. Si Kahn, *How People Get Power* (New York: McGraw-Hill Book Co., 1970), p. 10.
4. Edward B. Buxton, "Delivering Social Services in Rural Areas," in *Social Work in Rural Communities*, edited by L. Ginsberg (New York: Council on Social Work Education, 1976), p. 33.
5. Joanne Mermelstein and Paul Sundet, "Social Work Education for Rural Program Development," in *Social Work in Rural Communities*, edited by L. Ginsberg (New York: Council on Social Work Education, 1976), p. 25.

In the following article the author discusses how, in rural locali-
ties, "one's private and public lives merge." The professional in
the country is conspicuous and visibility is a factor with which
to deal. Professional relationships are affected when the parties
involved know each other in the larger context outside the helping
agency setting. There are both advantages and disadvantages
inherent in working in nonurban environments. The article fol-
lowing Fenby's expands on some of the points she makes.

23

BARBARA LOU FENBY

Social Work in a Rural Setting

Social work in a rural setting offers the practitioner a variety of delights and difficulties, because of the visibility of both client and worker. Schoharie County has a population of 29,288 spread over 622.9
square miles, and the largest village has 5,000 people. The mental
health center, where I have worked for 1½ years, averages 300 cases
per year. To give an idea of what that means for visibility of client and
practitioner, when I went to a son's Little League game, I found three
children on his team who were known to me through the clinic. As
the season wore on and my family and the clients' families spent
evenings at the ball park together, the usual professional image was
impossible to maintain. In a small community we are, above all, neighbors.

The face that the professional puts on in the office is difficult to
sustain as a discrete image in the rural community. Certainly the
well-dressed, poised Ms. Fenby at work is very different from the
distraught lady, shoeless and in cutoffs, who tries to recapture an
impish dog on the town's main street while holding up three school

Reprinted with permission from *Social Work*, Vol. 23, No. 2 (March 1978), pp.
162–163. Copyright 1978, National Association of Social Workers, Inc.

buses of laughing children. Yet both images are public, and the non-professional, neighbor image is reflected into the professional setting.

At times a client will be open about his or her knowledge "I hear you had oil burner problems this morning and Art sent his truck out." At times there is a subtle change in the therapy hour, and the therapist cannot discount the fact that information from the "outside" is affecting the interaction "inside." For example, a client who had been working well in therapy became evasive and distant, although nothing discernible had caused the change. Probing uncovered that the woman had discovered my husband was on a yearly contract at the college, and had surmised that therefore I would not be staying in the area. She thought that therapy would end in failure, uncompleted. In a small world it is essential to be aware of contamination from outside information in the process of the therapy.

Goffman writes of "defensive and protective practices" that are used to avoid embarrassing and discrediting the image a person would like to maintain.[1] What professional practicing in a small place cannot recall a time when she discreetly avoided a client in a public setting or altered her behavior slightly because she was being observed? Although such defensive practices may be used in behalf of the professional, we more commonly act in behalf of clients to protect their confidentiality.

Chance meetings on streets or in shops are common in small places, and often they turn into "sidewalk consultations." Family and close friends who observe the interaction soon tire of asking "Who's that?" There is a tacit understanding that the person has acknowledged being a client, and nothing more is said. With clients who are children, the acknowledgment is often more overt: "Hey, Fenby, your Mom is my shrink!" And this sets off a whole exchange in which the child has the opportunity to probe who I am in my more private life. It is not unusual to come home and find a young client sitting at my kitchen table. The strain in this instance is on the members of my family, who are called upon to act in a therapeutic manner to a child they do not know and about whom I can say little. When the professional intrusion on private family life becomes too pervasive, the family either suffers or begins to set limits for itself. "We are going to the movies tonight, just us," means that no tag-along clients will be tolerated.

Confidentiality is particularly tricky during crisis situations. Clients, hospital, or police feel free to call in emergencies—after all, I am a neighbor with expertise. The result is often evenings spent entangled on the phone, with names being mentioned as a local person is threatened with jail or hospitalization. Frequently my family will know the person involved or the children in the client's family; yet they cannot acknowledge this to others since they understand that they, too, are bound by confidentiality. The children have developed a code, saying to one another, "It's a charge-it-to-my-office call," meaning that this is a situation in which I and the crisis are to be considered invisible, and they are to act as if deaf.

In an area with such a small poplulation, there are complex marital and family interrelationships, so that the social worker's audience is often not whom she expects. An incident with one client gets played back weeks later by the client's distant cousin, also a client. This reemphasizes the need for discretion since, as the holder of many secrets, the worker is responsible for maintaining the client's confidences. Even heavily disguised case presentations are likely to be recognizable to a population tuned into their own and others' private lives.

Having a "native" on the clinic's staff is important in managing appointments so that former spouses and non-speaking in-laws are not scheduled to be in the waiting room at the same time—unless it is planned. This is one of the most obvious ways to protect clients' confidentiality. More than one client has been lost temporarily through careless scheduling that revealed their status as patients to neighbors or close relatives when they stepped into the waiting room.

'JUST NEIGHBORS'

On the positive side, one of the delights of being "just neighbors" is that I can feel free to bum a ride with my first appointment on mornings when my car is tied up. In exchange, the neighbor-client gets half an hour of free time as we ride across the mountains together. Often patients will telephone the house to offer me a ride so the car will be free for my family. When my son does not put corn into the family garden it is noticed, and we are the recipients of corn from the gardens of neighbor-clients. When a child needs to be driven to a performance at a distant school while I am at work, a client offers to take my child along with hers so I will not have to take off extra driving time. And when a family member has a picture in the local paper as the winner of a contest, I am deluged with compliments and copies of the paper. Former clients take the opportunity to call up and comment and to let me know incidentally how they are doing. In a rural community, just about everything gets into the newspaper, so our houseguests at Christmas time and our comings and goings are reported along with those of our neighbors. We are highly visible, even when we may not wish to be.

One obvious solution to the problem of visibility is to live outside the area and commute from the "city." But this brings further problems in its wake. There is the suspiciousness of the outsider, of *them* who remain apart from *us*. *Their* motives are more suspect, *they* are perceived as more aloof and distant, and consequently trust of *them* is not easily maintained.

Just as neighbors are often my clients, so also I am often theirs. When I go to a shop or for professional advice or to see my child's teacher, I am quite likely to run into someone I know as my client. The roles are reversed. Now I am the seeker and they are the helpers. Because of this, it is virtually impossible to maintain the role of the omnipotent therapist, the self-reliant person described in the early social work literature and projected by many patients. The clients see me as a person who, like themselves, plays many roles. For many clients this is a comforting insight; no longer must they see themselves as dependent and inadequate because they have sought help; the social worker, like themselves, simply provides a special service.

Clients' overall familiarity with the worker as a person apart from the professional leaves little room for the mystification that is at times useful to the traditional therapist.[2] Since the worker is seen more completely, the worker's personal deficiencies and problems become known and the myth of the therapist as the healer with all the answers loses credence.

Discussion of social work in a rural setting would be incomplete without at least a mention of the ubiquitous grapevine and gossip circuit, which involves not only the stories about the worker and her family, but also involves clients and their families. Just as clients hear stories about us, we hear stories about them. Often prospective clients are known by hearsay for months before they walk through the clinic door. When confronted by some local figure of notoriety, it is imperative to retain one's professional objectivity and allow the client to be an individual, apart from the rumors, that may be circulating. Social work in a small place may be different and, in many ways, more demanding, as one's private and public lives merge, but the standards of professionalism can be maintained despite the more intimate neighborly contacts.

NOTES

1. Erving Goffman, *The Presentation of Self in Everyday Life* (New York: Anchor Books, 1959), p. 13.
2. Ibid., p. 70.

In the previous selection there was discussion of the visibility of the professional helper who is rural. Another aspect of the visibility is noted in the following article, which observes that clients too are known in rural communities. Like so many other aspects of life in small communities, there are both positive and negative factors in being identified as a client. Rural conservatism may make it difficult for a public welfare client. The author also presents the case for a generalist social worker without using the term. Implications of the dearth of resources for attempting to serve people in need are examined.

Iowa, a state made up of ninety-nine counties, has much of the richest farm land in the nation. But as the author points out only a small minority of Iowans are farmers, that is, live on a farm. While the majority of the poverty in the state in 1970 was in rural communities, most of these poor persons lived in small towns. Poverty is most pronounced in the least populous counties. Problems of the elderly are also particularly significant in Iowa and the Midwest generally. Life in these small communities and their "welfare departments" is described and interrelated by the author.

24

MAX SCHOTT

Casework: Rural

While we normally think of poverty as being an urban problem, the 1970 federal census revealed that, in reality, more than one-third of our nation's poor live in rural areas. As one might expect, the percentage of rural poor is higher in an agricultural state such as Iowa. In fact

Reprinted from Max Schott, "Casework: Rural," *Iowa's People*, Vol. 1, No. 1, Fall 1974, pp. 9, 14–16, by permission of the author and the journal.

50.1% of the Iowans identified as living below the federal poverty guidelines live in rural communities.

This does not mean that these people—some 150,000 of them—live on farms. Federal and state statistics only differentiate between urban and rural areas; they do not distinguish between "rural" and "farm." Thus it is that although 42.8% of our state's population live in the 92 counties which the federal government classifies as "rural," only 19% of Iowa's residents actually live on a farm; and the vast majority of these make a fairly decent living from the land. Very few of Iowa's "rural poor" are to be found living in dilapidated, drafty, old farmhouses isolated miles away from anyone or anything. That might be true of the sharecropping regions in the South or the Appalachia area in the East. But the "rural poor" in Iowa live, for the most part, in the hundreds of small towns which are sprinkled throughout the state.

Whether this particular segment of Iowa's population presents special problems to the caseworkers in these areas depends on the context of the question. "If the question is whether the problems which rural people experience are any different from those in the city, then the answer is 'No'," commented an older caseworker who has had considerable social work experience in a metropolitan area before "retiring" to a far more sparsely populated region of the state. "We have old people who need help. We have housing problems. We have cases of child abuse. We have unwed mothers. We have kids into the drug scene. We have marital problems. We have crime. And we deal with these problems according to the same principles that an urban social worker uses. But while we do have the same generic problems here, we don't have the same numbers of people involved in them." And it is the fewer numbers of clients which account for many of the differences between doing casework in a rural as opposed to an urban setting.

Fewer clients mean fewer caseworkers; and fewer caseworkers mean a smaller county office. Usually tucked away in some corner of the county court house, these local offices often seemed to be cramped for space; desks are pushed together, files are piled one on top of another, and a hundred different kinds of forms are stacked everywhere. And yet despite their size and despite the fact that the ratio of cases to worker is pretty much the same as it is in the metropolitan areas, there is not the sense of confusion nor are there numbers of people waiting to be seen in these offices even on the first working day of the month when food stamps are purchased.

Moreover because many of these county offices are small, the staffs tend to be much closer. In addition, an observer is struck by the casual friendliness which exists not only between the workers themselves, but between the workers and clients; and not just between a given worker and his or her clients but between all the workers and all the clients. One worker (whose hometown had a population of over 100,-000 people) explained it this way: "I had always heard that in a small community everyone knows everybody else. And it's true. In talking over case problems with the other workers I found that eventually, even without trying very hard, I had learned a great deal of information not only about the clients on my own caseload, but about most of the cases in the whole county. In a small office, a face gets attached to a case record very easily. So now I know practically all of our clients on sight."

Nobody hides in a small town; and that simple observation has definite disadvantages and advantages for the caseworker in a smaller community. For one thing, rural communities tend to be fairly conservative in their attitudes towards public assistance. While the same negative attitudes are also present in an urban area, it is much easier for a client to remain fairly anonymous in a city. But in a small community everyone knows who is "on welfare." And the fact that this is common knowledge presents some brass tack problems to the caseworkers as well as the clients. One worker told of a case in which she had worked for six months trying to find a suitable house in town for a family who was living three miles outside of the city limits but had no car. "Our office gets the county newspaper the afternoon before it is delivered to the rest of the county so I always have a little bit of an edge in contacting people who advertise a house for rent. They were all pretty interested until I would tell them who I was calling for and then they shut off like a blown fuse. They had heard that the family was a bad risk; and they would rather let the house stand empty than take a chance on them. The unfortunate thing about this particular family was that the gossip about them was unfounded. They were good people. They did pay their bills. But that isn't what the people here in the community had heard. And once these people get something in their craw it is hard to convince them otherwise."

But the fact that no one can hide in a small town does have some advantages for the caseworker. "It's the greatest outreach system in the world," stated a county director. "If some older person in the community falls and breaks an ankle and is not going to be able to work for awhile, we'll hear about it. Someone will stop in to the office or call us at home. We might even read about it in the county newspaper. Once we hear about it, we find out if there isn't something we can be doing to help. In other words, we almost always know something about a person before he or she comes through our door for help or before we go out to knock on theirs."

Rural county workers and administrators like to feel that they generally are able to keep a little better track of the needy in their community and that they can "take a little better care of our own". "For instance," said one administrator, "we have a standing agreement with the utility company here in the county that they won't turn off anyone's gas or electricity without first contacting us and giving us some time to find out what's going on."

Another difference which rural social workers point to as being to their advantage is the variety of cases each of them handles in a smaller county. While most offices separate their service caseloads into those involving families and children and those involving adults, that is about as far as case specialization goes in a smaller county. Thus, for instance, a given family and children worker could talk to a delinquent youth, open a foster care case, conduct a home review for a couple wishing to adopt a child, visit a day care center to see how a given child is progressing and respond to a report of suspected child abuse ... all in the same day. The same variety is also evident in an adult caseworker's load. Now it could be argued that the lack of specialization retards the development of expertise in dealing with specific problems; but the rural workers think the advantages of general casework far outweigh the disadvantages. They feel that it is more important to them that they come fresh to each client and his or her problems; and they find that they can do this better if they do not have to work on the same kinds of cases all the time. Besides, they argue, in particularly complex and sensitive cases they can draw on the expertise of specialists attached to each of the district offices.

But while county workers can draw on departmental resources which are available to them through the central and district office as well as through the state institutions, they feel that the lack of more local resources is the single greatest disadvantage under which they must work. Of the many other service agencies and organizations—both private and public—which are operating in Iowa, very few have either the staff or resources to have an office in every county. They tend to concentrate their program operations to urban areas where they will be able to serve the greatest number of people. This means that for sophisticated and specialized resources—sheltered workshops, schools for the retarded, mental health clinics, vocational schooling, marital counseling, etc.—people must travel, and in some cases, travel a considerable distance. This lack of resource availability at the local level often works counter to one of the primary objectives of social work: to maintain the individual as independently and as close to his or her home community as possible.

This lack of service resources is indicative of the lack of resources of a more general and even more vital nature. Perhaps the most crucial of these relates to employment—or rather unemployment—and the failure of small communities to provide job opportunities for their residents. This lack has some rather alarming implications for the present as well as for the future. "What good does it do to send a client to secretarial school under WIN or under the Individual Training and Education Program unless the person is willing to relocate? How many secretarial positions do you think there are in a town of 3000? How many openings for anything in a town of 3000? And yet many times there are solid indicators that a client would be better off here in the community than in some unfamiliar urban setting. But, in most cases, if a client won't relocate it means he or she won't become employed. It also means that they are going to be the public's responsibility for some time."

The scarcity of employment opportunities has alarming implications not only for the present but for the future of these rural areas. The 1970 census revealed that during the previous decade, most rural communities lost a percentage of their population—in some cases as much as 15%. This population loss is a prime indicator that in these areas—as farms and farm related industries become more and more centralized—there has been no accompanying business or industrial growth. Thus, local tax bases have fallen. With the resulting migration of the unemployed labor force, the county's tax base becomes even further reduced. The resulting lack of a readily available work force and local markets further reduces an area's prospects of being able to attract new business or industry into the area and a vicious syndrome is established. The young must continue to migrate to the urban centers. In this regard it is hardly surprising to learn that 14 of the 25 counties in Iowa which have the highest percentage of persons living under the federal poverty guidelines are also among the 25 counties in the state with the lowest populations.

Moreover the fact that it is the young (particularly the educated young) which are migrating means that the median age within these counties is rising. While the median age for all of the people in Iowa is 28, in some of these rural areas, the median age is now over 40. Many of the elderly people living in these areas are able to exist independently, others are not. And for those who need help, the low tax base, the small population, the severe lack of resources all have a negative impact. Already rural counties are feeling the acute shortage of custodial homes as well as other care facilities. Health needs in general are not being met. There are not enough doctors, let alone medical specialists. There are not enough hospital beds. In some counties, there is not even a public health nurse.

But there have been recent developments which could be of inestimable value in helping the rural social worker cope with some client problems. The expansion of the Homemaker Services Program to all counties and the state's assuming what were formerly the county's costs in the program is an important development which should help take some of the pressure off the nursing and custodial home shortage by helping maintain the elderly and disabled in their own homes. There is also a new emphasis on developing purchase of service contracts in order that whatever resources do exist within a community can be mobilized to meet the needs of some of its residents. And federal dollars are available to local communities to help them develop resources: mental health clinics, day care centers, etc.

But these, important as they are in terms of meeting the needs of people right now, do very little in solving the long range problems besetting many of Iowa's rural counties. And it is these large systemic problems which present the greatest challenge today to the rural social worker. As professionals within their communities they must play a lead role in initiating, developing and supporting local projects and programs which take into account not only the needs of present clients but those of the future as well. Such advocacy activity offers an additional dimension to the role of the caseworker in any community be it urban or rural. But such activity is perhaps a little more crucial and vital for the rural workers. If they do not become involved on behalf of their clients, there are very few people in the community who could ... or would ... take their places.

*A comparative study of rural and urban attitudes relative to such
social welfare programs as public assistance, vocational training,
guaranteed annual income, and public day-care documents the
observation and impression that rural dwellers are conservative
on these issues and tend toward opposition to them. An interesting feature of this research is that it was conducted in Pennsylvania, a state with major metropolitan centers and highly rural
areas. Implications of the findings for social work are suggested.*

25

MARY H. OSGOOD

Rural and Urban Attitudes Toward Welfare

Rural poverty in the United States continues to be more acute, though
less visible, than urban poverty. As distance from an urban center
increases, so does the incidence of poverty. In the most distant and
sparsely settled counties, the poverty rate is 2½ times that in metropolitan areas; nearly half (44 percent) of the nation's poor reside in
nonmetropolitan areas.[1] Despite the high incidence of rural poverty,
however, urban areas receive a greater percentage of government
assistance funds than their rural counterparts. In 1974, nonmetropolitan areas received only about one-fourth of the federal outlay for
income security and other welfare programs.[2]

Reasons for lower outlays in rural areas relate both to program
characteristics as well as to certain rural behavioral tendencies. Some
programs have built-in biases against rural areas. For example, programs set up under the Comprehensive Employment and Training Act
(CETA) calculate benefits on the basis of unemployment rates, which
are particularly misleading indicators of poverty in rural areas because
of the way in which they are reported and computed. Furthermore,

because an area must have a population base of 100,000 in order for the local government to be a prime sponsor or administrator for CETA programs, rural areas usually fall into groupings administered by the state rather than by a local government more likely to be aware of local problems and needs.

However, behavioral tendencies and attitudes in rural areas may have even more influence than program requirements on the amount of government money going to these areas. Participation rates in welfare programs are lower in rural than in urban areas. In Pennsylvania, for example, four of the five counties with the highest percentages of families on welfare in 1970 were in Standard Metropolitan Statistical Areas (SMSAs). In many less urbanized areas, such as Butler County in western Pennsylvania, only 11 percent of the families having an income below the national poverty level as determined by the 1970 U.S. census received welfare, whereas in Philadelphia County, 35 percent of these families received welfare.[3] Because federal program allocations are usually based on current participation rates, low participation serves to lower the amount of federal money allocated to rural areas.

RURAL ATTITUDES

Why are welfare programs in urban areas used more heavily than those in rural areas? Implicit in many proposed explanations is the assumption that fundamental differences exist between rural and urban attitudes toward welfare. It has been suggested that these attitudinal differences are manifested in such ways as the following: adherence to the concept of local control may prevent certain rural areas from applying for federal grants; local governments may be unable—or unwilling—to master the bureaucratic procedures involved in getting projects funded; and administrative policies and case-by-case practices may tend to be more restrictive in rural than in urban areas.

Other explanations have attributed low rural participation rates to certain factors presumably found in nonmetropolitan areas, such as a lack of knowledge about available programs, inadequate financial support for local public assistance offices, scarcity of trained personnel, lack of confidentiality for the recipient (everyone knows and talks about the fact that a certain family is on welfare), apathy because the problem of poverty has been serious for so long that its existence becomes accepted as inevitable, and community attitudes of oppression and aggressiveness toward the poor.[4]

Are attitudes toward welfare programs in fact more negative in rural than in urban areas, thus reducing program participation rates and creating poverty problems of greater severity? The author examines this question by first reviewing previous studies of attitudes toward welfare and then by presenting data on rural-urban attitudinal differences from a study conducted in Pennsylvania. Conclusions and implications for welfare policy are then discussed.

PREVAILING PERSPECTIVES

Public welfare programs in the United States have been viewed from two perspectives, the residual and the institutional.[5] According to the residual outlook, welfare should be used only when usual sources—the labor market and the family—are unable to meet the individual's needs; welfare programs are viewed as providing temporary, emergency assistance. From the residual perspective, being on welfare carries a stigma. It is the poor person's own fault that he or she is poor. The institutional view, on the other hand, attaches no stigma to the receipt of welfare. The provision of public welfare is looked on as a proper and legitimate institution within society, and the need for comprehensive, continual support is recognized. Structural inefficiencies in society are seen as the cause of poverty; the individual is not blamed for being poor.

The residual view seems to be more prevalent in the United States, even among welfare recipients. In a study of 103 welfare mothers in Baltimore, many of the subjects perceived that a considerable degree of stigma was attached to being on welfare, and all subjects felt that there was some degree of stigma attached to being a welfare recipient.[6] Awareness of this stigma was found to affect the feelings of recipients toward themselves and others.

. . . . . .

It appears that a slight trend toward the institutional view of social welfare—that is, toward considering the provision of money and services as a major, normal part of society's functions—may be developing. Evidence of this trend can be seen when comparing responses to Gallup polls conducted in 1965 and 1969 concerning a guaranteed annual income. In 1965, 19 percent of a national sample favored the proposal; 67 percent opposed it; and 14 percent had no opinion regarding the matter. In 1969, 32 percent favored a guaranteed annual income; 62 percent opposed it; and 6 percent expressed no opinion.[7] Nevertheless, the trend toward a more institutional perspective in the

United States is still overshadowed by the prevalent, stigmatizing residual viewpoint, indicating a predominance of negative attitudes toward welfare.

RURAL-URBAN DIFFERENCES

[Several authors (Briar, 1966; Schiltz, 1970; Gans, 1972; Feagin, 1972; Kallen and Miller, 1971; Williamson, 1974; and Ogren, 1973[8]) have done studies relating to attitudes toward welfare, but these do not deal with rural-urban differences.] Few published studies have examined the differences between rural and urban attitudes toward welfare. Some of the most useful information on these differences is found in unpublished dissertations. These differences must be inferred from indirect indications, however, because researchers have used many different definitions of the term "rural" in their studies.

In a study of a rural county in Indiana, for example, Goudy found that those respondents who held the individual responsible for being poor were more likely than others to have negative attitudes toward public dependency.[9] When asked by Goudy whether they thought that "poverty is a problem in this area," these respondents were also more likely to state that they did not think so.

In a study of a traditional farming town in Colorado, Wooster applied the term "rural" to the following individuals: those who were currently living on a farm, those raised on a farm, those whose parents were farmers, those currently working in an occupation related to farming, and those married to any of the above.[10] He found that "rural" individuals had a higher degree of adherence to the Protestant work ethic than did "urban" individuals and that they also had more negative attitudes toward poverty.

Another unpublished dissertation surveyed the attitudes of social science teachers in Oklahoma, the study sample consisting of 140 cases.[11] In this study, which used mail questionnaires, the respondents themselves designated their respective backgrounds as either urban or rural. A discernible though not statistically significant tendency to be less sympathetic to the poor was found among those identifying themselves as having rural backgrounds.

Other investigators of attitudes have recorded similar findings. A case study of an area in Illinois undergoing industrialization found a "traditional rural reluctance to become involved in governmental expenditure on public health and welfare service, along with a presumed smaller need for such service where more traditional family aid is available."[12] In addition, the more rural counties in the study area spent far less per capita than urban areas on health and welfare services.

On the other hand, a study by Handler and Hollingsworth of Aid to Families with Dependent Children (AFDC) program recipients found that clients in rural and urban areas perceived a similar degree of stigma attached to the receipt of benefits.[13] Similar perceptions of community hostility were also shared by clients in the six counties studied, three of which were rural and three urban. In a similar vein, a summary compiled by Schiltz of national public opinion polls taken from 1935 to 1964 found that strong rural-urban differences were not evident on the question of support for government expenditures for welfare.[14] However, rural areas were less likely to support proposals for unemployment compensation and Medicare before they were enacted.

PENNSYLVANIA SURVEY

Data from the 1974 statewide sample survey of Pennsylvania residents conducted by the Pennsylvania Field Research Laboratory provide additional insights into rural-urban differences in attitudes toward welfare.[15] This statewide survey, known as the Continuing Social Survey of Pennsylvania, deals with a representative sample of all Pennsylvania households on a yearly or semiyearly basis. The reliability and validity of the data are increased by the systematic, periodic nature of the survey. The interview schedules for the survey were administered by skilled interviewers who are hired on an ongoing basis by the field research laboratory.

Counties and clusters of households within counties were selected at random to represent the population of the state. Responses were received from 1,426 households. To consider the rural-urban dimension of the responses, which was not part of the original sample design, data from the following three types of areas in the state were selected by the author for comparison: counties inside an SMSA with 95–100 percent of the population classified as urban by the U.S. Bureau of the Census.... (272 cases); counties inside an SMSA with 44–66 percent of the population classified as urban.... (154 cases); and counties outside an SMSA with 0–30 percent of the population classified as urban.... (155 cases). Survey questions dealing directly with attitudes toward welfare were selected for analysis....

Approximately 40 percent of the cases selected from the survey for analysis were male and 60 percent female. Respondents living outside an SMSA were slightly more likely to be female (62 percent). Few black respondents were included in the sample. Respondents living outside an SMSA tended to be older, and they were more likely than respondents living within SMSAs to be widowed, separated, or divorced. Levels of educational attainment were lower in areas outside SMSAs: those in rural areas were less likely to have attended college and much less likely to have been graduated from college. Correspondingly, income levels were lower in rural areas.

The confounding influences of income, education, race, and other variables on differences in attitudes among these groupings of respondents cannot be directly estimated. The issue at hand, however, is not to determine the degree to which rurality or urbanism per se, apart from other variables, influences attitudes but rather to identify any rural-urban attitudinal differences that exist. It is questionable, in fact, whether the concepts "rural" and "urban" have any sociological significance in modern society other than to denote distinctive distributions of socioeconomic and demographic characteristics.

FINDINGS

First Set of Indicators. Three different types of questions or indicators relating to attitudes toward welfare were used. In the first set of these, a statement was read to respondents, and they were asked if they agreed. The individual's response was to be selected from among the following: agree completely, agree mostly, agree partly, agree a little, or agree not at all. For the present analysis, the response categories of "agree completely" and "agree mostly" were combined into one category indicating agreement; the response category of "agree partly" was used alone to signify an in-between response; and the response categories of "agree a little" and "agree not at all" were combined to indicate disagreement.[16] On the basis of these three categories, chi-squares were computed.

As shown in Table 1, residents of rural and less urbanized areas were less likely to indicate support or sympathy for welfare recipients and programs. The first statement in the table, "Most people getting welfare are honest about their needs," deals both with the idea of the honesty of benefit recipients and with that of poor people's needs. These two topics may evoke opposite emotions in a person. Although he or she may feel that many "welfare cheaters" are on the public assistance rolls, the image of the needy may draw forth feelings of sympathy and support. This statement, therefore, ultimately elicits an expression of the feeling that is dominant within the individual. One-third of the respondents from less urbanized areas disagreed with the

TABLE 1
Responses Indicating Negative Attitudes Toward Welfare (percentage)

Statement	Response	Highly Urban (N=272)	Less Urban (N=154)	Rural (N=155)
1. Most people getting welfare are honest about their needs.	Agree a little or agree not at all[a]	24	33	29
2. Most welfare recipients would be willing to work if they could find jobs.	Agree a little or agree not at all[b]	32	47	46
3. Many people will stop working on jobs that need to be done if we make it too easy to get on welfare.	Agree completely or agree mostly[a]	59	71	74
4. It's the responsibility of the government to make sure that everyone has a good job.	Agree a little or agree not at all[b]	42	55	63

[a]p<.01
[b]p<.001

statement, and 29 percent of the rural respondents disagreed with it. However, only 24 percent of the persons in highly urban areas disagreed.

The second and third statements shown in the table relate to the work ethic prevalent in society. "Most welfare recipients would be willing to work if they could find jobs" was disagreed with by almost half of the respondents in rural and less urbanized areas (46 percent and 47 percent, respectively). Only about one-third (32 percent) of the residents of highly urban areas felt that welfare recipients would not be willing to work. Fearfulness of threats to society's continued functioning and of the possible erosion of society's work ethic may be elicited by the third statement: "Many people will stop working on jobs that need to be done if we make it too easy to get on welfare." Whereas 59 percent of respondents in highly urban areas agreed with this statement, 71 percent in less urbanized areas and 74 percent in rural areas agreed with it. These high percentages suggest that respondents living in more rural areas felt that strict eligibility requirements are essential and should be continued.

Respondents from rural and less urbanized areas displayed similar attitudes with regard to the first three statements shown in Table 1. When the responses to these statements are reviewed, a gradual shift to less sympathetic attitudes is not observable from urban to rural areas. What emerges instead is a dichotomy between the residents of cities and the residents of less densely populated outlying areas.

However, percentages relating to the fourth statement shown in Table 1 reveal a somewhat different pattern, with responses from less urbanized areas falling somewhere between the responses from highly urban and rural areas. The statement itself, "It's the responsibility of the government to make sure that everyone has a good job," implies the endorsement of a guaranteed employment plan. Those in rural areas were clearly more opposed to this idea, with 63 percent of the respondents disagreeing. The added dimension of federal government control implicit in this statement may have influenced the high percentages of negative responses in rural areas.

Second Set of Indicators.   A second series of attitude indicators used in the Pennsylvania survey involved the description of a hypothetical situation. After a situation was described to respondents, they were asked how often a person in the situation should be given help. Response choices for this series of indicators were the following: never, seldom, sometimes, usually, and always. For the present analysis, "never" and "seldom" were combined to indicate one extreme; "sometimes" was used as an in-between response; and "usually" and "always" were combined to indicate support.

TABLE 2
Responses Regarding Assistance in Situations Described (percentage)

	Never or Seldom		
Situation	Highly Urban (N=272)	Less Urban (N=154)	Rural (N=155)
1. A woman has had her fifth child; the father is not at home, and she can't work. She is asking for assistance in finding a larger place in public housing.[a]	14	14	20
2. A high school dropout can't find the kind of job he wants and applies for vocational training through a public program.[b]	7	8	12
3. A family of five has just moved here from Kentucky. The father can't find work and applies for cash income assistance.[c]	13	16	20

[a] $p < .001$
[b] $p < .10$
[c] $p < .01$

The first situation described dealt with someone wishing to find larger living quarters in public housing. (See Table 2.) In both highly urban and less urbanized areas, only 14 percent of the respondents were unwilling to offer assistance. Rural respondents were more likely to be unwilling: 20 percent indicated that assistance should "never" or "seldom" be given. Their response may have been influenced by the lower availability and awareness of public housing in rural areas.

The description of the second situation, in which a high school dropout wants to apply for vocational training, was met with widespread approval from respondents in all three areas. Only 7 percent of the respondents in highly urban areas and 8 percent of the respondents in less urbanized areas indicated that this type of support should not be given. Although not statistically significant at the .05 level, a trend in which rural areas revealed less sympathetic attitudes once more emerged: 12 percent of the respondents in rural areas were unwilling to provide vocational training to the high school dropout.

Similarly, rural residents were less willing to provide assistance to a family who had just moved into the area from another state, even though the father had tried to find work. Whereas 13 percent of the respondents in highly urban areas were unwilling to provide money to the family, 20 percent in rural areas were unwilling. The percentage for residents of less urbanized areas, 16 percent, fell between the other two percentages.

Third Set of Indicators. The final set of questions used to assess attitudes dealt with two proposals under discussion by the government, the establishment of a guaranteed annual income and of government-sponsored day care centers. Respondents were read descriptions of the proposals and then asked whether they favored or opposed such plans. Their responses were to be selected from among the following: definitely favor, favor somewhat, oppose somewhat, or definitely oppose. For the present analysis, the first two response categories were grouped together as a single category favoring a proposal, and the second two were grouped together as opposing it.

Responses to the first proposal, which related to a guaranteed annual income, show the largest percentage difference between residents of highly urban areas and residents of rural areas. (See Table 3.) Almost three-fourths (73 percent) of the rural respondents opposed such a plan, while less than half of the respondents in highly urban areas (45 percent) were opposed. This percentage difference probably again points to the prevalence of a stronger rural work ethic.

In all three areas, the concept of government-sponsored day care centers elicited more support than that of a guaranteed annual income. However, rural respondents were again much less likely to favor the

TABLE 3
Responses Opposing Proposals Described (percentage)

| | Oppose Somewhat or Definitely Oppose | | |
	Highly Urban (N=272)	Less Urban (N=154)	Rural (N=155)
Proposal			
1. There is much talk in goverment to-day about providing a guaranteed annual income. This means that whether a person had a job or not, the total amount of money he gets during the year would be at least enough to insure a minimum standard of living. Would you favor or oppose such a guaranted income plan?[a]	45	60	73
2. Another plan that's being talked about in government today is providing government-sponsored day care centers for children of all mothers who want to work, with parents paying for this service according to their income. Would you personally favor or oppose such government-sponsored day care centers?[b]	18	21	33

[a]$p<.001$
[b]$p<.01$

establishment of such centers. In rural areas, 33 percent opposed the setting up of government-sponsored centers, whereas only 21 percent in less urbanized areas and 18 percent in highly urban areas were opposed.

CONCLUSIONS

In response to all three sets of attitude indicators, residents of rural Pennsylvania were less likely than residents of highly urban areas to support welfare programs or be sympathetic to welfare recipients. Compared to respondents in highly urban areas, respondents in rural and less urbanized areas were less likely to trust the honesty of welfare recipients. They doubted to a greater degree the willingness of welfare recipients to work, and they were also more likely to feel that people would stop working if it became too easy for them to obtain welfare benefits. In addition, a larger percentage of respondents in rural areas disagreed with the idea that it is the responsibility of the government to make sure that everyone has a good job. Rural residents, moreover, were less likely to agree to the giving of assistance to persons in difficult situations. They were not as likely as urban residents to support the giving of help to someone seeking more adequate public housing or to support the giving of cash to an unemployed father and his family who had just moved from another state. A trend also existed in which rural residents were less likely to approve the supplying of vocational training. Finally, proposals for a guaranteed annual income and government-sponsored day care centers elicited the largest rural-urban attitudinal differences. Rural respondents were much less likely to support these two plans.

Taken as a group, these responses indicate that a residual view of welfare prevails in rural areas of Pennsylvania. The poor individual is distrusted and is held responsible for being poor. Rather than viewing poverty as the result of widespread unemployment and other structural inefficiencies in society, almost half of the respondents in rural and less urbanized areas felt that welfare recipients were not even willing to work.

Residents of less urbanized areas (those living in counties inside an SMSA but with only about half of the population classified as urban) exhibited attitudes more similar to those of rural respondents than to those found in highly urban areas such as Philadelphia and Pittsburgh. These data suggest that those in the cities have a more institutional perspective toward welfare than either those in the less densely populated SMSA counties or those in the very rural counties outside an SMSA.

. . . . .

To alleviate the problems of the poor in rural areas, social workers must recognize the persistence of certain attitudes in these areas and plan programs accordingly. Through local community action and changes in federal and state policies, problems of rural poverty can be reduced.

NOTES AND REFERENCES

1. Peter A. Morrison et al., *Review of Federal Programs to Alleviate Rural Deprivation* (Santa Monica, Calif.: The Rand Corporation, 1974), p. 1; and James Abourezk and George Rucker, "The Federal Budget and Rural America: Where Do All the Federal Dollars Go?" p. 9. Paper presented at the First National Conference on Rural America, Washington, D.C., April 1975.

2. Abourezk and Rucker, op. cit.

3. J. Patrick Madden, C. Shannon Stokes, and John R. Grossman,

Children in Pennsylvania, Vol. 1, State Summary (University Park, Pa.: The Pennsylvania State University, 1975), p. 56.

4. *See* Pennsylvania Panel on Rural Poverty, *Final Summary Report* (Harrisburg, Pa.: Department of Community Affairs, Commonwealth of Pennsylvania, 1971); and Janet Morton Derr, *Rural Social Problems, Human Services, and Social Policies*, Working Paper 13: Social Services (Denver, Col.: University of Denver, Social Welfare Research Institute, 1973), p. 7.

5. Harold L. Wilensky and Charles N. Lebeaux, *Industrial Society and Social Welfare* (New York: Russell Sage Foundation, 1958), p. 140.

6. Patrick J. Sullivan, "Perception of and Reaction to 'Welfare Stigma' and the Influence of Program Participation, Life Conditions, and Personal Attitudes," p. 101. Unpublished Ph.D. dissertation, The Catholic University of America, 1971.

7. Alan J. Hahn, "Helping the Poor: The Constraints of Public Opinion," *Human Ecology Forum*, 5 (Spring 1975), p. 1.

8. Scott Briar, "Welfare from Below: Recipients' Views of the Public Welfare System," in Jacobus tenBroek, ed., *The Law of the Poor* (San Francisco: Chandler Publishing Co., 1966), p. 59; Michael E. Schiltz, *Public Attitudes Toward Social Security, 1935–1965*, Research Report No. 33 (Washington, D.C.: U.S. Government Printing Office, 1970), p. 160; Herbert J. Gans, "The Positive Functions of Poverty," *American Journal of Sociology*, 78 (September 1972), pp. 275–289; Joe R. Feagin, "America's Welfare Stereotypes," *Social Science Quarterly*, 52 (March 1972), pp. 921–933; David J. Kallen and Dorothy Miller, "Public Attitudes Toward Welfare," *Social Work*, 16 (July 1971), pp. 83–90; John B. Williamson, "Beliefs about the Motivation of the Poor and Attitudes Toward Poverty Policy," *Social Problems*, 21 (June 1974), pp. 634–648; Evelyn H. Ogren, "Public Opinions about Public Welfare," *Social Work*, 18 (January 1973), pp. 101–107.

9. Willis J. Goudy, "Shoot Them If They Won't Work: A Study of Socioeconomic Status, Economic Aspirations, and Attitudes Toward Poverty, the Poor, and Public Dependence," p. 233. Unpublished Ph.D. dissertation, Purdue University, 1970.

10. John H. Wooster, "Attitudes Toward Poverty, Social Services, and Adherence to the Protestant Ethic in a Rural Colorado Community." Unpublished Ph.D. dissertation, University of Northern Colorado, 1972.

11. Dale O. Roark, "A Survey of Social Studies Teachers' Attitudes

Toward Poverty and Welfare Programs in Oklahoma." Unpublished Ph.D. dissertation, Oklahoma State University, 1973.

12. Gene F. Summers et al., *Before Industrialization: A Rural Social System Base Study*, College of Agriculture, Bulletin 736 (Urbana: University of Illinois, 1969), p.88.

13. Joel F. Handler and Ellen J. Hollingsworth, *The Deserving Poor* (Chicago: Markham Publishing Co., 1971).

14. Schiltz, op. cit., pp. 108, 145, 152.

15. These data were collected in the summer of 1974 by R. Richard Ritti and the staff of the Pennsylvania Field Research Laboratory of Pennsylvania State University in University Park, Pennsylvania. The author was given access to the data in June 1975.

16. Percentages relating to the original response categories are available from the author.

In the following brief statement an eminent American historian comments on certain myths about rural life and also notes some traditions and principles that are not myths. Both the myths and the traditions affect thinking about nonmetropolitan life. Hence they are important for those persons who wish to work in rural areas.

26

CLARKE CHAMBERS

Myths of Rural America

My first definition of myth is a body of beliefs, a social perception and ideology, a philosophy which serves to inform the cultural and political ethos of an America that remained rural in its majority until the recent past. In its secondary and second definition, I mean by myth a body of stories, images, dreams, stereotypes—most of them urban in origin—which very often presented distorted pictures of farmers and rural life. Yet, these myths had very real, live force because what people believe in their heads to be true, they act upon.

One perception traceable to the 17th, 18th and 19th centuries portrayed the American farmer essentially as a peasant who grubbed out a primitive existence that was debasing, destructive of human values and spirit. The peasants' life was marked by drudgery, ignorance, superstition. By this myth, all the finer, cultivated ways were urban. The image of the farmer as a hick and hayseed became an object of fun and derision.

A second myth portrayed an altogether opposite picture that I label romantic. Like the image of the farmer as a peasant and hayseed, it was chiefly urban in origin. I think its roots go back to classical Greece and Rome where there was kind of a romantic myth about the funda-

Reprinted from Clarke Chambers, "Myths of Rural America," *Conference on Rural America: Proceedings*, July 1976, p. 62, by permission of the author and the Minnesota Humanities Commission.

mental importance of the farmer, the economy, and the important contribution the country person made to citizenship. We found this idea expressed with our founding fathers. Rural folk lived close to nature and were presumed by that fact to be close to God. The farmer was in this perception peaceful, prudent, hard working, generous, the soul of integrity, innocence, and honesty. Neither of these images was very accurate, but both had enormous power on the imagination of the American people in perceiving rural life and the farmer.

The roots of the third myth are Jeffersonian. In part the Jeffersonian perception was romantic and idyllic, but it also included the notion that as long as farmers constituted a majority of the American citizenry, agrarianism and democracy were intimately interrelated. It was felt in this perception that the concentration of wealth, more than anything, would undermine, corrode and subvert the dream and hope of America. The strength of the nation rested socially, psychologically, culturally and politically on a wide diffusion of property, and on the family farm. All those virtues that are associated with that kind of structure—self reliance, cooperation, neighborliness, independence— were said to be an essential part of the American character.

But as the nation moved into the 20th century, the identity of America with its rural tradition was slowly eroded. Americans moved to the city. To be a successful farmer required education, ability, business acumen, managerial skills, access to credit, etc. The farmer was neither a hick nor a hero; he was and is a businessman, engineer, mechanic and agronomist.

There are principles and tradition, not myths, which I think are still viable for rural America and the nation. First, the traditional Jeffersonian dedication to the diffusion of property, the best representation of which may still be the family farm, is one indication of historical tradition that has meaning today. Second, I believe there is still strength in the dedication of rural America to the earth and land. It is that tradition of care, concern and love which now needs enforcement if we are to survive in a physical, social or cultural sense. Third, there is a historical tradition of rural America which remains alive and essential in the practice of neighborly cooperation. Fourth, there was and is a tradition in rural America which relates to education, to lifelong learning, and I do not mean formal school training. As we read the papers, we know how dependent the world is upon the productive capacity of rural America, and I think these four traditions are essential to survive on the planet earth in the next generation.

What is required to gain acceptance and be an effective practitioner in the rural human services is an important question. Mermelstein and Sundet in the next article suggest that the crucial consideration is the establishment of role in the entry phase of the helping process. They then develop the idea of a continuum or hierarchy of five roles, each with different demands for both the worker and the person(s) served.

27

JOANNE MERMELSTEIN AND PAUL SUNDET

Worker Acceptance and Credibility in the Rural Environment

When faced with entering social work practice in small communities and rural areas, the worker, particularly the inexperienced worker, is apprehensive about gaining acceptance and establishing credibility. The more aware the new worker is of the nature of rurality, the more acute the anxiety. All the well-known characteristics of rural communities such as clannishness, impermeability to outsiders, informal helping networks, and so on, are in the forefront of her or his thinking. And the anxiety is based in reality for all these can be and often are impediments for the worker entering rural practice.

The new worker's motivation for achieving acceptance is high, based on both the professional values of helping and the more pragmatic need for professional survival. If the worker is newly graduated from a social work program, "performance anxiety" is even higher and frequently the desire to demonstrate mastery of various clinical strategies is strong. As a consequence, the new worker in the rural environment often adopts a definition of her or his function, for example, therapist, that is at odds with the community expectations, and in-

From Joanne Mermelstein and Paul Sundet, "Worker Acceptance and Credibility in the Rural Environment," an original article, by permission of the authors.

deed, with the functions that the community will tolerate an outsider to perform. In other words, the very means the worker chooses to use to achieve acceptance and establish credibility are sources of the difficulty!

To deal with these twin problems of acceptance and credibility, the rural practitioner must address the basic tasks of the entry step in process. The fundamental tasks in "entry" are to establish roles and develop relationships. Of the two, the former is most problematic because few practitioners have analyzed either the range or implications of client role expectations or how the various roles complement and build on one another. The purpose of this article is (1) to provide the beginning practitioner in the rural community with a guide to sorting out the multiple roles that are required in rural social work practice; and (2) to demonstrate the hierarchical nature of these roles and how credibility and thus acceptance are established in them sequentially.

It is a well-argued postulate that there are indeed few professionally trained social workers in rural areas, just as there are few experts in any human service field practicing there. Scarcity influences role expectations of rural residents in several ways. The most obvious is expansion of the range of functions that the rural community seeks from an "expert." There is also a more subtle consequence of scarcity that is rooted in the ways that people try to familiarize themselves with a "new" experience. When the experience is that of understanding what a social worker does, they try to find role analogs—means of comparison within their own life experience—to measure social work performance against. Their experience with the community roles of friend, sister, minister, healer, and confidant do not always prepare them for the professional social work roles of mediator, negotiator, advocate, and manager of social change processes. Role clarification is, then, a crucial first task.

Demonstration of usefulness to the rural community must be predicated upon an understanding of what various professional roles may mean to the client-target population as well as upon the appropriateness of the role to the observed need.

It has been our experience, verified by colleagues in many fields of rural practice, that there are five essential social work roles that are central to rural practice. They are also appropriate for different systemic levels of a target population, from individual to group to an aggregate of persons (community). These roles are broker, technical expert, consultant, manager of change process, and advocate. Arranged on a continuum or ladder, this five-step range carries inverse gradations of risk and dependency for the worker and client system.

That is, for the professional worker, risk is highest on the bottom rung of the ladder—in demonstration of social brokerage, and secondly, in technical expertise—and is gradually reduced with progression to the higher rungs. The sources of risk lie in the nature of the main task: proving to the rural client system that the worker knows and can do something useful for it. If the proof is not forthcoming, that is, brokerage is not successful, the client system is no worse off than it was, but the worker has "lost ground" in a crucial, albeit "simple," test of competence. Risk for the client system, on the lower rungs of the ladder, is relatively low. To allow the worker to broker a service, the client system does not have to reveal data that are intimate or potentially damaging. The client is free to share only that which is necessary to secure the brokerage, and her or his control of data is firm. A broker is defined as one who makes linkage between a provider and consumer of a service; the bridge between need and resource. A tangible product, that is, receipt of goods or services is the outcome of the brokerage activity for the client-partner.

Because of the tangible nature of this professional exchange, the client system is often more willing to accept a more complicated role—the next on the ladder—that of technical expert in process. The technical expert is one who has special skill in or knowledge of a particular subject. In this instance, expertise is in the ability to construct a road map of change that serves as a guide to the worker and the client-partner in achieving mutual goals. Rooted in scientific methodology and employing the vehicle of relationship, the concept of process governs the social worker's approach to effecting social change with any social system. This "how to do it" advice is more complex than brokerage and requires more risk on the part of the client-partner who agrees to try the unfamiliar route. Risk is correlated with greater dependency on the worker as the client system ascends the ladder. The more knowledge is lodged solely in the worker, the less control and less assurance of success the client system has in agreeing to the partnership requirements.

The middle rung in the hierarchy is the role of consultant, equally applicable to a potential client of a therapeutic service as to another human service provider. To consult is to deliberate together. Consultation as an activity of practice implies technical expertise in one or a variety of content areas, a contractual arrangement with a less knowledgeable individual or organizational representative and a social change goal. Credibility in consultation derives from the authority of competence demonstrated in the activity, but the consultee has freedom to accept or reject the offering. The risk balance is approximately equal for both the client and worker at this level of helping, as the worker still faces the danger of "undoing" the acceptance gained in performance of the earlier roles if the consultation fails or backfires, and the client-partner is significantly more dependent on the worker and more revelatory of data about the problem in order to receive consultation.

The fourth role, and one that is a considerable "jump" in risk for the client system, is that of manager of the social change process—either therapist, in the case of an individual or family type problem, or organizer in the case of a group or community type problem. Permission to engage in this role is indication of fairly strong trust and acceptance on the part of the client system. Consequences of failure are primarily on the client-partner's side, not the worker's. Acceptance of the worker as therapist or organizer results in a power disparity in the relationship and thus is a major source of client risk.

Finally, the last and potentially most dangerous role for the client system to accept from the worker is that of advocate. An advocate is one who speaks on behalf of another; one who pleads the cause of another. Advocacy implies the public use of selected personal, family, or organizational data for intervention with other systems on behalf of the client-partner. Since the worker's judgment about systemic level, target, and mode of intervention is dependent on data not accessible directly to the client-partner, very high risk is inherent in the client's agreement to this arrangement. And advocacy is risky for the worker too, as the consequences can be exclusion from the rural human service network. A rich reservoir of relationships among other providers is required for effective advocacy, and then the occasion that prompted it does not become a reason to sever personal and organizational relationships between agencies. Advocacy presumes upon the respect that other providers have for the worker or the agency she or he represents. That respect is built and nurtured through the lower roles in this hierarchy: brokerage, technical expertise, consultation, and so on. In other words, the worker is reminded to have climbed the ladder of credibility with parallel human service systems in the rural area before attempting to ask them to accept her or him confronting their policies and programs. Confrontation and advocacy without acceptance and credibility to draw on usually lead to negative consequences for the client one is seeking to help and blocking of that worker from sources of information and resources.

Although the ladder of credibility and acceptance must be climbed a rung at a time, the process is not necessarily laborious or lengthy. This is so for two reasons: first, credibility and therefore sanction and acceptance of a particular helping role may meet the client system's need immediately and allow the process to move through the first several roles in a single contact; second, the well-known characteristic of rural clientele to quite freely discuss the content of professional intervention with family and friends often provides the worker with a reputation of credibility in specific roles, particularly broker and technical expert, so that they are assumed by successive client systems. Thus, community folklore has it that "... he got the medical center to see Uncle Jack," or "... she knows how to help you think through a problem!" In such situations, the client gives the worker permission to move to a higher role either by the way in which the request for help is phrased or, more commonly, by stating the basis for credibility, for example, "I know that you saw Mrs. Nelson and . . .," and so on. But in either case, it is the client who indicates that credibility and acceptance have been established and to what extent.

Before ending this brief discussion, it is important to emphasize one point about this hierarchy of roles. There is no particular merit in exercising all of the roles with each client. Nor is it necessary to have established the role of therapist to have had a professional social work relationship. It is both common and appropriate that in many interventions the relationship consists of brokerage or technical expertise, or both. If these roles are what the client wants and needs, they are the appropriate roles. Attempting to be a therapist or advocate is subverting the treatment process by meeting worker, not client, needs. And the new worker should be reminded that neither the broker nor technical expert is a simple role when performed adequately. In fact, if these roles were performed better there would be less need for the roles of therapist and advocate, for the client would have been able to solve her or his problem before reaching these more dependent levels.

In summary, then, the worker entering rural practice must have a clear conceptualization of professional role and should realize that client systems will view the various roles in a hierarchy, which requires that credibility be established in each in turn. The more the worker is conscious of this progression and at what rung on the ladder he or she is with the client, the more appropriate will be the interventions and the easier to establish both credibility and acceptance.

REFERENCES

1. Ginsberg, Leon H., ed. *Social Work in Rural Communities.* New York: Council on Social Work Education, 1976.
2. Mermelstein, Joanne, and Paul Sundet, "Social Work Education for Rural Program Development." In *Social Work in Rural Communities,* edited by L. Ginsberg. New York: Council on Social Work Education, 1976, pp. 15–27.

The issue pointed up in the next article has particular relevance for rural communities in that terms often take on special meaning there. Whether labels such as "client" or "patient" are used may make more difference in a rural way of life where there is less anonymity and more awareness of other people and their situations. It may also be true that traditional myths and stereotypes about personal problems and "mental illness" are more prevalent and persistent in nonmetropolitan areas. To the extent that this is the case, the need for rural professionals to be doubly conscious of the words they use is real. Terms both reflect and influence the environments from which they emanate.

28

ANDREW HINKLE

Patient vs. Client in Community Mental Health

The terms "patient" and "client" are often used interchangeably in the mental health profession. Do they mean the same thing and is it appropriate to substitute one term for the other? Let us examine the issue to determine if in fact there is any significant difference in meaning or preference of usage.

The term "patient" as used by mental health practitioners reflects the underlying professional orientation towards the medical model of mental illness. From this view point a "patient" is seen as one who suffers a disease in which a diagnosis, prognosis and treatment plan is provided. This procedure is widely followed in mental hospitals and adheres to orthodox medical practice.

However, the suitability of the term "patient" is brought to some question as a description of those who patronize the facilities of community mental health centers. The term "patient" carries connota-

Reprinted from Andrew Hinkle, "Patient vs. Client in Community Mental Health," *Human Services in the Rural Environment*, Vol. 3, No. 3, March 1978, pp. 5, 26, 32, by permission of the author and the journal.

tions that may not be consistent with the philosophy of community mental health.

According to the dictionary, a "patient" is a person passively affected and the object of external actions who is undergoing treatment for disease. This definition suggests that a patient has little control of his own condition and is dependent on the skills and knowledge of a therapeutic agent. Obviously from this perspective, a patient may accept little responsibility for his illness or not take any action for its treatment.

The touchstone of many contemporary therapies in community mental health is to help one help oneself. Whether in counseling, group therapy, or chemotherapy, a therapeutic goal is to encourage independence, self-reliance and personal responsibility. The term "patient" is hardly consistent with this objective.

The alcoholic who is often seen as dependent on his alcohol may, by the term "patient," fall into the comfortable position of replacing drug dependency with therapist dependency. The term "patient" is often unsuitable for other reasons. If a parent is seeking consultation for her child on behavior management, is it appropriate to refer to the mother as a "patient"? The term "patient" does not seem applicable for those seeking marriage counseling and may even be offensive to them. Recently at a community mental health center, a couple having marital problems were introduced as the doctor's new patients. They looked at each other, reassured the psychologists that they were not "mental patients" and did not return for the next session.

If the term "patient" is so often used in mental health practice, what accounts for its prevalence? The historical perspective of "mental illness" shows that those afflicted in ancient times were thought to be possessed by devils, a theological matter requiring exorcism. As medicine and science became more sophisticated, their condition was thought related to changes of the moon and the term "lunatics" was popularized. In the age of reason and enlightenment, the term "insane" was used to refer to those chained in dreary dungeons, elevated by the name "asylum." As Dorothea Dix and others began to fight these brutal and inhuman conditions over a hundred years ago with the establishment of mental hospitals, a tremendous leap forward was made in providing the medical model of care to those formerly treated worse than criminals.

Today current mental health philosophy has been shifted from focus on the hospitalization method to the orientation of community mental health with an emphasis on providing various out-patient services as an alternative to chronic hospitalization.

Just as this progress has influenced our methods of treatment and terminology in the past, they will continue to change. Those formerly termed lunatics would have been more appropriately called patients, just as those now called patients would be better called clients. The term "client" is preferable to that of "patient" because it implies some measure of personal responsibility, it does not carry the connotation or association of "mental patient," and it is a respectable reference to those who patronize community mental health services. Perhaps in a hundred years, this change will appear as significant as those of the last hundred years now appear to us.

Some of the changes demanded of the professional "helper" who moves from an urban to a rural community to practice are discussed in this selection. As is also noted by other authors, there are both advantages and disadvantages in using one's knowledge and skill in a nonmetropolitan area. The rewards are noteworthy but the challenges are considerable.

29

R. THOMAS RIGGS AND LINDA F. KUGEL

Transition from Urban to Rural Mental Health Practice

The opening of community mental health centers in rural areas in the past decade has coincided with an increase in the appeal of country living to some young professionals. In their transition from urban practice to rural practice, difficulties often arise as a product of an interaction between the naive expectations of city people as to what country living involves and the expectations of small town communities. In recent staff discussions of the authors' experiences as former city residents, they were struck by both the similarities and the differences in the experience of staff members in this New England agency. It was thought worth sharing with other professionals in the field.

In a recent survey of rural community mental health centers, Boris Gertz, Jill Meider, and Margaret L. Pluckhan identified a number of skills which clinicians working in rural centers have found to be important. Their findings appear valuable and are quoted extensively below:

> The personal qualities most frequently listed as desirable were good communication skills and the ability to function independently and to

Reprinted from R. Thomas Riggs and Linda F. Kugel, "Transition from Urban to Rural Mental Health Practice," *Social Casework*, Vol. 57, No. 9, November 1976, pp. 562–567, by permission of the authors and the publisher, Family Service Association of America.

have good interpersonal relationships. Other qualities listed were the ability to relate to minority groups and youths; to work with community organizations such as churches, schools, and granges; to tolerate isolation while still remaining visible to the community; and to develop trust and a sense of helpfulness.

Also considered to be necessary staff attributes were the potential for creativity, innovation, and flexibility in order to function effectively with limited resources.

Desirable general abilities included skills in teaching, consultation, public relations, management, and problem-solving. Sensitivity to signs of social change and the ability to understand networks of social interaction in the community were also cited. It was also considered important for staff to be able to do social planning and community organizing and to work with advisory councils from the community.

It is apparent from the responses that the uniqueness of the rural setting requires special skills and qualities of staff members. A number of respondents identified a knowledge of rural politics and power structures and the ability to develop informal patterns of communication with key community officials as essential to effective staff functioning. The importance of recognizing informal pressure groups that exert control in the community was also listed. Other necessary special skills and qualities included familiarity and empathy with the particular cultures, socioeconomic levels, values, and mores of the rural residents. Sensitivity to the community process and flexibility in adjusting program schedules to accommodate competing activities were also important.[1]

The authors of this article were not surprised to find that the results of this survey correspond quite strikingly to ongoing staff dialogue in their agency in response to the same questions. However, elsewhere in the survey, Gertz suggests that staff members reared in a small or rural community might be more successful than staff members with an urban background. The authors have found that a rural background may be helpful, but it is certainly unnecessary. They have turned to the staff process and experiences in a mental health agency in New Hampshire to find the reasons for these conclusions.

STAFF EXPERIENCES

It seems that most of the staff members, including the authors, underwent parallel processes during their first twelve to eighteen months of employment. The process included a number of identifiable stages which could be called euphoria, depression, and adaptation. This process is akin to that of culture shock.

A great deal has been written about the necessity of understanding transracial or transcultural experience in order to be helpful to, for instance, the black or Puerto Rican client. Very little has been written about the real differences in the practice of rural as compared to urban psychotherapy, what could be facetiously called the "only-garage-in-town syndrome."

In moving from urban to rural mental health centers, the authors discovered that the beauty of the physical surroundings, the realization of a kind of escape for which they had been longing, and other factors varying from person to person produced a sense of relief, accomplishment, completeness, even euphoria, extending for periods of time from weeks to months after arrival at the clinic. Later, however, the loss of city resources and stimulations, as well as the slow community acceptance of newcomers, resulted in the second phase—depression. Concurrently, the authors experienced a paradoxically claustrophobic yet anchorless feeling. During this period of time, many of the systems and relationships against and through which the authors had defined themselves were significantly changed or even removed. And with this identity difficulty comes the process of community testing and definition of the newcomer, just when the newcomer is least sure of himself.

During the initial stages of the development of a rural community mental health center, the community does not relate to a sense of clinic identity; rather, clinicians are viewed as individuals, responded to and tested individually. The Gertz article covers this point.

> The third most frequently identified problem was entry of the mental health system to the community. The respondents indicated that community acceptance was inhibited by general public attitude toward mental illness, superstitions, labelling and the stigma associated with being a patient. The difficulty with maintaining confidentiality in a small town setting was also listed. One respondent reported that when his patients walked into the mental health center they feel as though everyone in town sees them.[2]

The men and women on the clinical staff reported varying experiences, perhaps partly due to their differences in sex. Women professionals are still somewhat unusual in the small rural community. The women generally do not receive immediate recognition as competent professionals and therefore must spend time laying the groundwork with members of the community to establish their ability to function in the mental health field. In contrast, the majority of male clinicians are met with magical expectations as to what they should be able to accomplish; consequently, they must be able to tolerate the frustrations of being unable to meet these expectations. As a staff, personnel in this agency spent some time discussing which reception was more difficult to deal with. The conclusion was that they are simply different and each proves a difficult challenge

It will be apparent to the reader acquainted with crisis theory that there are some parallels between the experiences referred to above and the crisis state.[3] Specifically, the cultural change in moving from urban to rural community mental health can be perceived as a stress event. The initial period of euphoria might be considered the initial avoidance stage of grief work. Feelings of loss, threat, and depression had an impact on the authors' and other social workers' clinical practice; some clinicians chose to focus exclusively on outpatient work, the professional activity in which they felt most comfortable and competent. This decision contrasted with their initial expectations that they would be spending a great deal of time in community work. Other clinicians experienced diminished motivation and ability to function throughout their professional obligations. The working-through process as described in crisis theory was characterized initially by use of staff support and later by turning to community support.

NEED FOR STAFF SUPPORT

The authors and most of their colleagues did turn to and invest a great deal in the mental health center staff as a group. They felt strongly that gaining this support, shoring up their professional identity, and clarifying role issues were crucial to their success in the community. It is difficult to say whether the staff cohesiveness is a product of preselection factors or the needs experienced in response to initiation into the rural community. Nonetheless, the authors noticed distinct differences in the degree of support and sharing among staff members in this clinic as compared to their previous experience in other psychiatric settings.

A number of factors that the authors suggest are responsible for the need experienced by the clinicians for staff support are discussed below. An initial feeling was the sense of professional isolation. There are very few professional persons living in this county who have any formal training relevant to psychiatric practice. Although the clinicians on the staff were eclectic in their approach, a majority of them were trained in academic institutions where there was emphasis on ego-oriented analytic theory. Consequently, the authors' attempts to facilitate growth in patients by encouraging them to develop and utilize whatever strengths they have was often seen as withholding by the community, which would have felt pleased if the authors had engaged in more rescue missions. As a result, the clinicians often received negative feedback about their therapeutic stance, which furthered the feelings of alienation from the community.

A second factor influencing the need for staff support is the partial inapplicability of the therapy models which the authors were taught in urban psychoanalytically oriented schools. For example, in most academic settings, professionals learn that a therapist should be an anonymous personage to his or her patients. In addition, there should be a formality in the therapy relationship in order to ensure the therapist's ability to maintain a continuously objective stance. Living in a small town where social workers experience multiple role relationships with the other members of the community, it is impossible to remain anonymous and difficult to maintain any formality. One of the authors felt this problem keenly when she went to the bank with her first paycheck and handed it to one of her new patients who was the only teller available. The typical resident's feelings of awe and mistrust of psychiatric personnel have contributed to the authors' ability to maintain professional stances. However, many of their original precepts have had to be modified during this stay in a small town.

A third factor contributing to need for staff support has been each clinician's loss of personal privacy and ability to exercise control over his social contacts. Because a majority of the staff had been raised in a megalopolis, they had not previously experienced the kind of continuous exposure which one feels living in a small town. The authors soon recognized intellectually that if they maintained a consistent life style, the community would be accepting. However, consistently meeting patients in the towns where they and the authors live, in contrast to the anonymity experienced in the city, intensified feelings of loss of control over one's social life. A compounding factor is the reality of a clinician dealing with numerous emergencies with maximal exposure of his professional functioning and minimal clinical backup. Typically, when a person is on call he has one or two colleagues who are in the area. Sometimes, however, the closest clinician is forty-five miles away. The nearest psychiatric inpatient unit is an hour to two hours away, depending on which part of the county the clinician lives in. Consequently, the staff person frequently is working alone in emergent situations with only telephone backup available. This fact contrasts sharply with the kinds of situations most of the staff had dealt with in urban community mental health centers.

In response to the press felt by staff members, the staff developed a pattern of interaction which was simultaneously supportive and growth-producing. Those staff members who progressed through the stress stage to the working-through process uniformly displayed a willingness to subject their professional functioning to a close scrutiny by their colleagues. An openness and a sharing were expected of one another so that the staff could process clinical functioning and examine the decisions made by one another in both emergent and in ongoing therapy. Because small town clinicians are continuously involved in public relations work, this request for openness from one another was in part based on the fact that persons are subsequently able to experience comfort in dealing with issues with members of the community if they understand their colleagues' clinical functioning. In the process of such discussions, staff members developed respect for one another and received helpful information. The staff members who, for one reason or another, were highly resistant to the process of openness and sharing generally were the individuals who found living and working in a rural community mental health center unacceptable to them and eventually moved on.

A parallel process is suggested in the literature on the sociology of family and marriage relationships by Elizabeth Bott. She describes a correlation between the degree of role separation between husband and wife and the degree of involvement with surrounding social network. For example, husbands and wives who marry in neighborhoods in which they have many other relationship ties tend to have more separate and traditional role definitions within their relationship than those couples who have less outside ties and tend to share tasks. She also found that the closer the group network, the more norms are commonly accepted.[4]

If one considers a staff as a family and postulates parallel dynamics, the predictions would be that in new and different settings, staff would tend to share more commonality of roles and spend significantly more energy in social contact among themselves than staff in familiar settings, and that the close staff would tend to share more norms of behavior than the more distant, less-invested staff.

In actuality, the authors found both of these dynamics to reflect accurately their own personal experience. For instance, although various disciplinary backgrounds and values are represented, staff members felt more similar in viewpoint to each other than to the members of the community, at least during the initial stages of transition. Educational backgrounds familiarized them with the community mental health movement and produced an agreement with, even dedication to, the principles of community treatment. This shared experiential, educational, and value background is still new to the sociology of a small, rural community.

It is instructive to look at colleagues who made the decision not to continue living and working in rural communities. One-third of the staff hired in this agency during the past four years has left. This figure does not include two psychiatrists, each of whom served as consultants while stationed here on a two-year term of duty with the Public Health Service Corps. Most community mental health centers do experience a continuous turnover of personnel, but the fact that this group left, on the average, within the first year of their employment at the clinic reflects the difficulties posed by the transition process. For several persons, the main verbalized reason for leaving was that the clinician felt separate from, and not accepted by, the main body of the staff. A second, closely correlated reason, was the fact that the clinician wished to seek for further professional development, primarily educational, and that facilities were not available in the county. One could speculate about the individual reasons and the individual discomfort in each of these situations, but it would be tertiary to the main point: In every instance of staff's leaving the mental health center, the departure coincided with less comparative use of staff for support combined with increased dissatisfaction. Perhaps this situation perpetuated the depressive phase referred to above and caused staff to leave the center before becoming adapted.

CONCLUSIONS

Rural community mental health is a relatively young, challenging field. After a transition period which may be inevitable for clinicians coming from an urban to a rural setting, the rewards of this kind of work are unique. The authors had several experiences during the first year of practice in New Hampshire that could be characterized as abrupt and hostile rejection. From that starting point, they have each developed stimulating and most effective consultative relationships with groups varying from the local police department to the schools. Paradoxically, they have found that once the testing period was worked through to a level satisfactory to both the community and the professionals, there was a receptivity and availability for constructive change that is professionally quite exciting and unique to a rural setting.

As in many issues within the helping professions, the critical point is awareness and anticipation of the process. Too little attention has been paid to the transitional stages one experiences when moving from urban to rural social agencies in general, and mental health centers in particular. In contrast, a large body of knowledge has been gained along cross-cultural boundaries. As in any crisis, the growth and disorganizing potentials can be maximized and minimized respectively by an anticipation of the process. It has been found operationally that a different view of the function of a staff also facilitates this process. Although the sample covered for this article was limited and consisted mainly of upper New England mental health centers, in discussions with other rural mental health center clinicians the authors found that their experience of significant differences in staff needs occurs during the first year or two of employment. The authors would like to see a study undertaken to investigate these patterns in order to avoid the possibility of overgeneralization from their personal perspectives.

It is clear that the therapist's definition of and expectations of his own role are central to the transition process. Recent staff members have found the testing process somewhat less intense because the clinic is now established. Particularly in a relatively young mental health center, however, the more clearly defined the clinician's professional role, the more consistent and productive will be the testing process. Areas which deserve special consideration and thought are the areas of confidentiality and communication with other professionals and with the patient's relatives.[5]

Some very difficult decisions must be made in terms of how the individual professional and the agency define themselves as a community mental health center. When there are few or no private psychotherapy resources available, the luxury of being able to refer patients is nonexistent. There are also generally very few or no other psychiatric professionals available for consultations for schools and other social agencies. Some of the literature argues strongly and coherently for the use of the therapist's time in consultation and education services.[6] Much of that literature assumes that other professionals in the community will develop an expertise in handling cases without referral and that private practitioners are available. How much of the agency's clinical resources will be devoted to consultation and education must be carefully delineated.

The authors of this article believe that it was not accidental that the most important personal qualities listed in the Gertz survey were good communication skills and independent functioning ability. These factors are crucial, not only for clearly communicating decisions and rationale to the community, but also for the development of a staff interaction that is helpful, perhaps even necessary, in the transition of social work professionals from urban to rural practice.

NOTES

1. Boris Gertz, Jill Meider, and Margaret L. Pluckhan, A Survey of Rural Community Mental Health Needs and Resources, *Hospital and Community Psychiatry*, 26:816–19 (December 1975).
2. Ibid.
3. See, for example, Lydia Rapoport, The State of Crisis: Some

Theoretical Considerations, in *Crisis Intervention: Selected Readings*, ed. Howard Parad (New York: Family Service Association of America, 1965), pp. 22–32.

4. Elizabeth Bott, *Family and Social Network: Roles, Norms and External Relationships* (New York: Free Press, 1972), especially chaps. 3 and 7.

5. A clear delineation of these issues, though the authors would take issue with his conclusions, is presented in Allen S. Mariner, The Problem of Therapeutic Privacy, *Psychiatry*, 30:60–72 (February 1967).

6. See, for example, William G. Hollister et al., *Experiences in Rural Mental Health* (Chapel Hill, N.C.: University of North Carolina Press, 1973); or Hans Heussy, *Mental Health with Limited Resources: Yankee Ingenuity in Low-Cost Programs* (New York: Grune & Stratton, 1966).

The next article comes from the West where many traditionally small communities are now booming. Two case vignettes make the points that rural settlements have creative means of helping "their own," but that life in a recently changing, perhaps even newborn, growing town presents decided problems for some, if not all, of the populace.

30

CYNTHIA S. GUILLAUME AND HARRIETT HAYES

Preserving Family Life in Impacted Communities

"Wide, Wonderful Wyoming" reads the roadside sign as the traveler crosses the border of the ninth largest state in area. Wide, wonderful, and diverse is the land. Equally diverse small towns dot the plains, huddle in mountain valleys, and cling to the rims of rocky buttes.

It was always a pleasure to drive the brief twenty-five miles from the county social service office to the neighboring town. The drive passed through lovely farming land surrounded by gentle foothills. It was rare to receive a referral from this little town, with its population of 300 people. In this instance, the referral came from the county hospital on behalf of a single mother of two preschool-age children. She had been admitted to the hospital due to a serious heart attack. Her health had been poor for several months, making it impossible for her to work to support the family. The hospital nurse said the mother was deeply concerned over mounting bills and child care arrangements during her hospitalization. The children were temporarily left with a neighbor lady for care while the mother was hospitalized. I was prepared to obtain foster care for the two small children until the mother could return home, at which time a homemaker would be hired to care for the family. Day-care could be arranged for part-time supervision of the children. An emergency grant and food stamps would help the financial crisis.

From Cynthia S. Guillaume and Harriett Hayes, "Preserving Family Life in Impacted Communities," an original article, by permission of the authors.

Since there were very few marked streets in the town, it was necessary to stop and obtain landmark directions from a restaurant owner, who also was the town mail clerk. At the entrance of the restaurant was a sign announcing a community garage sale to raise money for this mother and her two children. The restaurant owner informed me that a local church had also taken donations to pay her overdue utility bills and rent, and that the children were being cared for by two neighbors; the neighbors had also arranged for several families to share meal preparation once the mother and children moved home. A group of people would also take turns visiting the mother, as soon as she would be allowed visitors, to reassure her and keep her informed of her children's situation.

I relayed the information to the hospital nurse and left my phone number in case I could be of assistance in the future.[1]

Energy development has brought a 23 percent increase in population since 1970, but the rural, small-town atmosphere of the state still remains. The growth connected with energy development (mining for coal and uranium, oil exploration, and construction of power plants) has produced the mixed blessings of economic growth and accentuated social problems for community residents. Median income for a family of four is about $20,000 in Wyoming, and the unemployment rate in the state in 1978 was 3.6 percent.

The pictures created by the words "boom town" are of crime- and divorce-ridden communities with many problems indicative of family breakdown. In reality, research suggests that such is not the case.[2] Divorce rates are no higher in impacted communities than in more slow-growing Wyoming towns, and the impacted communities have fewer women receiving Aid for Dependent Children.

As communities experience rapid growth, service delivery systems do begin to change, however. According to the U.S. Department of Housing and Urban Development (HUD), a growth rate of 10 percent per year for a small community begins to strain local service delivery systems; and above 15 percent these systems begin to break down.[3] Between 1971 and 1978, many Wyoming communities experiencing energy-related development had growth rates of 20 to 80 percent.

This referral sounded like so many others. . .an anonymous caller reporting three pre-school children being left unattended all day and early into the evening. . .

The caller gave me the mother's name and the mining site at which her trailer was parked. I left immediately, expecting to spend a great deal of time locating the trailer.

The mine site looked like all the others: small camper trailers backed up to the pits in some cases. The wind blew; there were no trees, grass, swings, or other signs of children. A quick-shop store and a laundromat were centrally located.

I knocked at several trailers attempting to find Mrs. R. Most people were not home; others were home, silently refusing to answer the door to someone driving a state vehicle; the few who were home had not heard of Mrs. R.

I returned later that evening, when more people were home and luckily located Mrs. R. I was amazed that none of the neighbors knew her or each other.

I explained the nature of the report to Mrs. R. Mrs. R. informed me that she had tried to locate day-care for her three children, but that none was available within the mine complex. The trailers were too substandard to be licensed for day-care; and too few women were willing to care for children when they could be making $600–900 per month working at the mine. Food and rent were very high, and it was necessary to work for as much money as possible. It was impossible to live on the state's AFDC grant of $305 per month, plus a food stamp bonus of $151 per month. The nearest day-care was fifteen miles away, and Mrs. R. was without transportation; a public transportation system did not exist. Mrs. R. was deeply aware of the danger in which she was placing her children. She wanted only to make enough money to move with her children to a more accommodating town.[4]

The restaurant owner, who knew his neighbors and a generation of local history, may find increasing numbers of new faces in the bar each evening. The neighbor who knew in intimate detail the problems facing the family across the street cannot even recognize the families in the trailers down the road. The informal resources and support networks of the community are no longer adequate. Increasingly, complex systems of formal service delivery begin to be developed to meet community needs.

Available research on the effects of rapid population growth on human behavior suggests that women and children are most adversely affected. Wives of workers at a power plant or mine fifteen miles from the nearest town lack the support systems that school and work provide their children and husbands. They may become isolated and alienated, and the stress of living in a new environment under uncertain conditions is increased. The profile of the average mental health center client in one energy-impacted community is a 35- to 44-year-old white female, a homemaker with a high school education, and with a husband who makes $15,600 to $20,000 a year. She comes on her own to the center for help with a "transient, situational disturbance."

Traditional means of getting acquainted often prove ineffective for the wife of the miner or construction worker. These women need support groups to help them adjust to the community in a short period of time. One young woman described her year in a trailer community of approximately 400 people whose only resources were a bar, a general store, and a service station in these words: "It was the strangest year of my life. I didn't know anyone and there didn't seem to be any way for me to get to know people. People weren't unfriendly, but they just didn't respond to my attempts to get acquainted. I nearly went crazy."

In another community the Newcomers Club is meeting with strong resistance from local residents who say, "We don't want those people getting involved in our community affairs." Support networks, whether informal or formal, must reflect the cultural diversity of the community members who use them. One mining executive seeking to help a struggling young clergyman in a community mushrooming on land that a year ago had been pasture, said, "Don't pay house calls on those families, just put a letter addressed 'occupant' in their letter boxes." The clergyman is still struggling with a congregation of four.

In some energy-impacted communities, informal resources and support networks have never existed. The community that springs up within commuting distance of a mine may bring in people who have no experience in the Koffee Klatching and backyard gabbing that help build a sense of neighborhood. Other communities are faced with the project of mobilizing and integrating formal resources as the old ways of coping with problems become more inadequate. A department of public assistance and social services director described his informal role as the local rental agent up to two years ago. Today that job has become too demanding to continue along with his regular job, and there is as yet no formal agency to help families find housing.

In spite of community planners and intervention projects, the prevailing attitude toward energy-related growth continues to be "let's not do anything until problems occur" or "until problems touch us."

To help preserve family life in energy-impacted communities, social workers need to use their skills not only as formal community organizers and program developers, but also to support existing informal helping networks. In towns where these do not exist the social worker must develop skills to help people recover and build a sense of community.

The challenge lies in the questions: What are the family needs? What informal resources exist to meet these needs? Who or what in the community exists already to meet these needs? And finally, what new resources would be acceptable to rural families?

NOTES

1. Adapted from a case handled by Cynthia Guillaume.
2. James Thompson, "The Gillette Syndrome," *Wyoming Issues* (Spring 1979), pp. 30–35.

3. "Rapid Growth from Energy Projects: Ideas for State and Local Action; A Program Guide" (Washington, D.C.: U.S. Department of Housing and Urban Development, 1976), p. 2. Quoted from "A Growth Management Case Study: Sweetwater County, Wyoming" (Denver: Denver Institute for Rocky Mountain Energy Company, December 1974).

4. Adapted from a student practicum case.

REFERENCES

1. "Rapid Growth from Energy Projects: Ideas for State and Local Actions; A Program Guide." Washington, D.C.: U.S. Department of Housing and Urban Development, 1976.

2. James Thompson. "The Gillette Sundrome." *Wyoming Issues* (Spring, 1979).

3. Leon Ginsberg, ed. *Social Work in Rural Communities: A Book of Readings.* New York: Council on Social Work Education, 1976.

4. John Harding and Edward C. Devereux, eds. "Leadership and Participation in a Changing Rural Community." *Journal of Social Issues*, 16, 4 (1960): 30–35.

5. Gwen K. Weber. "Preparing Social Workers for Practice in Rural Social Systems." *Journal of Social Work Education*, 12, 3 (Fall 1976): 108–115.

Social work or human service activity has both "micro" and "macro" aspects, work with individuals, families, and groups, on the one hand, and community approaches, on the other. Jacobsen's article which follows argues for a particular model of macro practice that has been termed locality or community development. This orientation is seen as especially pertinent and useful in nonmetropolitan contexts for reasons that are discussed.

31

G. MICHAEL JACOBSEN

Rural Communities and Community Development

Much of the literature about social work in rural areas suggests that there is a lack of adequate resources available to the rural practitioner. In combination with the fact that rural areas are also characterized by a further lack of human service professionals, one begins to understand the many references to the need for resource development in rural areas. Often, however, the professional located in rural areas does not have the luxury of devoting much energy to such developmental activities. Typically, rural social workers are also responsible for casework, groupwork, educational programs, administration, and so on—the generalist practitioner. The purpose of this article is to suggest that the most appropriate process available to the practitioner on the "community practice" or "macro-practice" side of generic practice is community or locality development. In the author's mind, community development is a preferable strategy largely because many of the goals, strategies, and techniques employed in community development are consistent with both the fabric of rural communities and

From G. Michael Jacobsen, "Rural Communities and Community Development," an original article, by permission of the author.

the resources available to rural social workers. It is also a process that has considerable potential for both resource development and fundamental social change in rural communities. Finally, it is a process that posits the role of the social worker as a *citizen* rather than an *organizer* or *expert*.

By consideration of some of the common characteristics of rural communities, one begins to understand the suitability of community development to the rural generalist practitioner. Briefly, rural communities have small populations, are more concerned about local issues than state or national issues, are somewhat traditional, and tend to emphasize self-pride and self-help. Other dimensions of the rural community often encountered by the practitioner include greater concern on the part of the community for internal rather than external relationships, which is often experienced as serious distrust or selective "ignoring" of regional or state bureaucracies; an orientation toward concern for the maintenance of common values and beliefs of the community; and mutual interdependence and concern for the continuance of long-standing (often familial) relationships among community members. Rural communities tend to be stable, slow to change, and very interested in taking care of "their own" so long as "theirs" do not offend local norms, values, and beliefs.

Edward Buxton while outlining some suggestions to rural social workers also provides further justification for community development as the "community" side of generic practice.[1] He suggests that it is helpful to remind ourselves and the rural community that the responsibility for solving community problems lies with the community and not the individual social worker or the social agency. Buxton also points out that all developmental activities must take place with proper sensitivity to local concerns and local etiquette or they are likely to be rejected by the community. Furthermore, local individuals and organizations often have an impressive "track record" of accomplishments in similar areas, and if an individual agency were to attempt to make changes, it probably would not have the resources necessary for success in an individual effort.

Various types of community practice have been utilized with differing degrees of success in many practice settings. A number of theorists have attempted to conceptualize modalities of community practice and analyze their relative effectivity in various settings. The conceptualization utilized in this article will be taken primarily from Jack Rothman.[2] He offers three traditional practice roles for the community practitioner—social action, social planning, and locality or community development.

The basic goal of the *social action* practitioner is to make fundamental changes in both communities and society. This necessitates shifts in traditional power relationships and decision-making processes in rural communities. Common change tactics for the social action practitioner include confrontation, initiation of conflict, and direct action such as strikes and boycotts. The social action practitioner often sees the power structure in a rural community as "the enemy" or as "the oppressors" who must be coerced or overturned. The basic change strategy of the practitioner includes crystallization of issues and polarization of the community as well as organization of the "oppressed" to take action against the "oppressor." Typically, the social action practitioner works cooperatively *only* with the "victims" in the community—those individuals and groups in the community who are seen as disadvantaged or suffering from the effects of social injustice, deprivation, and inequities. Frequently, the social action practitioner must spend large amounts of time "consciousness raising" with the "victims" because they may have difficulty conceiving themselves as "victims." Such suggestions may be seen as foreign or certainly very different from their previous understandings of their role in the community.

Within the *social planning* model of community practice, the practitioner role is largely one of the "expert" fact gatherer, analyst, program evaluator, and social problem solver. This so-called expert is often employed by a large regional or state organization. The social planning practitioner analyzes and diagnoses community problems (particularly specific mental and physical health, housing, or recreational problems) and provides possible solutions from a location typically *outside* the community. Power actors with this model are often approached as collaborators in a technical process of community problem solving. Often, only the power actors act as collaborators in the problem-solving process. Important members of the power structure for the social planner are often found *outside* the domain of the rural community such as in state offices, state and federal legislatures, and the federal bureaucracy.

The model for community change called *locality development* by Rothman has the practitioner working at the local level with a broad cross section of people involved in determining and solving their own problems. In this role the practitioner focuses upon facilitation of the process of community development. The critical elements in this process are a number of small task-oriented groups of community residents. The responsibility for the success or failure of the groups and the process rests with the community, *not* the practitioner. Characteristic change tactics of the community developer include a focus upon both consensus and communication among elements of the community. Members of the power structure in this model are approached as "fellow citizens" who might be interested in activities related to the growth and well-being of their own community.

Lee J. Cary discusses community development as a deliberate attempt by the community to work together toward altering the future of their community.[3] He also suggests several essential elements of a successful community development process. Cary stresses the importance of both community initiative and leadership as well as participation by as large a portion of the community as is possible. He suggests that salient practitioner roles include development and facilitation of small task-oriented groups in the community; efforts toward expanding participation of as many components of the community as is possible; working at the "boundaries" between external and internal community resources attempting to insure the "fit" with local needs; and the modeling of problem-solving and democratic group techniques for participants in the process.

It is hoped that by consideration of some of the salient practitioner roles in community development one may begin to appreciate the considerable "fit" between the rural community and the community development process. The emphasis upon community leadership and initiative found in the process of community development should enhance feelings of "local responsibility" as well as self-help and self-pride often found in rural communities. In this process the members of the community decide upon the nature of their community goals and problems as well as likely solutions. The practitioner participates as a *community member* and attempts to work *with* the community in ways determined by the community. Other methods tend to focus upon development of citizen support for *pre*established programs determined by *outside* groups or organizations in order to solve problems or raise issues determined *outside* the rural community. Rural community residents are sometimes resentful and rarely deeply committed to goals, solutions, and programs that others have determined for them. At times such activities are perceived as "meddling," are viewed with suspicion or distrust by community members, or are treated as representative of "outside" or "foreign" interests attempting to change the rural community.

The practice of employing internal resources supported by external resources secured upon the initiative of the local community further emphasizes community responsibility and control of the process. The rural community decides which external resources will be employed and how they will be utilized. The process draws upon the skills and interests of all involved citizens and not only upon the "more important," "better," or the "oppressed" as in other processes. Other methods tend to draw attention to the limitations of the local community in order to bolster inadequate local resources or radically alter traditional processes within the community. It is reasonable for many community residents to conclude that these *outsiders* perceive things as "terribly wrong" (unjust, sick, coercive, or deprived) in their home community. The "real," "just," or "more important" issues are defined by outsiders and suggest changes imported by outsiders rather than focusing upon the interest and ability of local citizens to set their own goals, define their own problems, and provide for their own solutions.

The concerns for multilevel participation and consensus found in community development are also consistent with the fabric of many rural communities. These concerns call for participation by as many members of the community as is possible so that a variety of viewpoints are brought up and fully considered. Agreements and decisions following from such discussions tend to be more satisfactory for all parties involved. The community development process tends to emphasize the participants' interdependence and their shared values and beliefs. Other methods tend to rely upon the use of conflict to settle differences, attempt to emphasize differences in community values and beliefs, or tend to simply ignore the need for comprehensive community participation altogether.

The concern for an organized comprehensive community approach on the community's terms helps to insure that the process does not move quicker than the rural community is able to accommodate. A focus upon inclusive participation can help to insure that all viewpoints are heard before decisions are made and that those decisions are based upon realistic goals and objectives. Other methods often encourage rapid, often fundamental changes, or the tempo of change is dictated by organizations located *outside* the rural community. Such emphases often tend to ignore the readiness of the community to change and may interfere with acceptance and integration of the changes by the rural community.

Finally, the community development process itself is not "foreign" to residents of rural communities. Although they may not have utilized this process in areas of concern to human service professionals, they certainly have done so in other areas. Evidence the development of swimming pools, parks, community buildings, libraries, ambulance services, and civic and fraternal organizations in rural areas. Additionally, the extension service has long employed methods of community development in its attempts to improve rural community life. Community development processes are often *the* processes employed by local organizations to solve their community problems.

In summary, community development is a process by which the local community establishes its goals for development, defines its own problems, and determines and acts upon its own solutions. The responsibility for problem resolution rests with the community, *not* with the social worker or the social agency. The professional social worker tends to act as a *citizen* who has both a right and a responsibility to address community needs and problems. The citizen social worker, however, is a social worker by profession who brings to the process certain understandings and abilities just as the local banker, teacher, factory worker, or farmer brings their own understandings and abilities. Important practitioner tasks within the community development process include development and facilitation of small task-centered groups; development of group and interpersonal problem-solving skills among participants; and mediation with regard to the utilization of extra-community resources.

Community development as a "community" or "macro-practice" process for the generic social worker has certain distinct advantages. The responsibility for change rests with the community, not with the practitioner. The time and person resources necessary for this more limited involvement in community change are more reasonable for the already overburdened practitioner. The practitioner is not seen either as the "expert" or as the "organizer." The community development process identifies and secures many "experts" and suggests that the community will "organize" itself. Skills necessary for effective community development are also typically within the repertoire of the generalist practitioner—group and interpersonal skills, knowledge of external resources, and "mediative" skills.

Involvement in community development processes may have more personal reward for the rural social worker. Many social workers located in rural areas complain of isolation or the lack of acceptance by the community. This separateness and differentness from the community can appear as a significant obstacle to both personal and professional satisfaction. Involvement in the community development process may suggest to the community that the worker is in fact a member of the community, is concerned about the future of the community, and is quite interested in working together with other residents around issues of common concern. Community meetings, group discussions, and personal discussions with members of the community involved in the process are all excellent ways for the isolated practitioner to form satisfying personal and professional relationships in the community.

NOTES

1. E. Buxton, "Delivering Social Services in Rural Areas," *Public Welfare* (Winter 1973), pp. 15–20.
2. J. Rothman, "Three Models of Community Organization Practice," from National Conference on Social Welfare, *Social Work Practice 1968* (New York: Columbia University Press, 1968).
3. L. Cary, *Community Development as a Process* (Columbia: University of Missouri Press, 1976).

REFERENCES

Biddle, William W., and Loureide J. Biddle. *The Community Development Process.* New York: Holt, Rinehart and Winston, 1965.

Cary, Lee J., ed. *Community Development as a Process.* Columbia: University of Missouri Press, 1976.

Cox, Fred M., John L. Erlich, Jack Rothman, and John E. Tropman, eds. *Strategies of Community Organization*, 2nd ed. Itasca, Illinois: F. E. Peacock, 1974.

Jacob, Nelson, Stephen Lilley, and Eddie Wynn. "An Action Scheme for Rural Community Development Practitioners." In *Second National Institute on Social Work in Rural Areas Reader*, edited by Edward B. Buxton. Madison: University of Wisconsin, 1978.

Johnson, Louise C. "Social Development in Nonmetropolitan Areas." In *Social Work in Rural Areas*, edited by Ronald K. Green and Stephen A. Webster. Knoxville: The University of Tennessee, 1976.

Morrison, Jim. "Community Organization in Rural Areas." In *Social Work in Rural Communities*, edited by Leon H. Ginsberg. New York: Council on Social Work Education, 1976.

Educational preparation for social workers to work in rural communities is the focus of this article. The need for professionals equipped to deal with the unique circumstances of the rural situation is developed, and various models for provision of practicum experiences are also discussed. This last factor is an important consideration in view of the large role for field, internship, and practicum types of learning in social work and human service educational programs generally.

32

GWEN K. WEBER

Preparing Social Workers for Practice in Rural Social Systems

America evolved from a rural economic structure that prevailed throughout its first 150 years of development. The patterns and qualities of life were primarily a result of agrarian determinants that still remain within the basic character of the nation. The era of industrialization encouraged migration to the city and by 1917 more people were living in urban centers than in rural areas. The urban structures were poorly prepared for such rapid expansion and soon social, economic, and political problems were growing at such a rate that the attention and energies of the nation were directed toward them and away from the rural areas.

The assessment of urban problems found many of their origins to be rural in nature—and understandably so, since many rural people were migrating to this "promised land." At the same time, emerging disparities in rural areas were found related to the by-products of urban economic development. Presently, the symbiotic character of

Reprinted from Gwen K. Weber, "Preparing Social Workers for Practice in Rural Social Systems," *Journal of Education for Social Work*, Vol. 12, No. 3, Fall 1976, pp. 108–115, by permission of the author and the journal.

the rural-urban quality of life is recognized. However, major disparities still exist in population growth, educational and health facilities,
housing conditions, social services, employment opportunities, and
income levels, with rural Americans consistently in a disadvantaged
position.

The professional commitment of social work to this one-third of the
nation's population cannot be accomplished by the few social workers
now practicing in rural communities. A survey by the National Association of Social Workers in 1969 found 16.8 percent of its professional (MSW-DSW) membership practicing in communities of 50,000
population or less, and 4 percent in communities of 4,000 or less.[1]

Providing and preparing social work manpower for practice in rural
social systems is the responsibility of social work education. A number
of schools already have excellent curriculums that relate to rural practice, and others have modified theirs to include more on rural issues.
Too often, however, these efforts are only superficial. As most schools
of social work, educators, practicum settings, professional organizations, and personnel are located in the city, the profession's concerns
quite naturally are directed toward urban issues. Theoretical concepts
and practice models are general and exclusive of the unique conditions
found in rural communities. Only a few social work educators are
located in rural settings to provide cogent feedback, thus we rely upon
borrowing information from other professions. It is the intent of this
paper to review briefly the character of rural America, its social problems, and its living conditions. From this, practical means to utilize
this information will be considered in the preparation of social workers
for rural practice.

DISTINCTIVE PATTERNS TO RURAL LIVING

Rural areas in each state have their own unique characteristics, and
to specifically define rural as it relates to population, occupation,
cultural background, and so on, is inadvisable, since what is rural to
some areas may not be to others. Generally, then, rural refers to the
environmental surroundings, the social systems, and the people who
reside in areas that have a relatively low population density, usually
either in the country or in small towns or villages. The Bureau of
Census defines rural Americans as the farm and nonfarm population
who reside in the country or in communities of less than 2,500 people.
They have a preference for minimal governmental involvement and
for local control over those regulations deemed necessary. Rural
people value their sense of independence, self-reliance, and privacy.

They often prefer the out-of-doors, a simplistic life style, and unstructured activities.

Voting patterns show that rural areas prefer traditionally established patterns and conservative values, and are more resistive to change.[2] Importance is placed on the family, and institutions such as the school, church, and local organizations usually provide the locus of community activity. Face-to-face, informal relationships are preferred and perhaps contribute to the fact that nonurban institutions have fewer problems in communication and relationship with people and with their community, than urban institutions.[3]

POPULATION FACTORS

Census Bureau figures show that population growth in rural areas is much below that of urban centers. The nation's population has doubled from 106 to 203 million over the past five decades, and the increase has largely been absorbed by urban areas, which increased from 54 to 149 million.[4] Annually, approximately 800,000 rural people migrate to the city.[5] Often these are either the young, educated, skilled individuals, or minority or indigent people seeking economic or social opportunities. The urban Black population rose from 12 percent in 1950 to 20 percent in 1966, with a similar decrease in small cities, towns, and farming areas.[6] Interestingly, a study by Lindley found that rural areas traditionally have treated the poor and minority groups with less compassion than cities, and that available community and public welfare services in urban areas attract minority groups.[7]

The Economic Research Service contends that outmigration of rural people will continue, especially in the Southeast, southern Appalachia, and the Great Plains. In the last ten years, 1,350 rural counties, many in these areas, actually declined in population. Others grew by only 6.7 percent as compared to the 16.6 percent growth in metropolitan counties.[8] The Department of Agriculture stated in the Agriculture Act of 1970 that a better balance in the distribution of the nation's population should be given a high priority in future policies and program planning.[9]

RURAL QUALITY OF LIFE

Income

Rural people are nearly twice as likely to be poor as are urban residents. These rural poor are neither as audible or visible as those in the urban areas, yet in many instances their problems are more acute. The President's Commission on Rural Poverty found 13 million rural poor, based on the index of a $3,000 income per family. This represents 30 percent of the total farm population and 24 percent of the rural nonfarm population. It compares with only about 13 percent, or 20 million, of the urban population.[10]

The severity of poverty is greater in rural areas, since more than 70 percent of the rural poor live on less than $2,000 per year and 25 percent exist on less than $1,000 per year. As recently as 1967, a government report estimated that about 35 percent of all farmers, often older and semi-retired, had annual cash incomes of less than $1,000.[11]

Although there are rural poor everywhere, there are proportionately more among certain minority and ethnic groups, and they are more prevalent in certain regions of the country. In 1969 more than half the total rural Black population was below the poverty level.[12] Migrant farm workers, Mexican-American farmers in the Southwest, and Indians also comprised the poor population. Poor regions often coincide with the location of this population, such as Appalachia, the Ozarks, parts of the South, the upper Great Plains, the coastal areas of the Pacific Northwest, parts of New England, and the upper Great Lakes.[13]

Housing Conditions

Rural communities have 60 percent of the nation's substandard housing. Many of these homes are occupied by the low-incomed, the aged, and minority families. In 1970 families with annual incomes of less than $3,000 occupied two-thirds of these homes, and most of the others were occupied by families with $3,000 to $6,000.[14] Three-fourths of both the homes of the rural Blacks and the Indian residences on reservations are substandard.[15]

Rural communities have utilized federal programs such as those administered by the Department of Housing and Urban Development, and the Department of Agriculture to develop new housing facilities, or to finance improvements on existing housing. Basic services such as water, waste disposal, electricity, and police and fire protection have, however, continued to be costly and difficult to provide to sparsely located rural dwellings.

Unemployment and Underemployment

Technological and scientific advances over the past 20 years have resulted in fewer job opportunities in traditionally rural occupations such as agriculture, forestry, mining, and fishing. The effects of mechanization have been profitable but clearly have affected rural employment trends. For example, less than half as many farmers are now able to produce approximately 40 percent more farm goods than in 1950.[16] With fewer man hours being required for farm production, farms sizes have been increasing. Those unable to compete or to adapt to these changes have been forced to leave their farms.

Similar events have occurred in the mining industry, with employment of miners dropping by one-third. Areas of the Great Plains, Ozarks, and Appalachia have experienced even greater drops.[17] In general, the unemployment rates are highest for the unskilled, and for those who have skills for which no jobs are available.

Fortunately the shifts in employment trends are stabilizing at the present. New job opportunities have been created by the increase of manufacturing and service industries now developing in rural communities. Agribusiness especially has been profitable. These enterprises have provided employment for women as well as men. Often they help increase the local population, and raise local income levels and the living conditions of the community.

Education

The quality of education in most rural school systems as a whole compares unfavorably to that of urban areas. Often teachers are less-qualified and paid significantly lower salaries. The curriculum offers less variety, and special educational programs are only beginning to emerge. Rural schools tend to resist or cannot afford outside instructional consultation, educational diagnostic services, or social services. The physical facilities are often inadequate and lack new instructional equipment.

Consolidation has improved many rural systems, and there is evidence to indicate that the level of educational attainment has improved over the past few years. But rural school districts have fewer funds to expend per pupil than do urban districts. With 25 percent of the nation's income, rural educational systems educate 36 percent of the nation's young people,[18] but spend only about three-fourths as much per pupil as urban areas.[19]

Fewer rural farm and nonfarm high school graduates plan to attend college than urban youth; 32 percent of the rural youth enroll in college, compared to 48 percent of urban youth.[20] As a whole rural youth tend to drop out of school earlier and are less successful in their chosen occupation.[21] Perhaps some of these factors are related to the fact that rural people often place less value on education. The average adult in a rural area has three fewer years of education than an urban adult.[22] In 1970, 65 percent of the adult farmers did not have a high school diploma and averaged an eighth- or ninth-grade level of education.[23]

Health Care Services

Rural communities in general have fewer health, mental health, and social service facilities than do cities. There is a lack of professional health personnel available, especially medical specialists. In 1969 the physician-patient ratio in rural areas was almost five times as many people per physician as the city. There were also 134 counties, with approximately 500,000 residents, without a physician. This was 36 more counties than in 1963.[24]

Rural people have a greater than average need for medical services but yet visit a physician less often and spend less on medical services than do urban residents. The occupational hazards of farm work rank next to the mining and construction industries, which have the highest death rate per person employed.[25] Rural people have higher rates of injury, lose more days from work due to illness and injury, and have more chronic diseases than their urban counterparts.[26] Statistics also show that rural nonfarm residents have higher rates of accidental death and injuries from motor vehicle accidents than urban residents.[27]

Rural populations include larger percentages of children, the aging, and the poor, all of whom have health needs greater than average. Minority and ethnic populations reflect a proportionately higher incidence of births. Good prenatal and postnatal instruction, free baby clinics, day care centers, and family planning and protective services are scarce in most rural communities.

Rural aged are found to have poorer physical and mental health, more chronic disease, smaller incomes, poorer diets, and homes that are deteriorated and unsanitary than the aged living in urban residences.[28] There are fewer supportive services such as home health care, public health, meals on wheels, and homemaker services available to them. Transportation problems often cause them to delay a visit to the physician until they are acutely ill.

Hopefully these distressing findings will alter with the emergence of comprehensive health planning efforts, improved accreditation standards for health facilities, regional rural mental health centers, and a federal medical insurance program.

FEDERAL PROGRAMS

Increases in federal government programming have provided an opportunity for rural development through multilevel structures. The Nixon Administration stated that the revitalization of rural America was one of its most important objectives.[29] Various rural development committees were established, such as the Rural Affairs Council, Rural Development Subcommittee, and Task Force on Rural Development. The latter identified as its goals job creation, improved community services, a better quality of living, and improved social and physical environment.[30] Title IX of the Agriculture Act of 1970 has aided in funding rural projects. In 1972 the rural development committee of the Department of Agriculture received $2.7 billion. This was two times greater than 1969, $1.4 billion, and four times greater than 1961, $5.75 million.[31]

RURAL PRACTICUM EXPERIENCES

Social work educators and schools of social work should utilize the gamut of potential resources in rural communities for practicum experiences for students. Students should be encouraged to pursue their interest in rural systems intervention and should have the opportunity to further integrate and individualize their theoretical conceptualizations and develop skills appropriate to the rural culture through a supervised experience. The curriculum should provide a generic base of information on the rural environment, and explore its problems. These efforts hopefully will inspire more students to enter practice in rural-based agencies.

An educator planning specific student assignments preferably should be located within the rural community and be familiar with its services, resources, problems, and current interests. Student placements often will be in an agency where social services are a secondary or ancillary service, since there are so few social service agencies in rural towns. Often this will demand that the educator be innovative in creating student projects and establishing a milieu conducive to learning. Many of these may be nontraditional types of assignments requiring a generalist practice approach.

Good interpersonal relations and a mutual regard among the educator, task instructor, and other community coordinators are essential. Responsibilities and expectations should be discussed prior to the students' arrival. The affiliate school of social work should also naturally provide support and assistance as needed. Some form of local public recognition of the students' activity and presence within the community will solicit the support of the local people, acknowledge students' and instructors' efforts, and promote the profession's capacities.

Three basic practicum models can be utilized in designing the placement. Students can be placed in a rural agency where the educator is located. Second, students can be placed in another community agency with a task instructor for all or part of their assignment, with the educator regularly providing supervision and consultation. Third, students can be assigned an identified social problem within the community and work independently in assessing it and involving local people in its resolution.

Each of these models has obvious advantages and disadvantages. Whichever is most effective for the situation should be selected. The first two are most useful in planning for a generic experience or for micro levels of intervention. They are also good for students who need a somewhat structured setting, experience with administrative procedures, a sense of local identity, or consistent support and supervision. Some sources to consider would include a public welfare agency, a community or veterans hospital, community action programs, housing development programs, a community mental health center, the YMCA or YWCA, an extended care facility, an alcoholic treatment program, church-related family and children services, the public school system, and cooperative extension services.

The third model is basically used to plan a community organization assignment directed toward larger social systems and the macro level of intervention. The educator should consider the current pressing social problems and interests of the community in defining a realistic project for the student. Additionally, a capable student should be selected who can work quite independently and without much given structure. For example, the student should have a good knowledge of research skills, be able to apply conceptual models in practice situations, and be goal-directed. The student should have a good sense of professional identity and the confidence and assertiveness to assume a leadership role.

Rural communities are especially good settings for community organization placements. The small, simplistic nature of the social structures enables students to form a comprehensive gestalt of them. Research skills or planned informal contacts can be utilized to acquire an understanding of the social problems, needs, and values of the people. Patterns of social interaction, organizational behavior, power structures, and problem-solving processes can be studied quite thoroughly and the support of appropriate social systems solicited to create a viable framework for joint action. Informal, personalized communication patterns help students in forming local task groups comprised of those being affected by the social problem and those interested in the well-being of the community. Usually students can operationalize their plan of action, evaluate its effects, make modifications as needed, and prepare for it to be self-supporting within the allotted practicum time. The completeness of this experience is especially good for student learning and evaluation.

Students also should be prepared to encounter barriers that traditionally have caused problems in providing social services to sparsely populated areas. Transportation problems, isolation, lack of professional staff support and consultation, and lack of adequate financial resources and service agencies often challenge students in a rural setting. They will discover that rural people tend to maintain their belief in the traditional structures and value systems and be quite resistive to change. Some may be slow to trust the students' leadership capacities due to their lack of knowledge of the profession, and the uncertainty of an outsider attempting to change their life-styles. Also, there is often a lack of consensus among the rural population.

Students may become frustrated in trying to define the rural community, since its boundaries are so diffuse. Even though those who live in a locality have a common identity and sense of belonging, not all of them rely upon the same resources for their needs. Transportation, consolidation of services, and employment outside of the locale often result in maintaining strong relationships beyond the community's natural area. This factor particularly makes it preferable for students to be given an assignment that is within a social structure or problem area of the immediate setting.

Utilizing this structure also enables students to acquire a good understanding of the systematic functional interrelationships of rural communities or the concept of "community of communities." This refers to the functional community or environment that provides institutional services to meet the needs of its rural members, that is, social, economic, political, religious, educational, recreational, physical, and protective services. This includes a hierarchy of towns of increasing size, service, and complexity, or a central city with surrounding satellite towns that consolidate for a community of communities.

The smaller towns provide the services demanded most frequently, and the larger towns or central city provide the more specialized services. This presumably leads to a higher quality of service, although it does reduce the number of services found in the smaller towns. This hierarchical arrangement reflects the consolidation, regionalization, or specialization efforts of current community development efforts and has enabled many smaller rural towns to exist economically.

Community planning is becoming a necessary way of life for rural areas. Especially as the local people work toward adjusting to the changes these structural modifications have caused, and as they develop and utilize their natural, human, and economic resources. The social work profession can provide leadership in assisting the community in assessing the internal and external forces that affect their living conditions. Assistance can be provided to help develop a systematic means of recognizing problems and those factors over which the community has some control. The social worker can implement various theoretical models to create problem-solving processes that are appropriate to the characteristics of the particular community.

Social work education must become more assertive in recruiting and preparing professional manpower for practice in rural settings. Curriculum content should be inclusive in considering the characteristics of rural environments and the disproportionate number of social problems that often oppress the rural population. These rural situations offer new and innovative practicum experiences for prospective professionals, and meanwhile provide services to the local community. The conceptualizations resulting from practice will enhance and contribute to the theoretical models of practice, and enable the profession to better carry out its commitments to this one-third of our nation's people.

NOTES

1. Alfred Stamm, "NASW Membership: Characteristics, Employment, and Salaries," *Personnel Information*, Vol. 12 (May 1969), pp. 1, & 34–35.

2. U.S. Department of Agriculture, *Contours of Change: Yearbook of Agriculture, 1970* (Washington, D.C.: Government Printing Office, 1970), p. 147.

3. K. G. Skaggs, "Education for Manpower: To Serve the People Better," in *National Growth: The Rural Component* (Washington, D.C.: Government Printing Office, 1971), p. 45.

4. U.S. Department of Agriculture, "Population of the United States, by Urban and Rural Residence, 1900–1970," in *The Economic and Social Conditions of Rural America in the 1970s* (Washington, D.C.: Government Printing Office, 1971), pt. 1. p. 2.

5. Donald L. Newport, "Health, Recreation, and Cultural Opportunities in Rural America," in *National Growth, op. cit.*, p. 49.

6. U.S. Bureau of the Census, *Social and Economic Conditions of the Negro in the United States*, Current Population Report, no. 332 (Washington, D.C.: Government Printing Office, October, 1967), p. 10.

7. Jonathan Lindley, "Projections on Location of Future Jobs and People" (Paper presented at the Eighth Annual Conference for Economic Projections, National Planning Association, April 28, 1967).

8. "U.S. Population Change, 1960–1970," in *The Economic and Social Conditions of Rural America in the 1970s, op. cit.*, pt. 1, p. 20.

9. Quoted by Henry Ahlgren in "Rural Development Is a Process," in *National Growth, op. cit.*, p. 9.

10. The President's National Advisory Commission on Rural Poverty, *The People Left Behind* (Washington, D.C.: Government Printing Office, October, 1967).

11. Rabel J. Burdge and Everett M. Rogers, *Social Change in Rural Societies* (New York: Appleton-Crofts, 1972), pp. 377 & 385.

12. "Persons by Poverty Status, by Type of Residence, 1969," in *The Economic and Social Conditions of Rural America in the 1970s, op. cit.*, pt. 1, p. 48.

13. The President's National Advisory Commission on Rural Poverty, *op. cit.*, p. 104.

14. U.S. Department of Agriculture, *A Good Life for More People: Yearbook of Agriculture, 1971* (Washington, D.C.: Government Printing Office, 1971), p. 73.

15. The President's National Advisory Commission on Rural Poverty, *op. cit.*, p. 104.

16. U.S. Department of Agriculture, *Contours of Change, op cit.*, p. 24.

17. U.S. Department of Agriculture, *A Good Life for More People, op. cit.*, pp. 275–76.

18. Newport, *op. cit.*, p. 49.

19. "Expenditures Per Pupil of Local Public School Systems by Metropolitan Status, 1967–1968," in *The Economic and Social Conditions of Rural America in the 1970s, op. cit.*, p. 104.

20. U.S. Department of Agriculture, *A Good Life for More People, op. cit.*, p. 162.

21. Lee G. Burchinal, *Career Choices of Rural Youth in a Changing Society* (St. Paul, Minn.: Minnesota Agricultural Experiment Station, 1962), pp. 24–25.

22. U.S. Department of Agriculture, *A Good Life for More People, op. cit.*, p. 162.

23. U.S. Bureau of Census, "School Enrollment: October, 1969," in *Current Population Reports*, series P-20, no. 206 (Washington, D.C.: Government Printing Office, 1970).

24. Paul M. Gottlieb, "The Migration and Distribution of Physicians," in *Reference Data on the Profile of Medical Practice* (Chicago: American Medical Association, 1971).

25. National Center for Health Statistics, "Types of Injuries: Incidence and Associated Disability," series 10, no. 57 (Washington, D.C.: Government Printing Office, 1969).

26. Tresa H. Matthews, *Health Services in Rural America*, bulletin no. 362 (Washington, D.C.: U.S. Department of Agriculture, 1973), p. 18.

27. Burdge and Rogers, *op cit.*, p. 392.

28. U.S. Department of Agriculture, *A Good Life for More People, op. cit.*, p. 200.

29. Quoted by T. K. Cowden in "Why Rural Development," in *National Growth, op. cit.*, p. 4.

30. The President's National Advisory Commission on Rural Poverty, *op. cit.*

31. Cowden, *op. cit.*, p. 4.

Afterword

The theme of this book has been change. "Rural" today, near the end of the 1970s, does not mean the same as it did early in this century or in the depression of the 1930s or after World War II. It is difficult to know what the 1980s will bring, but it is safe to predict that there will be social problems, old ones such as poverty or variations thereof, and new ones such as those emanating from the energy crisis, and that there will be efforts to cope with such changes and to help people cope. It has not been the purpose of this volume to present the last word on rural problems and services, even if that were possible, but to add to the necessary and growing thinking on this important subject at a time of profound change.

Contributors

Calvin Beale—Leader, Population Studies Group, U.S. Department of Agriculture, Washington, D.C.

Barbara Brown—Day Care Specialist, Wisconsin Department of Health and Social Services, Rhinelander

Phil Brown—Contributor, *Rural America*, Washington, D.C.

Clarke Chambers—Professor of History, University of Minnesota, Minneapolis. At the time of the presentation, Chairman, Department of History

Kenneth Coughlin—Assistant Editor, *Rural America*, Washington, D.C.

Jackie Denman—Formerly of Rural Department, National Council of Social Services, London, England

Barbara Lou Fenby—Unit Clinical Chief, Schoharie County Mental Health Center, Schoharie, New York

C. Scott Graber—Attorney and writer based in Beaufort, South Carolina

Susan Graber—Lives in Beaufort, South Carolina; has taught school in the area and written a research paper on correlations between physical isolation and intelligence

Cynthia S. Guillaume—Instructor, Department of Social Work, University of Wyoming, Laramie

Harriett Hayes—At the time the article was written, Assistant Professor of Social Work, University of Wyoming

Francis Hill—Professor in the Department of Government, University of Texas, Austin

Andrew Hinkle—At the time the article was written, in the Department of Psychiatry, Ohio State University, Columbus

Patricia Hutinger—Professor of Early Childhood Education, Western Illinois University, Macomb

Hideki Ishisaka—Associate Professor, School of Social Work, University of Washington, Seattle

G. Michael Iacobsen—Instructor, University of Iowa School of Social Work

H. Wayne Johnson—Professor and coordinator of the undergraduate program, University of Iowa School of Social Work

Louise Johnson—Director of the social work program, University of South Dakota

Ira Kaye—Transportation Specialist, U.S. Department of Agriculture, Washington, D.C.

Patricia Kelley—Assistant Professor, School of Social Work, University of Iowa

Verne Kelley—Director, Mid-Eastern Iowa Community Mental Health Center, Iowa City

Nick Kotz—Writer and author of several books and articles, Chevy Chase, Maryland

Linda F. Kugel—Coordinator, Carroll County Mental Health Service, Inc., New Hampshire; now lives in Conway

Joseph A. Leistyna—Director, Pediatric Ambulatory Services, University of Connecticut School of Medicine, Farmington

Nancy McKee—Project Coordinator, Early Childhood Education, Western Illinois University, Macomb

Joanne Mermelstein—Associate Professor, School of Social Work, University of Missouri

Gary R. Mooers—Director, Social Work Program, University of Mississippi

Jean Norris—Now lives in a rural area, Constable, New York; formerly on the staff of the Franklin County Office for the Aging, Malone, New York

Nancy J. Ormsby—Community Education Coordinator, Project Children, Quinco Consulting Center, Columbus, Indiana

Mary H. Osgood—Currently a homemaker; at the time the article was written, Instructor in Rural Sociology, College of Agriculture, Pennsylvania State University

David Powe—At the time the article was written, on the faculty of the University of Mississippi; now with the McComb Public Schools, McComb, Mississippi

Lynn Rhenisch—Contributor, *Rural America*, Washington, D.C.

R. Thomas Riggs—Currently lives in Somerville, Massachusetts; at the time the article was published, Coordinator, Carroll County Mental Health Service, Inc., New Hampshire

Max Schott—At the time the article was published, Information Specialist, Iowa Department of Social Services, Des Moines; now Director of Personnel, Woodward State Hospital School, Iowa

Thomas R. Sefcik—With the Quinco Consulting Center as Coordinator, Project Children, Columbus, Indiana

Paul Sundet—Associate Professor, School of Social Work, University of Missouri

Gwen K. Weber—At the time the article was written, on the faculty at the University of Nebraska School of Social Work; now a Ph.D. candidate

Index of Names

Index of Subjects